A Critical Systems Approach to Socio-Ecological Systems

Daniel D. P. McCarthy

A Critical Systems Approach to Socio-Ecological Systems

Implications for social learning and governance

VDM Verlag Dr. Müller

Impressum/Imprint (nur für Deutschland/ only for Germany)
Bibliografische Information der Deutschen Nationalbibliothek: Die Deutsche Nationalbibliothek verzeichnet diese Publikation in der Deutschen Nationalbibliografie; detaillierte bibliografische Daten sind im Internet über http://dnb.d-nb.de abrufbar.

Coverbild: www.purestockx.com

Verlag: VDM Verlag Dr. Müller Aktiengesellschaft & Co. KG
Dudweiler Landstr. 99, 66123 Saarbrücken, Deutschland
Telefon +49 681 9100-698, Telefax +49 681 9100-988, Email: info@vdm-verlag.de
Zugl.: Waterloo, University of Waterloo, Diss., 2007

Herstellung in Deutschland:
Schaltungsdienst Lange o.H.G., Berlin
Books on Demand GmbH, Norderstedt
Reha GmbH, Saarbrücken
Amazon Distribution GmbH, Leipzig
ISBN: 978-3-639-19489-0

Imprint (only for USA, GB)
Bibliographic information published by the Deutsche Nationalbibliothek: The Deutsche Nationalbibliothek lists this publication in the Deutsche Nationalbibliografie; detailed bibliographic data are available in the Internet at http://dnb.d-nb.de .

Cover image: www.purestockx.com

Publisher:
VDM Verlag Dr. Müller Aktiengesellschaft & Co. KG
Dudweiler Landstr. 99, 66123 Saarbrücken, Germany
Phone +49 681 9100-698, Fax +49 681 9100-988, Email: info@vdm-publishing.com

Printed in the U.S.A.
Printed in the U.K. by (see last page)
ISBN: 978-3-639-19489-0

Abstract

This dissertation builds on work that has applied complex systems thinking to socio-ecological systems as well as on research that explores critical and reflective approaches to planning. A broad, interdisciplinary literature review was undertaken to explore the implications of complex and critical systems thinking and critical social epistemology for environmental management, planning and policy research, governance and social learning. Building on the insights from this review, one of the key contributions of this research is a conceptual framework that explicitly integrates knowledge and learning into an understanding of socio-ecological systems. It is argued that in the highly complex and uncertain realm of environmental policy, planning and governance, we should begin to discuss such systems as socio-ecological-epistemological (SEE) systems. This research addresses the complexity, uncertainty, high decision stakes, power relations and plurality of knowledges involved in the process of social learning in environmental planning and governance.

The SEE systems conceptual framework for research and intervention was developed in the form of descriptive (Co-Evolution, Reflexive Uncertainty, Cross-scalar Considerations) and prescriptive (Critical Awareness, Pluralism, Power) principles. Based upon these principles, a critical systems-based approach to planning and policy research was developed and applied to two case studies of innovative, integrated environmental planning and governance: the Oak Ridges Moraine and the Long Point World Biosphere Reserve. A conceptual model for describing and refining the contributions of environmental movement organizations to social learning in the context of environmental governance emerged. The model describes the requirements of social learning as defined along three axes: typology of knowledge; levels of critical reflection; and, a scale axis from individual agent to larger social structures (institutions).

Through this work, it is evident that insights from complex and critical systems understanding have influenced thinking in environmental management, planning, governance and social learning. Through the exploratory application of the SEE systems approach to complex environmental planning and governance systems, the SEE systems principles appear to resonate strongly with the experience of environmental movement organizations. In particular, three key findings emerged from the two exploratory, empirical case studies. First, interviewees and workshop attendees in both case study contexts described the importance of various types of knowledge, especially scientific, local technical and governance knowledge in initiating policy change. Second, research participants stressed the importance of understanding the cross-scalar dynamics that affect their ability to influence policy as well as the need to develop policy and governance structures appropriate to the scale of the issue of interest. And finally, the need for individual as well as organizational critical reflection upon policy tools and implementation, policy goals as well as the power differentials embodied in certain policy and governance structures was also highlighted in the qualitative, empirical data generated through interviews and workshops. This research reaffirms the importance of the collaboration and the collective contribution of academic researchers, civil servants and volunteer members of environmental movement organizations to fostering social learning for sustainability in the context of complex SEE systems.

In memory of Professor James J. Kay

Table of Contents

List of Figures and Tables

Chapter 1: Introduction

1.1 Introduction and Context for Research

By the mid- to late-1980s, development in the Greater Toronto Area (GTA) had expanded north and begun to threaten the fragile hydrogeology, geomorphology and ecology of a major glacial moraine landform that served as an important green space corridor, the Oak Ridges Moraine (ORM). It took over a decade but the Ontario Provincial government eventually passed moraine-specific, conservation legislation in 2001 protecting almost 92% of the moraine from urban development. More impressive is that this important and restrictive environmental policy was enacted during an era of far-reaching neo-conservative, political economic trends that emphasized smaller government and market-based policy. Furthermore, many of the regional conservation movement's most ardent advocates initially became involved in ORM-related issues for local interests only to later learn of the importance and sensitivity of the moraine as a natural landscape feature. Such an impressive, if not unlikely, conservation success could have only resulted from knowledge sharing and learning on a large, social scale, among other factors.

In a somewhat different social and economic context but only a couple of hundred kilometers away, learning on a social scale is enabling community members in an internationally designated and protected landform to foster sustainable development within their economically depressed local area. The Long Point World Biosphere Reserve is an internationally recognized geomorphological and ecological system, historically protected as a sports fishery and game reserve surrounded by a primarily rural, agricultural landscape. The Point itself has been actively protected by various conservation and preservation organizations and agencies since 1866; in 1982 it was recognized as a RAMSAR site, and in 1986 was designated as a UNESCO World Biosphere Reserve (Kickert, 1993; Francis and Whitelaw, 2001). The rural communities surrounding this internationally recognized landform have been economically depressed as a result of international agricultural policies and the collapse of tobacco-growing industry. Despite the broad, sustainability-focused mandate of the UNESCO designation, the Long Point World Biosphere Reserve Foundation (LPWBRF) has primarily been a preservation- or conservation-oriented organization. Recently, however, the LPWBRF initiated a series of workshops to engage the local community on issues of sustainability in the Long Point area. The results of these workshops centre on learning about new opportunities to foster fruitful connections among the Long Point ecological stewardship, the local economy and community building.

In spite of the differences in the ORM and Long Point contexts, there appears to be evidence that the phenomenon of learning on a social scale (social learning) has been a crucial component for fostering joint attention to the environmental protection and economic aspects of sustainability. Social learning can be defined as an on-going, adaptive, communicative process of local, scientific and governance knowledge creation and synthesis undertaken by individuals and groups with inherently limited and biased perspectives that results in changes to social structures (e.g. policy, mandate, social norms) fostered by an understanding of the importance of scale (spatial and temporal) and critical reflection on various levels from the pragmatic to the ethical. Policy change in both of these environmental planning and governance contexts has required stakeholders to address complexity, uncertainty, multiple perspectives and cross-scalar dynamics through the use of a variety of knowledges and a measure of critical reflection.

1.1.1 Complexity and the Planning and Governance Context

There are emerging approaches to addressing the complex, uncertain and inherently pluralistic nature of socio-ecological systems based on the "new science" of complex systems theory. The "new science" or complexity theory refers to a group of interrelated theories (catastrophe theory, chaos theory, information theory, hierarchy theory and self-organization theory) that have been derived in several scientific disciplines, including chemistry and physics. Despite their traditional scientific disciplinary origins, they have provocative implications across disciplines and fields and, more generally, for the way we understand various types of phenomena as well as the role of learning in planning and policy making.

Complex and critical systems thinking is a mode of reasoning based on the formal theory that can be applied to a variety of practical contexts. A complex and critical systems thinking-based approach to planning and policy making, such as the one developed in my dissertation work, provides a broad, integrated, cross-scalar, multiple perspective counterpoint to more conventional planning and policy approaches. It is not meant to replace traditional planning approaches such as rational comprehensive planning, but rather to complement them.

Rational comprehensive planning is basically procedure-driven. A survey is conducted to collect information, analysis is undertaken and a comprehensive master plan is produced. Issues and problems are compartmentalized, a suite of alternative solutions is identified and the "best" alternative is selected. Decisions are made according to technical rules, generally using quantifiable data coupled with a set of empirically established probabilities about the external world (Faludi, 1982; Thomas, 1982). Rational comprehensive planning is "based on a technocratic ideology that accepts the scientific legitimacy of the planner's expertise" (Alexander, 1992: 75). This approach has been criticized because of its assumption of full, "objective" knowledge on the subject environment, alternatives, and values of citizens (Forester, 1987), and reinforcement of the political and economic status quo (Alexander, 1992).

Conventional planning and policy approaches, such as rational comprehensive planning, have attempted to study complex phenomena by simplifying them through analytical reductionism (describing them as simple systems, machines) or by aggregating and averaging through statistical analysis (describing them as unorganized complex systems). However, complex systems, such as socio-ecological systems, exist at a threshold between order and chaos, too complex to be treated as machines and too organized to be assumed random and averaged (Figure 1).

Reductionist and statistical tools, for the sake of mathematical tractability, seek to eliminate the very complexity and uncertainty that characterize complex systems by assuming mechanistic linear causality (Region I on Figure 1) as well as macro-level order by assuming chaotic or random distribution (Region II on Figure 1). The types of errors that result from the potentially inappropriate application of these tools have to some extent come to be expected by the general public in policy matters and are often justified away by citing the inadequacy of the data or limitations of a particular technique. The underlying epistemology and ethics of the use of knowledge for decision making are not often considered.

Figure 1: Machines, Aggregates, Systems

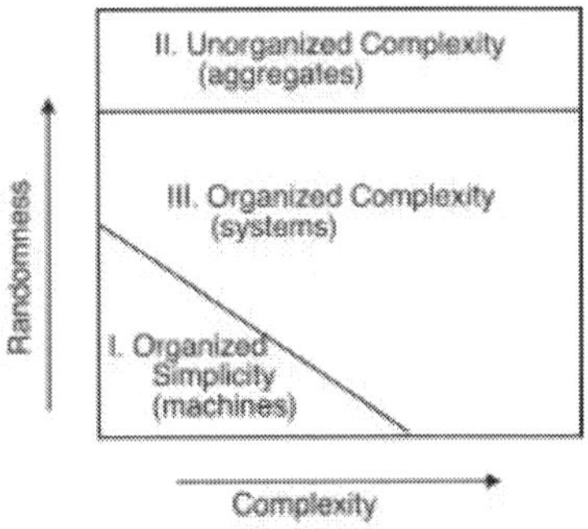

Region I – 'Organized Simplicity' the region of machines, or mechanisms
Region II – 'Unorganized Complexity' the region of populations, or aggregates.
Region III – 'Organized Complexity' the region too complex for analysis and too organized for statistics – this is the region of systems.
- Weinberg (1975)

Another way of viewing the distinction between complex and critical systems-based approaches and conventional approaches to planning and policy making is to distinguish between different types of decision making based on the level of system uncertainties and the scale of decision stakes (Funtowicz and Ravetz, 1992, 1993, 1994) (Figure 2). As opposed to the search for "objective", scientific truth

Figure 2: Post-Normal Science

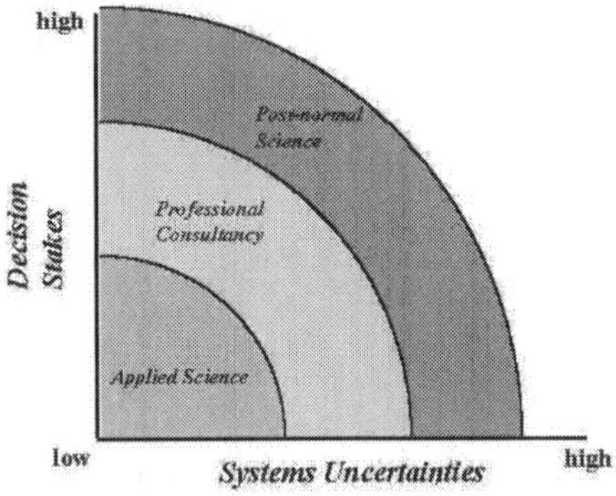

- Funtowicz and Ravetz (1993)

(applied science) or in the interest of a client (professional consultancy), post-normal science's "theoretical core is the task of quality assurance; it argues the need for new methods, involving 'extended peer communities', who deploy 'extended facts' and take an active part in the solution of their problems. It is already being realised in many initiatives; for those it provides a theoretical basis and legitimation" (Ravetz, 1999: 647).

It can be argued that other approaches, such as transactive, collaborative and critical planning, address the need to reflect on the assumptions embedded in a particular approach and for the inclusion of non-expert, extended peer communities in decision making. And while there are examples of critical, reflective approaches to planning (Section 2.5.1) and even of systems-based approaches to collaborative planning (Section 2.5.2), there are few examples of critical systems-based approaches to environmental planning, policy making and governance (Forsyth, 2003; Fuchs, 2004; Keen et al. 2005). As a result, my dissertation research begins with the assumption that socio-ecological systems are too complex to be analyzed as machines and too ordered to be aggregated through statistical analysis; and, exhibit extreme uncertainty and high decision-stakes (Funtowicz and Ravetz 1992, 1993, 1994; Ravetz 1999). Therefore, it is assumed that complex and critical systems thinking is a useful approach to address planning and governance issues related to ecosystems, human social/institutional systems, human knowledge and learning and especially for systems that represent the integration of all three. The approach developed in my dissertation work explicitly begins with generic critical, reflective, systems-based principles to problem solving, then tailors these for use in the planning and policy domain and finally illustrates their utility and begins to test them in two empirical case studies of social learning in environmental planning contexts.

A wide variety of academic literatures provide insight into the complex, systemic and political process of social learning and its implications for environmental planning and policy making. There also have been efforts to develop and apply the concept of social learning for use in environmental planning contexts. However, there have been few attempts to acknowledge explicitly the complexity, perspective dependence and need for critical reflection in the concept of social learning (Sections 2.5.6, 2.5.7, 2.5.8). Complex and critical systems thinking and critical social epistemology could provide the necessary systemic and critically reflective tools to buttress the concept of social learning theoretically.

1.1.2 Research Approach

This dissertation research provides a rich, interdisciplinary overview of the relevant conceptual and applied fields of study and synthesizes these into a generic complex and critical systems-based conceptual framework for research and intervention (Section 3.2). This framework is then tailored into a methodological approach to planning and policy research (Section 3.3) and a model for fostering social learning in environmental planning emerged through the application to two instrumental case studies (Chapters 6 and 7). This dissertation work will provide environmental policy and planning researchers and practitioners with an explicit means to integrate knowledge and the complexity of the learning process into an enhanced understanding of complex socio-ecological systems. It is argued that in the highly complex and uncertain realm of environmental policy, planning and governance, we should begin to discuss such systems as socio-ecological-epistemological systems (SEE systems), the subject of this dissertation.

The SEE systems conceptual framework, developed through this work (Section 3.2), brings together aspects of complex and critical systems thinking to describe the dynamic relationship between individual knowledge (agency) and institutionalized knowledge (structure) as originally expressed in Giddens' (1984) structuration theory. Three Aristotelian intellectual virtues (*episteme*, *techne* and *phronesis*) more recently highlighted in the work of Flyvbjerg (2001) are then incorporated to enrich further the description of the self-organizing nature of knowledge for environmental decision making. The integration of complex and critical systems thinking, structuration theory and the three Aristotelian intellectual virtues provides a dynamic, integrated, and socially-embedded view of learning for environmental decision making within socio-eco-epistemological systems.

My dissertation work explicitly builds on interdisciplinary, complex systems-based research that explores resilience within socio-ecological systems (Gunderson et al., 1995;

Gunderson and Holling, 2002; Holling, 2001; Berkes and Folke, 1998, 2003). Such studies involve large, long-term, in-depth case studies and are often expert-driven (Section 4.3). My research is meant to develop and explore the potential of a framework for integrating social learning into an understanding of complex, socio-ecological systems. It is also intended to focus on the feasibility of including insights from a broad, extended peer community of non-government, environmental movement organizations (Funtowicz and Ravetz, 1992, 1993, 1994; Ravetz and Funtowicz, 1999). While stakeholder involvement in environmental planning and management is now common, Reed and McIlveen (2006: 591) argue that "stakeholders can contribute to a pluralistic civic science that incorporates local knowledge directly into environmental decision making and research". My work develops a complex and critical systems-based conceptual framework for describing the contributions that stakeholders from environmental movement organizations make to social learning.

This exploratory research differs from explanatory (establishing causal linkages through standardized protocols) or descriptive (in-depth, case study description for inductive or simply descriptive purposes) research (Robson, 1993). Robson (1993) characterizes exploratory research as inquiry that assesses phenomena through a new perspective or conceptual lens. The SEE conceptual framework is a new perspective and requires this type of exploration, illustration and initial testing. It is argued that case studies are the most appropriate strategy for exploratory research (Robson, 1993). Two instrumental case studies (the Oak Ridges Moraine and the Long Point World Biosphere Reserve) are utilized to begin to explore the potential of this emerging conceptual framework for integrating expertise and social learning developed in environmental movement organizations. Instrumental case studies are designed to provide insight into a specific issue as well as to refine a conceptual explanation (Berg, 1998), in this case the SEE systems conceptual framework. The Oak Ridges Moraine case is a long-standing, contentious, land-use planning process in one of Canada's most affluent areas, while the Long Point case focuses on the linkages between an internationally recognized protected landscape and its depressed, local rural economy. Both case studies are examples of civil-society led, innovative, sustainability-focused policy-making processes in the province of Ontario.

These two instrumental case studies will provide the SEE systems framework with the type of illustration and initial testing required to begin to ground this abstract conceptual framework. Further research proposed in the recommendations (Section 8.4) will continue to test the utility and transferability of the conceptual tools developed in this dissertation.

1.2 Research Goal and Objectives:

1.2.1 Goal

This dissertation seeks to develop and then illustrate and begin to test the utility of a complex and critical systems-based framework for research and intervention by describing and refining the contributions of environmental movement organizations to social learning in the context of complex environmental policy making and governance systems.

1.2.2 Objectives

Five objectives underlie the discussion:

1. to develop a complex and critical systems-based conceptual framework for research and intervention based upon an interdisciplinary literature review;
2. to develop, based on the framework above, a complex and critical systems-based methodological framework for research and intervention in the planning and policy domain;
3. to apply the frameworks to two instrumental case studies of innovative examples of social learning in environmental policy making and governance in Ontario to illustrate and begin to test their utility;
4. to develop a complex and critical systems-based conceptual model for describing the contributions of environmental movement organizations to social learning in the context of environmental policy making and governance in Ontario; and,
5. to develop theoretical and practical research contributions as well as recommendations for further research and for the practice of environmental planning, policy making and governance.

1.3 Justification for Research and Research Contributions

Justification for this research comes from both conceptual, and more pragmatic, policy and action-oriented levels. Conceptually, this dissertation seeks to fill a research gap, identified through a comprehensive, interdisciplinary literature review, in the application of a complexity-based, socially-embedded perspective on knowledge creation and social learning for environmental policy, planning and governance. On a more practical, policy level, this work seeks to explore the knowledge and social learning requirements for a UNESCO World Biosphere Reserve designation for the Oak Ridges Moraine and to provide a framework for fostering social learning in the context of an existing Biosphere Reserve, the Long Point World Biosphere Reserve.

1.3.1 Conceptual Justification

The conceptual tools and philosophical implications of complex and critical systems thinking appear to provide a suite of conceptual and pedagogical tools useful in fostering reflection and learning within environmental policy, planning and governance systems. As a result of the literature review, my work points to a research gap in the application of a reflective, socially-embedded view of knowledge creation and learning within a framework that explicitly integrates social, ecological and epistemological complex systems for the purposes of environmental policy, planning and governance intervention and research.

1.3.2 Pragmatic Justification

On a more pragmatic policy level, this research describes a loose, three-part typology of knowledge required for effective intervention and social learning within environmental policy, planning and governance. The application of this typology and the SEE systems framework to the two case studies highlights the politically contentious and often ideological nature of the environmental planning and policy process. Environmental conservation and stewardship measures often require legislative and regulatory changes that trigger contentious, time-consuming and costly judicial or quasi-judicial processes which rely on scientific, expert-oriented knowledge. With legislative and regulatory conservation measures in place, as occurs in both case studies, other non-regulatory approaches, such as the UNESCO World Biosphere Reserve designation, can serve to foster "big picture", systemic thinking and the development of three types of knowledge (scientific, local technical, governance), including a measure of critical reflection.

The UNESCO World Biosphere Reserves serve three main functions: conservation, promoting sustainability of local economies, and providing logistical functions such as education, research, monitoring and demonstration projects (Francis, 2004). The non-regulatory nature of the biosphere reserve designation seems particularly appropriate to the highly political context of land use decision making and overlapping policy in southern Ontario. Lessons and the results of social learning processes from the existing Long Point World Biosphere Reserve may be transferable to other areas within Southern Ontario, especially the Oak Ridges Moraine, a potential candidate for biosphere reserve designation. Such a designation would provide the ORM with non-regulatory recognition of the significance of the moraine, as well as its existing and potential contributions to the local economy and as a model for innovative, integrated and sustainable land use and governance.

1.4 Case Studies

As previously mentioned, two case studies were chosen. Both the primary case, the Oak Ridges Moraine, and the secondary case, the Long Point World Biosphere Reserve, were chosen based upon the following criteria:

1. Innovative approach to land use planning
2. Evidence of social learning leading to policy change
3. A strong role for civil society, non-government organizations in policy change
4. Regional in scale and bioregional or ecological boundaries to ensure cross-jurisdictional interactions
5. Sufficient documented history
6. A venue for action-oriented outcomes
7. An opportunity to examine social learning in both a potential and existing UNESCO World Biosphere Reserve
8. Availability of funding to conduct the research
9. Proximity to the University of Waterloo

1.4.1 Oak Ridges Moraine

The Oak Ridges Moraine (ORM) is located to the north of the City of Toronto and extends from the Niagara Escarpment in the west to the Trent River in the east. The Moraine is approximately 190,000 hectares in size, 160 km in length and between 3 and 24 km wide. It rises some 229 meters above Lake Ontario (Government of Ontario, 2002). This case study focuses on the ORM land use planning process from 1988 to 2005. The ORM case involved a civil society-led advocacy and planning movement that led to the area specific legislation, the *ORM Conservation Act* in 2001 (Government of Ontario, 2001), and development of the land use plan *ORM Conservation Plan* in 2002 (Government of Ontario, 2002).

1.4.2 Long Point World Biosphere Reserve

Long Point is a 32 km long sand spit located on the north shore of Lake Erie, in Norfolk County, and is an example of the Great Lakes coastal ecosystem. The Long Point complex is an important staging area for migrating waterfowl, is renowned for exceptional bass fishing and birding, and is home to the largest number of endangered, threatened and species of concern in Canada (Craig et al., 2003). The Long Point World Biosphere Reserve was designated by UNESCO in 1986. Biosphere reserve projects are administered by the Long Point World Biosphere Reserve Foundation (LPWBRF), a charitable, not-for-profit, volunteer organization. In 2006, the LPWBRF Board initiated a process to extend its mandate from a conservation and stewardship focus to a broader notion of sustainability. This process demonstrated considerable social learning within the Long Point community (McCarthy et al., In Press).

Taken together, the two case studies provide an empirical basis for an exploration of the implications of a SEE systems conceptual framework, an application of the SEE systems description, an explanation of some of the key causal linkages between components of SEE systems, and a venue for action-oriented research outcomes.

1.5 Empirical Case Study Methods

Critical systems planning and policy research is a reflective, systems-based, participatory and action-oriented approach to the study of policy development (Section 3.3). When making methodological decisions, the critical systems policy researcher should ensure that the research interventions are socially and theoretically critically aware, complex systems-based, pluralistic, focused on governance structures, and empirically grounded.

In the context of this application of critical systems policy research (Section 3.3), various research methods were utilized. For the primary case study, the Oak Ridges Moraine integrated land use planning process (1988-2005), key informant interviews, policy document analysis and participatory, observational research were undertaken. For the secondary case study of the Long Point World Biosphere Reserve, key informant interviews, participatory, observational research through a workshop series and policy document analysis were undertaken.

1.6 Outline of Chapters

Chapter two provides a comprehensive overview of an interrelated, interdisciplinary literature which includes complex and critical systems thinking, environmental planning, governance, social learning, knowledge management and critical, social epistemology. Areas of conceptual overlap between and among these various fields are examined. This review identifies a research gap and the opportunity to develop a view of social learning for environmental policy, planning and governance using complex and critical systems-based heuristics.

Chapter three presents a conceptual framework that provides researchers and practitioners with three descriptive and three prescriptive principles for studying and intervening in complex socio-ecological, epistemological systems.

The descriptive principles are:

- Co-Evolution - Social, ecological and epistemological systems self-organize and co-evolve.

- Reflexive Uncertainty - systems are inherently complex and perspective-dependent.
- Cross-scalar Considerations - SEE systems are hierarchically nested, exhibiting both top-down and bottom-up causality.

The prescriptive principles are:

- Critical Awareness – within SEE systems, intervention should be undertaken with a measure of critical awareness, reflexivity and openness to different perspectives.
- Pluralism (Knowledge, Perspectives and Methods) – Intervention within SEE systems should incorporate multiple perspectives, methods and types of knowledge (e.g. epistemic, technical, phronetic).
- Power – Intervention within SEE systems should acknowledge issues of power in the form of structural constraints and opportunities for individual agents to reach their potential.

Based on the SEE systems conceptual framework, a methodological frame of reference known as critical systems planning and policy research is developed. Critical systems planning and policy research is a reflective, systems-based, participatory and action-oriented approach to the study of policy development and implementation. Through the application of the SEE systems framework and critical systems planning and policy research to the two empirical case studies, a conceptual model of social learning is developed.

Chapter four provides a description and justification for the use of the two instrumental case studies as well as the empirical methods for qualitative data collection. Chapter five provides general background on the social, ecological and epistemological facets of the environmental policy, planning and governance system in Southern Ontario. Chapters six and seven then outline the empirical results of the two case studies and provide analysis based on the SEE systems description and critical systems policy framework. Chapter eight outlines conceptual and action-oriented conclusions and recommendations for further research and potential policy changes.

Chapter 2: Literature Review

2.1 Knowledge and Social Learning for Decision Making in Complex Socio-Ecological Systems

To fulfill objective #1 (Section 1.2) of my research a broad-based, interdisciplinary literature review was undertaken. The intent was twofold. First, it is meant to demonstrate that insights from critical, reflective and systems-based perspectives pervade fields of research related to environmental planning and policy making. And second, it is intended to begin to synthesize some disparate fields of study into a reflective, systems-based framework for approaching research and intervention and, more specifically, for describing the process of social learning in environmental planning and policy making.

The conceptual and methodological frameworks that result from this literature review (Sections 3.2 and 3.3) are meant to provide environmental management researchers and practitioners with a means to integrate knowledge and the complexity of learning explicitly into an understanding of complex socio-ecological systems. The conceptual model (Section 3.4) is intended to describe the knowledge requirements of social learning as it leads to policy change within socio-ecological systems. It is argued that we should begin to discuss such systems as socio-ecological-epistemological (SEE) systems.

Mitchell (2004) draws a distinction between theoretical and conceptual frameworks, based on their relative capacity for generalization and their ability to explain and predict. A theoretical framework is intended to be universal in its capacity for generalization and is intended to explain and predict, often quantitatively, the behaviour of a system of interest. In contrast, a conceptual framework is meant to characterize what are believed to be the key components and relationships of a particular problem or a system. The SEE systems perspective is meant to provide a set of tools and a perspective that describes and emphasizes the tight interelationships among social, ecological and epistemological components of a complex system. Applied to social learning, the SEE systems perspective facilitates development of a conceptual framework that is meant to be generalizable across a variety of system types and scales; however it is not intended to predict system behaviours especially not in a quantitative sense. While this framework appears to have elements of both theoretical and conceptual frameworks, it will be referred to as a conceptual framework hereafter.

This chapter begins with a brief summary of the notion of sustainability that provides the ethical compass for this dissertation. Following this, the chapter focuses on providing a critical overview of some key fields of study relevant to the conceptual framework. A review of the literature from practice-based fields such as planning, governance and social learning is complemented by literature from theoretical and philosophical fields, including complex and critical systems thinking and critical, social epistemology.

Given the vastness of the fields of research and scholarship that this work draws upon, this chapter also highlights some of the main areas of conceptual or thematic overlap among planning, governance, and knowledge management with complex and critical systems thinking and critical, social epistemology. General background overviews are provided on each of these fields. They are then followed by sections documenting cross-cutting works such as those that apply complex and critical systems thinking to planning (for instance, Innes and Booher, 1999), environmental management (for instance Kay et al., 1999) and / or knowledge development and management (for instance, Stacey, 2001; Fuller, 2002b). A number of works integrate several of these fields to varying extents. Berkes and Folke (1998, 2003) for example, discuss the importance of knowledge and learning (in particular traditional ecological knowledge) for environmental decision making in complex socio-ecological systems, and Fuchs (2004) reviewing the process of learning to integrate insights from complex systems thinking and Giddens' (1984) Structuration Theory. However, these works that integrate knowledge and environmental decision making with complex systems thinking are relatively rare.

2.2 Sustainability as an Ethical Foundation

One of the main assumptions here is that in making decisions related to environmental issues there is a need to consider a plurality of perspectives on what is considered to be economic viability, social inclusiveness and ecological sustainability across spatial and temporal scales (Francis, 2004: 1). Generally, this ethical frame of reference has its basis in the notion of sustainability.

The Brundtland Report, *Our Common Future*, 1987 brought the concept of "sustainable development" to the broad attention of the world. The report defined sustainable development as "meeting the needs of the present generation without compromising the ability of future generation to meet their own needs." Despite the intuitive logic of providing for the needs of future generations, the concepts of sustainable development and sustainability appear to some as so vague, "as to be consistent with almost any form of action (or inaction)" (Pearce et al., 1994: 457).

Robinson et al. (1996: x) note that sustainability is "not a wholly objective concept, and contains desired as well as necessary components". This view is reflected in their definition of the term, "the persistence over an apparently indefinite future of certain necessary and desired characteristics of the sociopolitical system and its natural environment". Explicitly acknowledging the perspective dependence of any notion of sustainability makes the concept more robust from a complex systems perspective as it allows for the consideration of a plurality of differing, even incommensurate, perspectives. Allen, Tainter and Hoekstra (2003: 26) take a more explicitly systems-oriented view of the concept, identifying the need to maintain the context of the system to maintain the system itself. And they too acknowledge the perspective dependence of sustainability in their definition of the term, "maintaining, or fostering the development of, the systemic contexts that produce the goods, services, and amenities that people need or value, at an acceptable cost, for as long as they are needed or valued". The value of this definition is that it acknowledges the complex, self-organizing dynamics that underlie any notion of sustainability and thus the need to maintain the context for the system to continue to adapt and evolve.

Gibson et al. (2005) observe that sustainability has emerged as three things: a critique, a set of principles implying positive objectives and a focus for strategies for change. Sustainability has emerged as a critique of the continuous environmental degradation and growing inequities at various local to global scales as a result of relentless global economic development and population increase. This critique of conventional thinking and practice acknowledges the paradox of the need to preserve ecological integrity while allowing for continued development to alleviate the existing economic inequities providing an impetus for change. "Together, development with sustainability demanded initiatives designed and pursued in ways that would protect resources and ecological integrity over the long term while greatly improving human well-being, especially among the poor" (Gibson et al., 2005: 20). Lastly, Gibson et al. (2005: 95-114) present a set of principles developed from the extensive sustainability literature. These are:

Socio-ecological system integrity - Build human-ecological relations that establish and maintain the long-term integrity of socio-biophysical systems and protect the irreplaceable life support functions upon which human as well as ecological well-being depends.

Livelihood sufficiency and opportunity - Ensure that everyone and every community have enough for a decent life and opportunities to seek improvements in ways that do not compromise future generations' possibilities for sufficiency and opportunity.

Intragenerational equity - Ensure that sufficiency and effective choices for all are pursued in ways that reduce dangerous gaps in sufficiency and opportunity (and health, security, social recognition, political influence, etc.) between the rich and the poor.

Intergenerational equity - Favour present options and actions most likely to preserve or enhance the opportunities and capabilities of future generations to live sustainably.

Efficiency - Provide a larger base for ensuring sustainable livelihoods for all while reducing threats to the long-term integrity of socio-ecological systems by reducing extractive damage, avoiding waste and cutting overall material and energy use per unit of benefit.

Socio-ecological civility and democratic governance - Build the capacity, motivation and habitual inclination of individuals, communities and other collective decision-making bodies to apply sustainability principles through more open and better informed deliberations, greater attention to fostering reciprocal awareness and collective responsibility, and more integrated use of administrative, market, customary, collective and personal decision-making practices.

Precaution and adaptation - Respect uncertainty, avoid even poorly understood risks of serious or irreversible damage to the foundations for sustainability, plan to learn, design for surprise and manage for adaptation.

> **Immediate- and long-term integration -** Attempt to meet all requirements for sustainability together as a set of interdependent parts, seeking mutually supportive benefits.

This broad conception of sustainability provides a useful ethical scope or compass for posing questions about the nature and use of knowledge for environmental decision making and governance. The SEE systems framework has been developed explicitly to aid in understanding the types of knowledge necessary for, and the role of social learning in, the definition and pursuit of sustainability.

The two case studies were also in part chosen as they reflect environmental movement organizations actively pursuing sustainability. Sustainability is reflected in both the Oak Ridges Moraine Conservation Plan and the United Nations Educational, Scientific and Cultural Organization (UNESCO) Biosphere Reserve concept.

The Oak Ridges Moraine Conservation Plan utilizes the notion of sustainability with reference to natural resource use by noting that an activity is "sustainable" if "the natural resource is able to support a particular use or activity without being adversely affected" (Government of Ontario, 2002: 14). The plan also makes specific use of the concept of sustainability with reference to a water budget.

The UNESCO World Biosphere Reserve Program also embodies sustainability. Biosphere Reserves serve three main functions: conservation, promotion of sustainability for local or regional economies, and logistic functions such as research, monitoring and education (Francis, 2005). As such, the Long Point Biosphere Reserve is meant to promote sustainability and the LPWBR Foundation has demonstrated its commitment to this goal through its sustainability workshop series. The Oak Ridges Moraine has also been discussed as a potential Biosphere Reserve. Efforts to begin the UNESCO nomination process for the moraine so far have included an exploratory committee consisting of stakeholders on the moraine, including STORM, formed in April 2004, and this will be explored further through an Oak Ridges Moraine Foundation project based at the University of Waterloo. Consequently, this research on knowledge and social learning for environmental governance with the normative goal of sustainability is salient and timely.

Given the assumption that sustainability is a worthwhile, foundational ethical basis for intervention within complex SEE systems, the following sections provide background regarding practice-based fields of planning, environmental management, governance and social learning. These are followed by sections outlining relevant insights from the more abstract, theoretical and philosophical fields of complex and critical systems thinking and critical, social epistemology.

2.3 Relevant Areas of Applied Research and Scholarship for the Proposed Conceptual Framework

2.3.1 Planning

In considering fields relevant to the use of knowledge and social learning in environmental decision-making decisions and interventions, planning is perhaps the most obvious. Planning has been defined as "future-oriented, public decision making directed toward attaining specific goals" (Fainstein and Fainstein, 1996: 265). Its philosophical and theoretical basis is broad but loose, expanding from modern, positivist, rational comprehensive planning, to a more recent post-modern-inspired "communicative turn" in the form of communicative or deliberative planning theory. As such, planning theory, as Campbell and Fainstein (1996: 2) indicate, "is not easy to define ...; the subject is slippery, and explanations are often frustratingly tautological or disappointingly pedestrian". Not only is planning theory broad, ambiguous and even incommensurate, as a practice-based profession it has experienced a pronounced "theory-practice gap" (for instance, Allmendinger, 2002; Watson, 2002). In fact, "to bemoan the theory-practice gap is now *de rigour* for an exploration of planning theory" (Allmendinger, 2002: 20).

In a seminal work, Hudson (1979) developed a classification scheme for planning's various theoretical traditions and discussed them under the rubric SITAR (Synoptic, Incremental, Transactive, Advocacy, Radical). Synoptic planning or the rational comprehensive approach, conventionally the dominant planning tradition, has four basic elements: 1) goal setting, 2) identification of policy alternatives, 3) evaluation of means against ends, and 4) implementation. Incremental planning, as originally advanced by

Charles Lindblom, criticized the synoptic approach as unrealistic and put forth the notion of "planning" (or non-planning) by "mutual adjustment", "learning by doing" or "disjointed incrementalism". Transactive planning, in contrast to incremental planning, placed more emphasis on process, in particular the process of personal and organizational development and not only the achievement of objectives. Generally associated with decentralization, transactive planning "consists less of field surveys and data analysis, and more of interpersonal dialogue marked by a process of mutual learning" (Hudson, 1979: 389). Hudson's (1979) fourth planning tradition, advocacy, surfaced in the 1960s in response to power inequities in traditional planning processes. Modeled after the legal system, it was used to defend the interests of community groups, environmental causes and the poor. Finally, Hudson's radical planning is an ambiguous "catch-all". Many recent ecological, humanistic and communicative planning theories would have fit under Hudson's radical planning rubric.

Hudson (1979: 387) argued that while they are "often strongly at odds ... parallel application of more than one theory is usually necessary for arriving at valid, three-dimensional perspectives on social issues and appropriate action implications". Using six criteria (public interest, human dimension, feasibility, action potential, substantive theory, self-reflective), Hudson (1979) highlighted the strengths and weaknesses as well as the complementary nature of the various planning schools.

More recently Fainstein and Fainstein (1996) describe four planning traditions (traditional, democratic, equity, incremental), linking them to facets of political theory: technocratic, democratic, socialist and liberal. Traditional planning, as Fainstein and Fainstein (1996) see it, would be similar to Hudson's synoptic planning in that the planner describes both the "goals" and the "means" for the plan. Democratic planning, in contrast, called for a more participatory approach to planning, explicitly incorporating the goals of the community into planning. Equity planning can be seen to parallel both Hudson's (1979) advocacy planning and Friedmann's (1987) social mobilization planning tradition, reflecting the need to increase fairness in the planning process. Finally, Fainstein and Fainstein's (1996) incremental planning tradition frames planning as a series of "successive approximations".

In one of the most highly regarded and most-quoted works on planning theory, Friedmann (1987) traces the origins of four traditions in planning: policy analysis, social learning, social reform and social mobilization. Social reform focuses on the role of the state in societal guidance, framing planning as a "scientific endeavour" and seeking to institutionalize it as a process. Policy analysis can be directly linked to Hudson's synoptic tradition as it shares its distinctive method (see above). Social learning can be characterized as, "learning by doing" and can be likened to Hudson's incremental planning. Finally, the social mobilization planning tradition "departs from all the others by asserting the primacy of direct collective action 'from below'" (Friedmann, 1987: 83). He concludes that all four traditions revolve around one main concern: "how knowledge should be properly linked to action" (Friedmann, 1987: 74).

Allmendinger (2002: 20) argues that "each development in theory fills a gap in retrospect; that is, practice develops apace and different theories emerge with champions who say 'no, this theory best explains planning's raison d'etre and how to do it'". This allows planners to pick and choose theories to guide or justify their actions or approaches. Allmendinger (2002) argues that theory is nothing more than elaborate social constructions, an instrument of power, or a rhetorical device. He concludes that what is required is a critical, political perspective on theory, locating it in an appropriately "political context".

Allmendinger's conclusion resonates with two concurrent and related trends in planning: the "practice movement", characterized by "an epistemology of practice implicit in the artistic, intuitive processes which some practitioners do bring to situations of uncertainty, instability, uniqueness and value conflict" (Watson, 2002: 180) and the recent communicative, collaborative (Innes and Booher, 1999; Healy, 1997), deliberative and critical planning based on Habermasian or Giddensian communicative theory (McGuirk, 2001; Yiftachel and Huxley, 2000). "Communicative planning theory builds its case for renewing planning practice on a critique of the epistemological foundations of planning" (McGuirk, 2001: 196).

Planning does not seem to lend itself to identification with a single philosophy or method. If this is the case, then what are the defining characteristics of the process and practice of planning? Klosterman (1996) has identified four main functions of planning in light of his analysis of economic, pluralist, traditional and Marxist arguments for and against planning. These include promoting common or collective interests of the community, considering the external effects of individual and group action, improving the information base for public and private decision making, and considering the distributional effects of public and private action (Klosterman, 1996). Given these characteristics, the relevance of Friedmann's (1987) assertion that, despite their disparities and incommensurabilities all traditions of planning are concerned with the linkage between knowledge and action, should be obvious.

Linking knowledge to intervention (any purposeful action by an individual agent to create change) is a defining characteristic of systems thinking and will be the focus of much of what follows. The development and diversity of planning theory has paralleled that of systems thinking. In fact, Allmendinger (2002) notes a tendency to conflate systems thinking and rational planning as they both rose to prominence in the late 1950s and early 1960s. Elements of complex systems thinking, in particular autopoietic theory (Section 2.4.1.2) and critical systems thinking (Section 2.4.1.3), can lend credence to a critical, process-oriented view of the linkage between knowledge and action or intervention and so can be directly relevant for planners, practitioners and theorists alike (see next section).

If planning is indeed, as Friedmann (1987: 74) describes, concerned with "how knowledge should be properly linked to action", then it is one logical avenue for exploring the implications of a complex SEE systems-based perspective. There have already been attempts to integrate critical theory and systems thinking into the discourse on planning through the works of Healy (1997), Innes and Booher (1999) and Yiftachel and Huxley (2000). There remains, however, an opportunity to explore further the complexity of integrated social, ecological and epistemological systems through planning research and scholarship.

2.3.2 Environmental Management

Environmental management is another field of research and practice integral to any discourse on knowledge and social learning for environmental policy and decision making. Mitchell (2004: 108) defines environmental management as "actual decisions and action concerning policy and practice regarding how resources and the environment are appraised, protected, allocated, developed, used, rehabilitated, remediated and restored". This broad field of research, policy and practice has roots that extend across the natural and social sciences. In fact, much of current environmental management focuses on the integration of social and ecological systems.

As our understanding of environmental issues has evolved, we have come to realize that environmental decision making has to address both the complexity of ecological systems and the complexity of interdependent human organizational and institutional systems (White, 1945; Berkes and Folke, 1998; Kay et al., 1999; Holling, 2001; Gunderson and Holling, 2002; Mitchell, 2002, Francis, 2003). White (1945) and more recently Berkes and Folke (1998, 2003), Gunderson and Holling (2002) and Mitchell (2002) have set a profound and necessary precedent with their work, explicitly integrating the study of natural resources with human organizations and institutions to focus research and intervention on integrated socio-ecological systems.

In recent decades, efforts to address some of the paradoxes in resource and environmental management (Holling et al. 2002) have required an evolution in our thinking about environmental science and decision making. The result has been a shift from reductionist, command and control science and management to a more integrated, adaptive, systems-based approach (Gunderson et al., 1995; Gunderson and Holling, 2002; Mitchell, 2002; Berkes and Folke, 1998, 2003). Integral to this more systemic approach to environmental decision making has been the incorporation of an emerging body of theory often referred to as complex systems theory, or the "new science" (Allen and Hoekstra, 1992; Ulanowicz, 1997; Kay et al., 1999). Complex systems theory has offered a more sophisticated understanding of the structure and dynamics of both social and ecological systems than the relevant "normal" scientific disciplines (Section 2.5).

Even this integrated, systemic view of socio-ecological systems does not explicitly acknowledge the complexity of the process of social learning for decision making within socio-ecological systems. The integration of planning and governance theory with complex and critical systems thinking, as well as with social learning and epistemology, points to new opportunities in the study of environmental decision making. Building on the integration of social, institutional systems into an understanding of ecological systems, this work seeks to also integrate the learning or the epistemological system as well.

Attempts to extend insights from the field of social learning to the practice and study of resource and environmental management have also contributed to the discourse on social learning for environmental planning and decision making. Sinclair and Diduck (2001) have taken Mezirow's (1994, 1998) transformative theory of adult learning and applied it to understanding how public participation in environmental assessment processes provides opportunities for social learning. Jamison (2001) has explored the politics of the environment and the development of environmental knowledge for cultural change in his book, *The Making of Green Knowledge*. In this dissertation I seek to add to this discourse by integrating conceptual tools from complex and critical systems thinking with insights from critical, social epistemology for understanding knowledge for environmental planning and management.

The evolving field of environmental management provides another practice-based field through which to explore the implications of a SEE systems conceptual framework. Already, work in the field of environmental management has highlighted the importance of integrating social and ecological systems for the purposes of environmental decision making (Gunderson et al. 1995; Gunderson and Holling 2002; Mitchell 2002; Berkes and Folke 1998, 2003). As well, some in-roads have been made in the application of complex systems thinking to environmental management (Allen and Hoekstra 1992; Ulanowicz 1997; Kay et al. 1999). And finally, the importance of understanding social learning for environmental decision making has been highlighted (Sinclair and Diduck 2001; Jamison 2001). This provides the opportunity for this dissertation research to further the integration of social learning into an understanding of complex socio-ecological systems through the development of the SEE systems framework.

2.3.3 Governance

Another main field of inquiry and practice in which the linkage among knowledge, learning and intervention in the realm of environmental decision making is prevalent is governance. Governance focuses directly on the political side of the decision making, or knowledge-to-action, equation. Whether referred to as approaches to elements of theory or conceptual themes the governance literature points to a set of key characteristics that define the term. Stoker (1998) described five interrelated propositions of governance theory: reference to a complex set of institutions; identification of the blurring of boundaries and responsibilities for tackling social and economic issues; identification of the power dependence involved in collective action; the importance of autonomous self-governing networks of actors; and, recognition of the capacity to get things done which does not rest exclusively on the power of government to command or use its authority. Rhodes (1996) discusses six uses of the term "governance": minimal state, corporate governance, the new public management, good governance, socio-cybernetic system, self-organizing networks. And Rosenau (1995) describes conceptual themes of governance, which include command and control, interdependence and proliferation, dissaggregation and innovation, and emergence and evolution.

However, all of these overviews from the governance literature speak to a conception of political economy, and more generally decision making and knowledge for intervention, that is more broad-based, flexible and evolving than traditional models of public decision making through govern*ment* intervention. There is also either an implicit or explicit understanding that the political-economic environment is changing fundamentally (not necessarily for the first time) and that the prevalent hierarchical, especially nation-state level forms of governance (e.g. bureaucratic government structures) have become insufficient.

Some literature points to trends that represent a changing style of governance associated with a shift in political-economic regime in response to economic globalization. This shift is from a Fordist to a post-Fordist accumulation regime (Jessop, 1995b) and from a Keynesian welfare state to a more neo-conservative, Schumpeterian workfare/competition state (Cerny, 1997; Jessop, 1993). The term governance (vs. government) has become popularized in reaction to what has been termed the "hollowing out" of the nation-state (Rosenau, 1995). Whereas the activities of governance have traditionally been associated with government and in particular governments of nation-states, the current literature (emanating from several disciplines, including International Relations, Urban Studies, Organizational Behaviour, etc.) broadens the notion of governance beyond that of traditional government.

Insights from the governance literature point to a changing political-economic context for public decision making, and a new context for relating knowledge to intervention. It is one that is rich with opportunities for experimenting with various planning approaches, including communicative or deliberative planning processes in which governance coalitions made up of cross-sectoral groups could engage. It is, however, also rife with uncertainty over, for instance, planning processes becoming co-opted by corporate, consumer-driven interests as opposed to more equitable, civic and citizen-oriented ones (for instance, Jessop, 1993; Cerny, 1997; Fitzgerald, 1997).

Complex systems approaches could provide, and are already providing, governance stakeholders with philosophical and methodological underpinnings and practical heuristics to look critically at the interface of learning and intervention (see for instance, Ulrich, 1987; Kickert, 1993; Jessop, 1995a; Dunsire, 1996; Swyngedow, 2000; Nelson, 2001; White, 2001). While many have argued that the application of natural scientific models, such as autopoiesis, in the social sciences can be hazardous (most notably Varela, 1992), the usefulness of the complexity-based heuristics employed here do "not seem to lie in the strict adherence to the original and literal translation, but rather in their power as a source of creative lateral thinking" (Kickert, 1993: 276).

The governance literature highlights the importance of politics and pluralism in decision making. The literature reviewed here points to the necessity of understanding the political-economic context of decision making and the broader trends that act to constrain decision-making choices. This brings to the fore the need to extend the decision-making community, for instance beyond that of traditional govern*ment,* and integrate the various components into a coherent, efficient and effective whole. While there have been attempts to gain insight into governance as a complex system, the governance literature does little to integrate the complex process of learning into decision making. The field of social learning, however, is meant to address explicitly the process of collective learning for decision making.

2.3.5 Social Learning

The literature on social learning attempts to operationalize many of the complex epistemological issues around the nature of knowledge and the process of learning. Webler et al. (1995) provide an excellent overview of the origins of the concept of social learning, and document the tension within the literature between psychological and sociological views. The psychological or pedagogical perspective on social learning, as represented by Bandura (1971, 1986, 1991), is based on the work of social-psychologist Kurt Lewin and revolves around the individual process being dependent on social interactions. In contrast, the sociological perspective moves beyond individuals learning in a social context to learning within social structures such as organizations or institutions (e.g. Argyris, 1993) or viewing social learning as an expression of coordinated cognitive and normative adjustments resulting in social change (e.g. Wynne, 1992).

Webler et al. (1995) provide a useful starting point for a discussion on the nature and definition of social learning. They note that "social learning means more than merely individuals learning in a social situation ... (they) envision a community of people with diverse personal interests, but also common interests, who must come together to reach agreement on collective action to solve a mutual problem" (Webler et al. 1995: 445). And they define the concept as "the process by which changes in the social condition occur - particularly changes in popular awareness and changes in how individuals see their private interests linked with the shared interests of their fellow citizens" (Webler et al. 1995: 445).

Webler et al. (1995) recognize two general components of social learning, "cognitive enhancement" and "moral development". Cognitive enhancement is the acquisition of knowledge while moral development refers to how individuals come to make decisions about what is right and wrong (Webler et al. 1995). Webler et al.'s (1995) conception of social learning, in this sense, fits nicely with the critical epistemological view of socially embedded view of knowledge creation and learning explored in my dissertation research.

Other work (Sections 2.5.5, 2.5.6, 2.5.7, 2.5.8) grounds the notion of social learning in the field of environmental management (Simon, 2004; Pahl-Wostl and Hare, 2004; Bouwen and Taillieu, 2004; Tippett et al., 2005). Other authors seek to provide the concept of social learning with a critical, reflective philosophical basis (Mezirow, 1994; Mezirow, 1998; Flood and Romm, 1996). Sinclair and Diduck (2001) and Fitzpatrick and Sinclair (2003) have integrated Mezirow's transformative theory of learning into a conception of social learning for environmental management. And finally, Keen et al. (2005) explicitly integrate elements of systems thinking and critical reflection into their conception of social learning in environmental management providing a useful precedent for this work. The SEE systems conceptual framework is intended to provide a complex and critical systems-based perspective on the underlying dynamics of social learning to aid in fostering the process through research and policy interventions.

2.4 Relevant Areas of More Theoretical Research and Scholarship for the Proposed Conceptual Framework

2.4.1 Complex and Critical Systems Thinking

The literature on complex and critical systems thinking provides various approaches to dealing with or embracing complexity. And, as will be demonstrated in this section, systems thinking provides conceptual tools for understanding complexity within a variety of systems: ecological, human institutional, and epistemological or learning. The self-organizing, uncertain, multi-scalar and perspective-dependent nature of complex systems highlights the need to include the observer of the system in any analysis. Critical systems theorists in particular pick up on this need and call for principles such as critical awareness and emancipation or improvement and pluralism as one approach to dealing with the assumptions and biases associated with the knowledge of any system observer (Jackson, 2000; Midgley, 2000). Systems theorists have also developed approaches to understanding the nature of knowledge, conceiving it as a self-organizing process (Maturana and Varela, 1980, 1987; Stacey, 2001; Fuchs, 2004).

2.4.1.1 Complex Systems Thinking

A body of concepts has emerged since the early 1980s that explicitly addresses the complex, uncertain and inherently pluralistic nature of human socio-economic and biophysical systems. The "new science" or "complexity theory" refers to a group of interrelated concepts (catastrophe theory, chaos theory, information theory, hierarchy theory, self-organization theory) that have been developed in several scientific disciplines including chemistry, physics, mathematics, biology and ecology.

It is argued by some theorists that complex systems exist at a threshold between order and chaos, where phenomena are too complex to be treated as machines and too organized to be assumed as random and averaged. Newtonian and stochastic conceptual tools, for the sake of mathematical tractability, seek to eliminate the complexity and uncertainty (by assuming mechanistic linear causality) as well as macro-level order (by assuming chaotic or random distribution) that characterize complex systems. The interrelated ideas about complexity – catastrophe theory (esp. Thom, 1975), chaos theory (esp. Lorenz, 1993; Stewart, 1989), hierarchy theory (esp. Pattee, 1973; Simon, 1973; Allen and Hoekstra, 1992; Ahl and Allen, 1996), and the theories of self-organization (esp. Prigogine and Stengers, 1984; Haken, 1978; Eigen, 1979; Maturana and Varela, 1980, 1987) – do not attempt to reduce the complexity or uncertainty inherent in complex phenomena by either mechanistic, reductionist analysis or statistical aggregation.

The implications of complexity theory are as numerous as the individual interpretations of it. Nevertheless, as a theory, some common themes and heuristics have been highlighted in, for instance the discipline of ecology and the field of environmental management (see examples including Ulanowicz, 1997; Holling, 2001). These heuristics are described briefly below and are illustrated through a discussion of Holling's model of ecosystem dynamics (Section 2.5.3). In spite of the powerful insights from this type of interpretation of the implications of complex systems thinking, it appears to miss the broader philosophical implications that, for instance, autopoiesis (esp. Maturana and Varela, 1980, 1987) and critical systems theory (esp. Jackson, 2000; Midgley, 2000) highlight.

Complex systems *thinking*, for the purposes of this work, can be defined as a mode of reasoning that has emerged from the formal complex systems *theory* (as previously noted, actually a set of interrelated concepts, some of which have also been called theories) and applied to the study of a variety of phenomena in a number of disciplines or interdisciplinary fields. My understanding of complex systems thinking has come to include, not only the properties and heuristics noted below, but also a critical realist, process-oriented philosophy with methodological pluralism. On an operational level, a set of principles for the practice of intervention reflects a process-oriented relationship between knowledge and intervention.

Properties of Complex Systems

Listed below are several of the key properties of complex systems. From these properties, several key heuristics can be gleaned:

Properties of Complex Systems

- Non-Linear: Behave as whole, a system. Cannot be understood by decomposing into pieces which are added or multiplied together.
- Hierarchical: Are hierarchically nested. The "control" exercised by a specific level always involves a balance of internal or self-control and external, shared, reciprocating controls involving other hierarchic levels in a mutual causal way that transcends the old selfish–altruistic polarizing designations. Such nestings cannot be understood by focusing on one hierarchical level (holon) alone. Understanding comes from multiple perspectives of different types and scales.
- Internal Causality: Non-Newtonian, not a mechanism, but rather is self-organizing. Characterized by goals, positive and negative feedback, emergent properties and surprise.
- Window of Vitality: Must have enough complexity but not too much. There is a range within which self-organization can occur. Complex systems strive for optimum, not minimum or maximum.
- Dynamically Stable: There may not exist equilibrium points for the system.

- Multiple Steady States: There is not necessarily a unique preferred system state in a given situation. Multiple attractors can be possible in a given situation and the current system state may be as much a function of historical accidents as anything else.
- Catastrophic Behaviour: Is the norm.
  - Bifurcations: Moments of unpredictable behaviour.
  - Flips: Sudden discontinuity.
  - Holling four-box cycle: Shifting steady state mosaic.
- Chaotic Behaviour: Our ability to forecast and predict is always limited, for example to about five days for weather forecasts, regardless of how sophisticated our computers are and how much information we have.

(Kay et al., 1999: 23)

In subsequent sections (Sections 2.4.1, 2.5.2, 2.5.3, 2.5.4, 2.5.10), the implications of these properties of complex systems will be explained for ecological, socio-ecological and also to learning or epistemological systems.

2.4.1.2 Autopoiesis

Maturana and Varela's (1980) theory of autopoiesis (self-creation) was originally developed as a theory of living systems, essentially exploring the qualifying factors of life itself. Maturana notes that the origins of the notion of autopoiesis can be traced back to 1960, when a first year medical student asked the question, "what began three thousand eight hundred million years ago so that you can say now that living systems began then?". Beyond this seemingly fundamental question, Maturana and Varela's work goes on to address interrelated questions regarding the nature of reality (ontology) as we as humans experience it and the implications for knowledge and learning (epistemology) given that relationship. Maturana and Varela (1987: 78-79) defined the process of autopoiesis through a definition of "living machines":

> an autopoietic machine is a machine organised (defined as a unity) as a network of processes of production (transformation and destruction) of components that produce the components which: (i) through their interactions and transformations continuously regenerate and realise the network of processes (relations) that produce them; and (ii) constitute it (the machine) as a concrete unity in the space which they (the components) exist by specifying the topological domain of its realisation as such a network.

Thus, it is the organization of an autopoietic system that defines it as such. Its structure or its bits and pieces are the result of its organization. Varela (1992:5) clarifies this by stating, "the autopoietic mechanism will maintain itself as a distinct unity as long as its basic concatenation [chain] of processes is kept intact in the face of perturbations, and will disappear when confronted with perturbations that go beyond a certain verifiable range which depends on the specific system considered". It is through these self-creating processes and boundaries that the autopoietic entity "self-separates" from its environment, "the living system must distinguish itself from its environment, while at the same time, maintaining its coupling; this linkage cannot be detached since it is against the very environment from which the organism arises" (Varela, 1992: 7). Thus, autopoietic systems are structurally open but organizationally closed.

While autopoietic systems must maintain their organizational closure in order to maintain their identity, they must also maintain a relationship with their environment. Maturana and Varela (1980, 1987) describe this necessary interaction as structural coupling. Maturana (Draft Manuscript: 13) describes two types of structural change that autopoietic systems can undergo:

- Structural changes through which the organization of the changing system is conserved; Maturana refers to these as changes of state
- Structural changes through which the organization of the structurally changing system is lost, not conserved; he refers to these as disintegrative changes

Structural coupling is described by Maturana (Draft Manuscript: 13) as a process in which

> the structure of the living system and the structure of the medium change together congruently as a matter of course, and the general result is that the history of interactions between two or more structures becomes a history of spontaneous recursive coherent structural changes in which all the participant systems change together congruently until they separate or disintegrate

The typical examples used by Maturana and Varela are the idea of a foot in a shoe mutually adjusting to fit each other, or the frog's eye being the evolutionary result of the structural coupling of the frog and its environment (a frog can only see things in motion and it only eats what it can see). Thus, structural coupling is a process whereby the structure of the system and the environment both change or co-evolve as the result of iterative, mutual, non-destructive changes. Autopoietic theory and its tenets such as structural coupling have compelling implications for our understanding of ecological, social and even knowledge systems. While an autopoietic view of physical and cognitive structural coupling may imply a measure of biological determinism, it is not the intent of this work to promote such a perspective.

It is appropriate here to highlight the field of socio-cybernetics and the work of Luhmann (1984). Luhmann's autopoietic-based Social Systems Theory and his focus on reflexivity in communication systems have provided insight into how communication systems or communities (Connell, 2003) self organize in relation to other systems. He describes the process of communication as social structural coupling between two autopoietic systems.

It is the philosophical implications of applying an autopoietic perspective to cognition and the process of knowledge generation itself that are, for the purposes of this work, most compelling. Should we view ourselves as autopoietic systems, biological, cognitive beings, interacting and structurally coupling with complex environments? If we are, the nature of inquiry into complex systems and more broadly, the process of knowledge generation, change fundamentally. While the physical structures that emerge from the process of structural coupling (eyes for instance) remain relatively fixed and consistent across humans, cognitive and even social structures that emerge through the process of structural coupling can be more fluid. The dynamic tension between physical structural coupling (through physical senses and measurement) and interpretive or cognitive structures result in the emergence of a plurality of perspectives.

Knowledge does not, of course, emerge in a vacuum and, aside from physical constraints there are social or institutional constraints on how knowledge emerges. It is here that the work of Anthony Giddens (1984) and his structuration theory have been instrumental in understanding how individual agents' knowledge emerges in dynamic tension with social structures (Section 2.4.2.4). As well, the work of Steve Fuller on social epistemology has contributed to the view of knowledge emerging in a social context (Section 4.3.1). It is also helpful to note that Jackson (2000) and Midgley (2000) have developed a systems-based approach that provides a logical extension for exploring the philosophical implications of autopoietic theory for action or intervention.

2.4.1.3 Critical Systems Thinking

Critical systems thinking has emerged from what Jackson (2000) calls "emancipatory" and "post-modern" systems approaches and what Midgley (2000) calls the "third wave" of systems thinking. Jackson (2000) notes that critical systems thinking has three main tenets or "commitments": critical awareness, emancipation or improvement, and pluralism.

Critical Awareness, according to Jackson (2000), involves both theoretical critique and social awareness. First, what I have labeled theoretical critique, Jackson (2000: 375) describes as "critiquing the theoretical underpinnings, strengths and weaknesses of available systems models, tools and techniques". And secondly, Jackson highlights the need to contextualize this critique with an understanding of social awareness, a grasp "of the organizational and societal climate which determines the popularity of use of particular systems approaches at different times, and the kind of impact that use has" (Jackson, 2000: 375-376).

The second commitment of critical systems thinking is improvement or emancipation. Jackson (2000) sees this tenet of critical systems thinking as "part of a much broader dedication to human improvement – defined ... in terms of bringing about those circumstances in which all individuals could realize their potential" (Jackson, 2000: 376). Jackson notes that critical systems thinkers realize that a universal notion of emancipation is untenable and somewhat contrary to the post-modern bases of critical systems thinking. Instead, the less universal notion of improvement (Midgley, 2000) is presented and linked to critical awareness and pluralism.

This leads to the third tenet of critical systems thinking, pluralism. Jackson (2000: 365) interprets pluralism "in the broadest sense as the use of different methodologies, methods, models and techniques in combination". He notes three reasons for the recent interest in, and need for, a more pluralist approach. The first is that a great deal of critique has been undertaken of many scientific disciplines and older notions of single, totalizing approaches. The second reason for the increased interest in pluralism is the pervasive resonance with relativism that preceded, but is generally associated with, post-modernism. And thirdly, Jackson notes, quite pragmatically, that pluralism just seems to be necessary. "It is inevitable that practitioners will try to buttress traditional approaches with some of the newer thinking" (Jackson, 2000: 377).

Midgley (2000) also discusses a version of critical systems thinking not unlike Jackson's. However, Midgley focuses on the notion of boundary critique or boundary judgments, which relate to a process of knowledge creation or learning (Section 2.7.2.2). However, for the purposes of this brief overview, Midgley (2000) describes two foundations for critical systems thinking, what I refer to as critical reflection and methodological pluralism. Critical reflection, much like Jackson's "critical awareness", points to the "need to be critical of the value and boundary judgments made by planners. Those involved in and affected by planning are encouraged to reach agreement on key assumptions upon which planning ought to be based" (Midgley, 2000: 205). The other cornerstone of critical systems theory for Midgley is methodological pluralism (Section 4.3.2). What the reader should take from this overview of critical systems thinking are two key interrelated themes: critical reflection of assumptions (reflexivity), and methodological pluralism albeit in service of some notion of improvement or emancipation.

Complex and critical systems thinking provides a unique set of conceptual tools or heuristics for understanding the dynamics and tight interrelationships between social and ecological systems. And it has also led some scholars to a provocative set of questions about the nature and role of science and, more generally, knowledge in socio-ecological systems (Maturana and Varela, 1980, 1987; Jackson 2000; Midgley 2000,). Complex systems thinking is the entry point utilized in this dissertation into questions about the nature and role of knowledge for environmental decision making. It is the potential of its heuristics to explicate the nature of knowledge and its role in environmental decision making that have drawn me to it.

2.4.1.4 Complex and Critical Systems Thinking and Knowledge for Environmental Planning and Decision Making

"Whenever we want to compel somebody else to do something according to our wishes, and we cannot or do not want to use brutal force, we offer what we claim is an objective rational argument. We do this under the implicit or explicit pretense that the other cannot refuse what our argument claims because its validity as such rests on its reference to the 'real'" (Maturana, 1988: 26). The problem, it would seem, appears to be that if we follow the logic of complex systems thinking, and particularly autopoietic theory (Section 2.4.1.2), the objective, rational perspective resulting from the subject-object dualism allows for the autonomous, autopoietic observer but denies the corollary of congruent, mutual change or structural coupling between the observer and the observed (system and environment). In a 1978 work on autopoiesis and cognition, Maturana (1988:28) addressed this very issue and began to reconceptualize the relationship between the observer and the observed, viewing cognition as a biological phenomenon.

> That we cognate seems to us self-evident. In the very process of doing what I am doing, cognition appears to me as my immediate experience ... The cognito ergo sum of Decartes grasps this and gives to the experience of knowledge a central role: the cognato, the act of cognition, is for Descartes the starting point. Or, in other words, cognition is a human property and no question arises about cognition as a phenomenon.

Instead, Maturana (1988) would prefer to pose the question, "what kind of biological phenomenon is the phenomenon of cognition?". Maturana's reconceptualization of cognition as a biological, autopoietic phenomenon has profound philosophical implications for science and science for policy making. Cognition, as Maturana (Draft Manuscript: 23) defines it is, "the capacity that a living system exhibits of operating in dynamic structural congruence with the medium in which it exists". In this sense, according to Maturana, whether we are talking about instinctive (phylogenic) knowledge or learned (ontogenic) knowledge, it is acquired through the process of structural coupling. Just as autopoietic systems are organizationally closed but structurally couple with their environment, so too, it would seem, the autopoietic, observing, human being, is structurally coupled to what it might be observing in its environment.

We as biological, autopoietic beings do not experience reality (either the physical or the mental). Or, to use Kant's distinction between the noumena (things in themselves) and phenomena (appearances of things as they are presented by our senses), we do not experience the noumena (realism). We only experience the phenomena that our autopoietic structures provide us access to. What we experience is the result of centuries of congruent change with our environment, resulting in specific sensory and cognitive structures, as well as years of individual cognitive coupling, that allow us to maintain our organization.

Maturana and Varela (1987) reason that biology shows us the uniqueness of being human lies in what they refer to as a "social structural coupling" which they, in a similar fashion to many post-modern thinkers, argue occurs through language. They explain that social structural coupling generates two key responses: 1) the regularities appropriate to the human social dynamics, for example, individual identity and self-consciousness, and 2) the recursive social human dynamics that entail a reflection, enabling us to see that as human beings we have only the world which we create with others - whether we like them or not (Maturana and Varela, 1987: 246). Knowledge is generated through the experience of being (various forms of structural coupling) but is always demonstrated to others in a relational context. That is, knowledge can be seen to be demonstrated whenever we observe an effective (or adequate) behavior in a given context. In other words, any act of being that preserves a system's organization and conserves structural coupling demonstrates knowledge (Maturana and Varela, 1987). Thus, an autopoietic view of knowledge calls into question the notion of objectivity.

Instead of relying on and giving primacy to hard scientific knowledge in decision-making processes, an autopoietic view of knowledge requires an explicit, critical reflection on knowledge and its use in decision making. It can also lead an observer to turn that view of complexity back upon the process of her own observation, back upon her own understanding of how she creates the knowledge of the systems she is observing. It is this view of the pervasiveness of complexity that has led some systems thinkers to espouse a critical view of their thinking, of systems thinking. Utilizing the work of Habermas and Foucault, systems thinkers such as Jackson (2000) and Midgley (2000) have developed different approaches to critical systems thinking. As previously discussed, critical systems thinking has three key principles: critical awareness of one's theoretical assumptions and of the social context in which the observer is developing and utilizing them; pluralism of both method and perspectives; and, emancipation or improvement, that is to say that individuals should be able to work towards their potentials.

2.4.2 Critical, Social Epistemology

Epistemology is one of the core areas of philosophy and is concerned with the nature, sources and limits of knowledge. Therefore, a discussion of epistemology is especially salient in the context of this research on the nature of knowledge for social learning in environmental planning and policy making. While I cannot address the full breadth and complexity of this philosophical discipline, it is helpful to situate my work generally within the main traditions of the field, and acknowledge the influence of key philosophers.

The traditional empirical interpretation of epistemology (e.g., Hume and Locke) holds that knowledge is gained through sensory exploration and experimentation. Traditional rationalism (e.g., Descartes, Leibniz and Spinoza) holds that much of knowledge comes from rational intuition and *a priori* conceptualization. Rather than viewing knowledge or learning as either innate or empirically objective, I embrace a view of knowledge creation as a human and socially-embedded process. This is discussed below with reference to Jurgen Habermas' and Michel Foucault's critical theory, Anthony Giddens' structuration theory, Bent Flyvbjerg's typology of knowledge and Steve Fuller's social epistemology.

2.4.2.1 Critical Theory

The epistemological underpinnings for much of the work that has informed this dissertation came from Jurgen Habermas and Michel Foucault. It is well beyond the scope of this dissertation to cover the evolution of critical theory in the works of either Habermas or Foucault. I would, however, be remiss not to acknowledge the influence of their collective work in this discourse on the nature of knowledge for environmental decision and policy making.

The influence of the Frankfurt School and its most influential thinker Habermas (1973 and 1984) on this work should not be understated. In his encyclopedic work on critical systems thinking, Jackson (2000) directly incorporates the work of Habermas and his three human interests and three types of knowledge as the underlying principles of critical systems thinking. More specifically, Habermas's attempts to distinguish an emancipatory interest for knowledge development have provided some of the philosophical basis for Steve Fuller's (2002) work on social epistemology and Tim Forsyth's (2003) critical political ecology.

According to Habermas, three fundamental cognitive interests drive attempts to acquire knowledge: technical, practical, and emancipatory. He links these human interests to three types of knowledge. Tied to the technical interest are what Habermas referred to as the "empirical analytical" sciences. The knowledge produced by these sciences is objective, law-like hypotheses based on observable events. Historical hermeneutic sciences produce knowledge about meanings and understandings of intersubjective or mutual understanding among humans. This is the practical interest. Finally, tied to the emancipatory human interest are the critical sciences. The critical sciences recognize the inherent limitations of the other two sciences and the dangers of acting on embedded assumptions. Critical scientists attempt to synthesize and evaluate knowledge by providing tools for self-evaluation or self-reflection to allow people to liberate themselves from the limitations caused by their assumptions (Habermas, 1973, 1984; Jackson 2002). This categorization of knowledges parallels an Aristotelian typology of knowledge referenced by Flyvbjerg (2001) (Section 2.4.2.3). These three types of knowledge, as evidence from the case studies will demonstrate, are critical to fostering social learning within environmental planning and policy processes.

Michel Foucault's discourse on power and the role of knowledge in decision making has also been influential on critical theory and disciplinary descendants such as critical political ecology and social epistemology. In an historic view of the "Art of

Government", Foucault (2000) describes three fundamental types of government, each relating to a particular science or discipline. The art of self-government is connected to morality; the art of properly governing a family is associated with economics; and, the science of ruling the state is connected to political science. Foucault's typology of knowledge provides a more cross-scalar view of decision making than that of Habermas. While they both highlight three similar types of knowledge, Foucault describes the nested nature of knowledge for decision making from the individual agent to the state. Foucault's (2000) conception of knowledge for governance also explicitly highlights the moral and political facets of decision making. A conceptual model of social learning will be presented (Section 3.2) based on an integration of critical systems thinking (Jackson, 2000; Midgley, 2000), Gidden's (1984) structuration theory and Flyvbjerg's (2001) Aristotelian typology of knowledge.

2.4.2.2 Structuration Theory

Anthony Gidden's (1984) theory of structuration explicitly addresses the relationship between individuals (agents) and institutions that constrain and/or facilitate them (structure). Giddens' work focuses attention on the role of knowledge and the issue of power within social systems. Structuration is a theory of social systems that sets neither the individual actor nor the existence of a societal totality as more real. Instead, Giddens (1984: 2) argues that human social structures are self reproducing and recursive in that they are not brought into being by individual actors but are continually recreated through repeated behaviours and decisions. That is, agents continuously recreate social structures through their actions and this process of structuration allows for the continuation or reproduction of social activities. Structure or "structural properties" are the rule systems by which individuals organize themselves. They are "instantiations" of the repeated practices that orient the conduct of knowledgeable human agents (Giddens, 1984:17). The time-space extent of such "structures" or structural properties varies. The most extensive or pervasive structural properties are referred to by Giddens (1984:17) as "structural principles" and are usually associated with the behaviour of social institutions.

Giddens' structuration theory provides a view of social systems that acknowledges both the action and knowledge of the individual agent as well as the existence of social institutions and the knowledge embedded in "structural principles". It explicitly acknowledges that the rules or structural properties individuals recreate and live by express forms of domination and power. Given this, Giddens' (1984: 18) theory can empower the individual agent but also acknowledges his/her responsibility and contribution to the continuous recreation of the structural properties and institutions that can act to constrain him/her.

In Giddens' view of social systems, knowledge resides in both the individual agent and also in structural properties. Giddens argues that knowledge creation is tightly coupled with the relationship between human agents and social structure. He states that "all human agents know a great deal about the conditions of their activity, that knowledge being not contingent upon what they do, but constitutive of it" (Giddens, 1996: 69). Therefore, he concludes our knowledge is always bounded institutionally by the structural constraints we constantly recreate. It is the role of the social sciences, Giddens (1996: 69) argues, to reflect upon these boundaries and give discursive form to what we already know but cannot necessarily describe. It is the role of the researcher studying social systems to explore the dynamic, dialectical (two-way, mutually reinforcing) relationship among the individual and social structure, the knowledge created, and the assumptions embedded in a given social structure.

Giddens' (1984) Structuration Theory points to an innovative perspective on the concept of social learning. Giddens' notion of a dialectic tension between individual agents and social structures speaks to a complex emergence of learning on an organizational or social level as well as at the individual level. The work of Bent Flyvberg provides a loose typology of knowledge necessary for social learning.

2.4.2.3 Phronetic Social Science

In his discourse on the "science wars", Flyvberg (2001) describes how to make social science "matter" by providing an alternative approach to emulating the natural sciences' "episteme" or epistemic knowledge. Flyvberg (2001: 55-56) invokes the Aristotelian distinction among three intellectual virtues: "episteme", "techne" and "phronesis".

- *Episteme* – Scientific knowledge. Universal, invariable, context-independent. Based on general analytical rationality. The original concept is known today from the terms "epistemology" and "epistemic".
- *Techne* – Craft/Art. Pragmatic, variable, context-dependent. Oriented toward production. Based on practical instrumental rationality governed by a conscious goal. The original concept appears today in terms such as "technique", "technical" and "technology".
- *Phronesis* – Ethics. Deliberation about values with reference to praxis (practical application of theory). Pragmatic, variable, context-dependent. Oriented toward action. Based on practical value rationality. The original concept has no analogous contemporary term.

The goal of the natural sciences, Flyvbjerg argues, is to develop epistemic knowledge that is, universal, invariable, context-independent knowledge. His argument is that the social sciences have erroneously been attempting to emulate the natural to develop "epistemic" knowledge when the real strength of the social sciences is the development of "phronetic" knowledge. He argues that to require social science to attempt to develop universal explanations of social phenomena or develop predictions of social dynamics is an impossible task. Phronetic social science, in contrast, "requires an interaction between the general and the concrete; it requires consideration, judgment and choice" (Flyvbjerg, 2001: 57). Social science, Flyvbjerg argues, should play to its strengths by exploring phronetic research questions such as "where are we going?", "is this desirable?", "what should be done?" and "who gains and who loses?".

Delanty (2002) contrasts Flyvbjerg's conception of phronetic social science with Wagner's (2001) "Theorizing Modernity" and Nowotny et al.'s (2001) "Knowledge and the Public in an Age of Uncertainty". All of these works describe recent trends in the social sciences toward more communicative and reflexive thinking. Delanty (2002) notes that Notwotny et al.'s (2001) and Wagner's (2001) works more directly address epistemological issues, while Flyvbjerg focuses on the methodological and redirects his discussion specifically to issues of power. Solesbury (2002), in his review of Flyvbjerg's work, argues that how social science gets used is not addressed in Flyvbjerg's work and from a phronetic view this should be addressed.

Flyvbjerg's use of a three-part typology of knowledge, based on the Aristotelian intellectual principles, appears to resonate strongly with the experiences in both case studies (Sections 4.4.3 and 4.5.3). Based on insights from the case studies, there appears to be great utility in highlighting the relative importance of knowledge pertaining to power relations, ethics and normative issues.

2.4.2.4 Social Epistemology

Fuller (2002a: ix) defines social epistemology as an intellectual trans-disciplinary movement that attempts to reconstruct the problematique of epistemology once knowledge creation is regarded as a socially-embedded process. The fundamental question posed by Fuller's (2002a: 3) social epistemology is:

> how should the pursuit of knowledge be organized, given that under normal circumstances knowledge is pursued by many human beings, each working on a more or less well-defined body of knowledge and each equipped with the same imperfect cognitive capacities, albeit with varying degrees of access to one another's activities?

Fuller's question places the development of knowledge firmly in a social context. Even "objective", value-free science as a knowledge pursuit is not immune to its social context. "Scientific thinking consists of rhetoric; which is to say, of attempts to influence other scientists to take one's argument seriously" (McCloskey, 1987: 73). Science, as with other knowledge, evolves in a human, social context. It has been argued that scientific paradigms maintain their status and power by producing rhetoric that manipulates the historical record so that it appears that the current paradigm is the logical outcome of scientific inquiry up to that point (Fuller 2002a). Fuller's claim explicitly links knowledge creation and power. He argues that the granting of "epistemic warrant" is a covert form of distributing power (Fuller, 2002a: 10). Fuller clarifies this statement however, noting that the former (granting epistemic warrant) is not *identical* to the latter (distributing power). Instead, he argues that granting epistemic warrant "has the effect of" distributing power (Fuller, 2002a: 12). This perspective allows for such provocative questions as who are the groups that developed the knowledge claim, who are the groups that are benefiting from the knowledge claim's acceptance, and who are the groups that can build on this acceptance to further their own knowledge claims?

While the notion that the development of knowledge is a socially-embedded process and has explicit implications for power distribution is not new (Foucault, 2000), what is new and highly relevant to this dissertation is Fuller's (2002b) use of this perspective to critique knowledge management. His book, *Knowledge Management Foundations*, addresses what the management mentality does to knowledge and not *vice versa*. Fuller (2002b) focuses on the tension and power relations between knowledge workers and knowledge managers. He notes that the challenge of knowledge management, that is, the necessity for knowledge producers to justify themselves, should be welcomed. Fuller's (2002a, 2002b) work, which socially embeds the process of knowledge creation and links it explicitly with human power relations, underlies the perspective on environmental knowledge creation developed in this dissertation.

2.4.2.5 Critical, Social Epistemology and Learning for Environmental Planning and Decision Making

Taken together, the works of Giddens (1984), Flyvbjerg (2001) and Fuller (2002a, 2002b) emphasize the need for a critical, socially-embedded view of knowledge. Giddens describes social systems and the knowledge creation process as a tension between individual knowledge and institutionalized knowledge. Flyvbjerg's typology of knowledge highlights the significance of epistemic (scientific) and technical knowledge, but also the importance of phronetic or political or ethical knowledge. If one sets this loose typology of knowledge within Giddens' dialectic tension between the individual agent and institutions or structures, one can see how individual technical and phronetic knowledge feed into the development of epistemic or institutionalized scientific knowledge and how this would then feedback, providing structure for and influencing power relations between individual agents. Fuller's work on social epistemology can be utilized to describe the whole dialectic process as socially-embedded and to emphasize the importance of phronetic knowledge in relation to technical and epistemic for providing a critique of knowledge systems.

2.5 Areas of Thematic Overlap Among Components of the Proposed Framework

2.5.1 Planning and Critical Social Epistemology

2.5.1.1 Collaborative Planning

Collaborative planning brings together the concepts of power, equity and quality of process in the discipline of planning. One name synonymous with collaborative planning is Patsy Healy. Her seminal work, *Collaborative Planning: Shaping Places in Fragmented Societies* (Healy, 1997), was based on her research on the role of planning policies on development in 1980s neo-conservative, Thatcherite England. The political climate of the day was "inherently hostile to the idea of planning and of managing land and property markets to achieve wider economic, social and environmental goals" (Healy, 2003: 102).

While many have concluded that the work of Habermas underlies Healy's collaborative planning, Healy herself argues it is the work of Anthony Giddens on structure and agency that most closely resonated with her practical experience (Healy, 2003: 106). Giddens' work provided Healy with a framework for situating the work of participants in planning or governance within a process through which institutional structures and processes are continuously formed (structuration). Giddens' work focused attention on the quality of interactions and relations within this process. In the early 1980s, at the height of Thatcherian neo-conservatism, the need for a critical evaluative framework to assess the interactive qualities of processes became urgent as governments came under pressure to restructure their systems and practices in the name of efficiency and financial accountability (Healy 2003: 106). In her approach to "understanding and evaluating governance processes, and especially those that focus on developing qualities of place and territory" (Healy 2003: 107), she identifies two lines of critique about collaborative planning. First, it focuses too much on agency and not enough on broader structuring forces. Second, collaborative planning is really an unachievable ideal, given issues of power and quality of process in planning and decision making. This dissertation strives to extend this pluralistic, Giddensian approach to planning to integrate explicitly a complex systems and socially-embedded view of knowledge creation into the focus of planning.

2.5.1.2 Critical Planning – the "Dark Side"

Inspired by the work of Michel Foucault (1977, 1980), a group of planning theorists has explored the implications of critical theory for planning (Boyer, 1983; Huxley, 1994a; Huxley, 1994b; Allen, 1996; Lewi, 1996), and especially Yiftachel (1998) and Flyvbjerg (2001). Yiftachel (1998) illuminated the "dark side" of the theory and practice of planning. He describes planning as a tool of "social control" (Yiftachel 1998: 400) that represents a paradox in that planning was introduced to assist in social reform and to improve society's quality of life but can also be used to repress peripheral groups. Yiftachel (1998: 401) argues that urban and regional planning is a key tool in the imposition of control and oppression of the "other", but concludes that planners often avoid examining this problem. He explores four dimensions of control exercised by planning: the territorial (spatial), the procedural (power relations and decision making), the socioeconomic (long-term material consequences), and the cultural (its repercussions on identities and ways of life and thinking) (Yiftachel 1998: 401). The implications for planning are that its theorists and practitioners should reevaluate their conceptualizations of planning to view it as a double-edged endeavour, having both positive and negative as well as intended and unintended consequences. Yiftachel's work explicitly links critical theory and issues of power to the issues and practice of land use planning.

2.5.2 Planning and Complex Systems Thinking

2.5.2.1 Collaborative Planning and Complex Adaptive Systems

It would be remiss not to mention the work of Judith Innes in the context of complex systems-based approaches to planning and governance. Innes' work brings insights from complex systems thinking and Habermas' communicative rationality to the research and practice of consensus building (Innes and Booher, 1999; Connick and Innes, 2003; Innes, 2004).

Consensus building, a broad term used for many types of collaborative efforts, is best understood as an *ad hoc* and self-organizing process, embedded within a complex evolving system (Connick and Innes, 2003). Innes sets this complex, adaptive systems-based world view to contrast it with a mechanistic view that, she argues, underlies the "modernist paradigm of governance in the USA" (Connick and Innes, 2003: 179). Innes has argued that a mechanistic view assumes a level of predictability, predicated on adequate information and expertise that will lead to policies, programs and regulations to meet social objectives and produce desired outcomes (Connick and Innes, 2003: 179). Innes asserts that the assumptions embedded in a mechanistic view of planning and governance systems are "a poor match with reality" (Connick and Innes, 2003). She concludes that a complexity-based view of collaborative planning and governance systems leads to policy making that is adaptive, innovative and intelligent (Connick and Innes, 2003: 180).

Innes' work bears a striking resemblance to Habermasian communicative rationality. Habermas' communicative rationality is an idealized process of knowledge creation in which a kind of truth emerges as interests engage in dialogue, undistorted by power and information disparities and where assumptions are challenged (Innes, 2004: 10). While Innes concedes that communicative rationality does provide an appropriate epistemological and ethical underpinning to consensus building, she clearly states that unlike communicative rationality, consensus building is neither an epistemological view nor an ideal process (Innes 2004).

Innes' work provides an innovative synthesis of complexity-based thinking, empirical research and Habermasian epistemology. Her work addresses the practical need for a planning and decision-making process that acknowledges the "speed of technological and social change, the fragmentation of power, and the juxtaposition of more and more conflicting values and views in public life" (Innes 2004: 16). Innes highlights the need to alter our view of decision-making systems from mechanistic to complex and adaptive.

2.5.3 Environmental Management and Complex Systems Thinking

2.5.3.1 Integrated Environmental Management

In his work on integrated and adaptive environmental management, Mitchell (1997, 2004) describes two key themes in natural resource management: uncertainty and conflict. As will be noted in the case study for this dissertation, these arise from complexity and inherent indeterminacies as well as the implications (often taking the form of conflict) of change and fundamentally different perspectives on the issues involved in environmental decision making. Mitchell (2004: vii) characterizes the problematique of resource management as "different understandings, values, interests, and contexts lead to varying preferences regarding goals and objectives, alternative interpretations of information and evidence, and various ideas regarding appropriate strategies and actions". This acknowledges the complexity and uncertainty of socio-environmental issues, and acknowledges that rarely are there adequate solutions to the complex problems of environmental management. Instead, as Mitchell concludes, we must decide among a suite of imperfect responses. Several of the chapters in his most recent volume explicitly address a number of the themes of this dissertation, including governance (Dorcey, 2004) and complexity and an ecosystem approach (Slocombe, 2004). However, the notion that learning and social learning should be explicitly addressed as part of the system of interest is something this dissertation work adds to the discourse on environmental decision making and governance.

2.5.3.2 Ecosystem Dynamics

Holling's conceptual model has been influential in changing how ecologists and environmental managers view the dynamics of ecosystems (Holling, 1973; Holling, 1978; Holling, 1995; Gunderson and Holling, 2002). Incorporating both Clementsian linear succession as well as Gleasonian independent, species-level behaviour, Holling integrates these into a complexity-based model utilizing insights from catastrophe theory, chaos theory and self-organization theory. Holling et al. (1995, 2001) have documented evidence of these "figure-eight" dynamics in various types of social and ecological contexts and noted their implications for resource management.

The four-phase dynamic is an example of self-organization within a complex, open system. Based on the work of Ilya Prigogine, James J. Kay (Kay, 1991; Kay, 1993; Kay, 1994; Boyle et al., 1996; Kay et al., 2002) has described ecosystems as large "dissipative structures" similar to, but far more complex than, the vortex that self-organizes in any bathtub as it empties. Ecosystems dissipate energy gradients with the spontaneous emergence of macro-level organization typified by the Holling figure-eight model. These self-organizing systems can also be characterized by abrupt changes or "flips" between the domains of "attractors".

The exploitation- and conservation-phases can be seen as attractors. Events such as fire, storm or pest outbreaks can be seen as "natural" bifurcation points between attractors. The cycle itself can also be seen as an attractor. If the context of the ecosystem is altered in any way (i.e. a change in the amount or quality of energy, nutrients or in species diversity – information), the system may "flip" into the domain of another, equally viable attractor, in this case another Holling loop (with a different type of "climax" community). In this sense, there is no attractor or system-state that can *a priori*, especially without consideration of the system context, be described as objectively "preferred". And while prediction of system states, even qualitative or very limited quantitative ones about the behaviour of a system around a single attractor, are possible and can be very useful, Schneider and Kay (1994: 14) indicate that,

> the form of expression this self-organization takes on is not predictable in advance because the very process of self-organization is by catastrophic (in the catastrophe theory sense) change ... (that is) systems may have several possible behavioural pathways available at a catastrophe threshold.

Although quantitative predictions are possible over a very limited range, long-term quantitative predictions about the behaviour of ecological systems are impossible. Ecosystems in this sense can be seen as self-organizing entities, existing at "the edge of chaos", "in a middle ground of enough, but not too much" order (Schneider and Kay, 1994: 35) or in a dynamic tension between order and disorder. Holling's work describing ecological systems as complex and self-organizing has had profound implications for environmental management and planning, highlighting the co-evolutionary nature of human social (institutions) and ecological systems.

2.5.3.3 Complex Socio-Ecological Systems

The work of Holling et al. (1995, 2002) in books such as *Barriers and Bridges* and *Panarchy* describes not only the complex dynamics of ecological systems but also the complexity and self-organization of the human institutional systems coupled with them. Examples of the integrated and co-evolutionary nature of social and ecological (socio-ecological) systems are explored through examples in the Great Lakes, Chesapeake Bay and the Florida Everglades (Gunderson et al. 1995). And the implications of the figure-eight model for ecosystem dynamics are further explored in *Panarchy* (2002), where Gunderson and Holling (2002) again engage the paradoxes of environmental resource management. They conclude that new and innovative policies may eventually lead to myopic and rigid institutions meant to uphold and defend the status quo. The authors also illustrate how expert advice can often lead to crisis and political gridlock (Holling et al., 2002).

2.5.3.4 Self-Organizing, Holarchic, Open (SOHO) Systems and Ecological Integrity

Kay et al. (1999) characterize SOHO systems descriptions as scenarios of how a self-organizing, holarchic, open system might evolve. These scenarios include the following components:

- The human context for the narrative
- The hierachical/holonarchic nature of the system
- The attractors which may be accessible to the system
- How the system behaves in the neighbourhood of each attractor
- The positive and negative feedbacks and self-reinforcing loops and associated gradients which organize the system about an attractor
- What might enable and disable these loops and hence might promote or discourage the system from being in the neighbourhood of an attractor; and
- What might be likely to precipitate flips between attractors

(Kay et al,. 1999: 8).

SOHO scenarios are intended to inform decision and policy makers about:

- Possible future states of organization of the system
- Understanding of conditions under which these states might occur
- Understanding of the tradeoffs which the different states represent
- Appropriate schemes for ensuring the ability to adapt to different situations
- Appropriate level of confidence that the scenario deserves, that is, the degree of uncertainty

(Kay et al., 1999: 8-9).

There are no unique or correct perspectives on self-organizing phenomena. Rather, a diversity of perspectives is required to develop a SOHO systems description (Kay et al., 1999). From a self-organizing perspective, the properties of uncertainty and emergence limit our capacity to predict how a situation will unfold. Generally, it is not possible to construct an objective, accurate quantitative model to forecast the future of a system (Kay et al., 1999).

Kay et al. (1999) provide an innovative protocol for describing the structures and dynamics of complex socio-ecological systems while emphasizing the perspective and context dependence. However, the SOHO description, as described above, does not explicitly integrate the production of knowledge or the associated influence of power relations.

Aside from integrating insights from non-linear thermodynamics into understanding ecosystems, there are provocative questions about how to engage or "embrace" the complexity of ecological systems in environmental decision making (Kay, 1984, 1991; Kay et al., 1999; Mánuel-Navarrete et al., 2002). The concept of "ecological integrity" integrates the concepts of ecosystem health and resilience as well as an understanding of ecosystems as self-organizing entities with multiple, possible steady-states. This means that the notion of integrity is perspective and context dependent. That is, the integrity of an ecosystem has as much to do with human values and interventions in ecosystem contexts as it does with the thermodynamic realities of the ecosystem in question. The traditional, "objective" scientific perspective on ecological integrity was a "necessary but not sufficient" foundation upon which to base environmental decisions. Thus, the decision making, management and governance systems should begin to reflect this by allowing for the inclusion of as many perspectives as possible. Kay's work was truly interdisciplinary and integrated explicitly the social and the ecological in environmental decision making. His later work began to explicitly address the role of human agency and knowledge as integral to understanding ecological integrity (Manuel-Naverrette et al., 2002). However, the need to conceive socio-eco-epistemological systems as integral to environmental decision making was never addressed.

2.5.3.5 Self-Organizations and Ecosystem-based Management

The work of Slocombe on self-organization in socio-biophysical systems and ecosystem-based management is another example of an approach to resource management issues utilizing aspects of complex systems thinking and explicitly integrating social and biophysical or ecological systems (Gryzbowski and Slocombe, 1988; Slocombe, 1990; 1993; 1998). Slocombe's early work integrated insights from self-organization theory to explicate the complex dynamics of socio-biophysical systems. His work on the development of ecosystem-based management helped to clarify the need for flexible but clear goals as well as the need to avert the institutional tendency towards territoriality (Slocombe, 1998).

In his most recent summary of an ecosystem approach, Slocombe (2004: 423) describes ecosystem approaches as similar to systems approaches generally. That is, they are different things to different people. He describes some of the common or fundamental similarities of ecosystem approaches, including:

- the use of some kind of systems analysis
- a focus on interactions flows, processes (matter, energy, information)
- an interest in both biophysical and socio-economic aspects of a system
- an attention to institutions and management options
- an integrative, holistic, interdisciplinary perspective
- an orientation towards anticipation and adaptive responses
- an ethical perspective on action and decision making

Slocombe has explored the practical challenges and opportunities provided by an ecosystem approach to environmental management through several case studies including the Kluane/St. Elias region along the Yukon, Alaska border, and the Great Lakes bioregion. From these examples, Slocombe has distilled several practical challenges to implementing an ecosystem approach:

- Bringing institutions together
- Developing, managing and disseminating the necessary information base so all stakeholders have the same information
- Better using and integrating new governance and conflict resolution ideas
- Balancing the substantive, research aspects with the consultative, participatory, goal-setting, and deliberative processes

Slocombe's work has clarified the theoretical foundations and the practical implications of an ecosystem approach to environmental planning and decision making. His work highlights the challenges and benefits of a systems approach to environmental management and the need to view sociobiophysical systems as integrated wholes. He also highlights the importance of information in environmental decision making. This dissertation builds on Slocombe's notion of an ecosystem-based approach as it integrates the complex process of knowledge creation into the understanding of socio-ecological systems as integrated wholes, and explores more explicitly and critically issues of power in environmental decision making.

2.5.3.6 The Resilience of Socio-Ecological Systems (SES)

Berkes and Folke (1998, 2003) have explored the implications of complex systems thinking in the context of the resilience of socio-ecological systems. Berkes and Folke (1998: 20) begin their 1998 work *Linking Social and Ecological Systems* with the assumption that, "social-ecological systems which have survived over extended periods of time are sustainable. This assumption is consistent with Ostrom (1990), and will facilitate the search for mechanisms for the resilience of the integrated social-ecological system". They define "resilience", a key normative goal in their book, as "the buffer capacity or the ability of a system to absorb perturbations; the magnitude of the disturbance that can be absorbed before a system changes its structure by changing the variables and processes that control behaviour" (Berkes and Folke, 1998: 6). They assert that, "maintaining resilience may be important for both resources and social institutions – that the well-being of social and ecological systems is thus closely linked" (Berkes and Folke, 1998: 21). Through several case studies, Berkes and Folke (1998: 21) depict social mechanisms and practices based on local ecological knowledge that they cite as evidence of a "co-evolutionary" relationship between local institutions and their ecological system.

In their 2003 work *Navigating Socio-Ecological Systems,* Berkes and Folke focus more directly on the social side of socio-ecological systems, such as governance, property rights and access. Still exploring insights from complex systems thinking and the influence of different systems of knowledge, they explore how human societies deal with change and how capacity can be built to adapt to change.

Operationalizing an understanding of socio-ecological systems for planning, policy making and governance requires a comprehensive, interdisciplinary understanding of the SES developed collaboratively with researchers, practitioners and local representatives. Walker et al. (2006) and Abel (2001) provide examples of the types of conceptual tools and research and planning protocols required to undertake such comprehensive and collaborative studies. My research extends the exploration of sustainability within socio-ecological systems to integrate the development and use of knowledge and the importance of social learning.

2.5.3.7 Supply-Side Sustainability

Allen et al. (2003) also explore the implications of complex systems thinking for socio-ecological systems. However, instead of resilience, they utilize sustainability as their normative goal. They recognize that resiliency and sustainability can conflict. They differentiate between sustainability and resiliency, describing "sustainability as the capacity to continue a desired condition or process, social or ecological" whereas resiliency is the "ability of a system to adjust its configuration and function under disturbance". Given that "the problem of sustainability is as much a matter of understanding social dynamics and human nature as it is an environmental crisis" (Allen et al., 2003: 8), they conclude that pursuing resiliency can mean abandoning sustainability goals and the values that underlie them. Allen et al. go on to refine the notion of sustainability as the maintenance of system context versus maintaining system outputs. In so doing, the authors define this "supply side" sustainability as "maintaining, or fostering the development of, the systemic contexts that produce the goods, services, and amenities that people need or value, at an acceptable cost, for as long as they are needed or valued" (Allen et al. 2003: 13).

My work will not seek to resolve the differences or apparent incommensurabilities between sustainability and resiliency as a normative goal for socio-ecological systems. Trade-offs or compromises will be required across systems and scales to move towards ecological resilience or sustainability. The focus thus is not to critique these normative goals but to develop an approach for explicitly including the learning processes that are integral to socio-ecological systems.

While the above works cite the importance of different types of knowledge, information and learning as critical in understanding and sustaining socio-ecological systems, they do not explicitly acknowledge the integral, systemic relationship of knowledge to socio-ecological systems. Learning should not simply "stand equal to the production of resources" in a discussion of sustainability (Allen et al. 2003: 83). Learning and specifically social learning *is* our discussion of sustainability, it *is* our understanding of the production of resources. It is not enough to acknowledge the importance of different types of knowledge from local, practical, "indigenous", or tacit to explicit and scientific (Berkes and Folke, 1998: 51-53), without acknowledging that knowledge and learning themselves are as much a part of the socio-ecological system as the social and ecological.

2.5.3.8 Adaptive Methodology for Ecosystem Sustainability and Health (AMESH)

In their work on the development of an Adaptive Methodology for Ecosystem Sustainability and Health (AMESH), Waltner-Toews et al. (2003, 2004) utilize aspects of complex adaptive systems thinking and participatory action research to develop practice-based principles for addressing the complexity of human and ecosystem health in socio-ecological systems. Growing out of experience studying disease vectors between animals and humans in developing nations, Waltner-Toews, an epidemiologist, quickly realized that to address human health in these circumstances required a refocus of medical research attention to include human social institutions as well as ecological systems. Waltner-Toews et al. (2004) offer four guiding principles: 1) methodological pluralism and locally grounded perspectives, 2) hierarchical and cross-scale interactions, 3) self-organization, and 4) unpredictability and uncertainty. The authors have developed AMESH as a loose, five-part, adaptive planning protocol based on these principles:

1. Documenting the present situation
2. Analysis of stakeholders, issues and policy, politics and governance
3. People and their stories
4. Systems descriptions and narratives: developing a systemic understanding
5. Collaborative learning and action

Like Berkes, their work highlights the need to explicitly integrate local knowledge of complex socio-ecological systems to address problems such as human and ecosystem health.

2.5.3.9 Post-Normal Science

Funtowicz and Ravetz (1992) coined the term "post-normal" in contrast to Kuhn's (1970) concept of "normal science". The term also was chosen in part to take advantage of the links to post-modern philosophy but at the same time to distinguish post-normal science from post-modern deconstruction (the process of continuously questioning the assumptions embedded in a process/structure). More recently, Ravetz (1999: 647) has defined post-normal science as:

> (g)oing beyond the traditional assumptions that science is both certain and value-free, it makes system certainties and decision stakes the essential elements of its analysis. It distinguishes between "applied science" where both dimensions are low, "professional consultancy" where at least one is salient, and Post-Normal Science where at least one is severe.

The authors distinguish among applied science, professional consultancy and post-normal science using two criteria: system uncertainties and decision stakes. As opposed to the search for objective, scientific truth (normal and applied science) or in the interest of a client (professional consultancy), "the theoretical core (of post-normal science) is the task of quality assurance; it argues the need for new methods, involving "extended peer communities", who deploy "extended facts" and take an active part in the solution of their problems" (Ravetz, 1999: 647).

In this post-normal decision-making context, what is the role of the expert in policy making? Kay et al. (1999) indicate that "a scientist's role in decision making shifts from inferring what will happen, that is, making predictions which are the basis of decision, to providing decision makers and the community with an appreciation through narrative descriptions, of how the future might unfold". Such descriptions might include plausible attractors and the structures and processes within the domain of a given attractor; and, potential methods of enhancing or de-coupling the self-organizing system's feed-back loops in order to "push" the system towards a democratically-derived vision.

This is a far more ethically sound position for scientists or "experts" such as planners. Post-normal science provides an alternative framework for decision making in the face of complexity and uncertainty as it takes seriously what appear to be implications of complex systems thinking and takes into account the ethics of irreducible uncertainty in decision making within complex systems. There is a critical, post-modern edge to post-normal science that requires the expert to question the assumptions underlying decision-making structures; and to be critical of the information that she as an expert provides and, of the process by which that information is developed. It is this critical edge to a post-normal perspective that should be highlighted. What is key is the critical view of knowledge generation for action or intervention. A post-normal perspective views knowledge, even scientific knowledge, as a human construction and one that requires constant, critical review. There is a strong sense of the structures and dynamics of complex systems, of what science is and should be, and of a changing role for experts represented in post-normal science. And it does emphasize a phronetic aspect, that is, the extension of the decision-making peer community. However, post-normal science does not explicitly address the question of how we as humans, as biological entities, relate to our environment and develop knowledge, translate that knowledge into social learning and embed that learning into decision-making structures.

This aspect of thematic overlap between environmental management and complex systems thinking draws to the fore the complex – self-organizing, holarchic, uncertain – nature of integrated socio-ecological systems. It also highlights the importance of the context- and perspective-dependent nature of our knowledge of such systems. And finally, it points to the need to include multiple perspectives in environmental decision making.

2.5.4 Governance and Complex Systems Thinking

2.5.4.1 Post-Normal Governance

In an earlier exploration of environmental governance and decision making, I attempted to bring together insights from three bodies of interrelated thought – complexity, governance and civics – in order to begin to develop the notion of "post-normal" governance as an option to traditional environmental management theory and practice (McCarthy, 2003). Conventional environmental management can be characterized as top-down, "command and control", often implemented through bureaucratic structures which can be seen to short-circuit more participative, democratic decision making. I argued, based on insights gleaned from complex systems theory, that due to the high uncertainty and high decision stakes associated with making decisions within complex systems, a "post-normal" approach to science and decision making, in which the "peer community is extended", should be explored (Funtowicz and Ravetz, 1992; Funtowicz and Ravetz, 1993; Funtowicz and Ravetz, 1994; Ravetz and Funtowicz, 1999).

The essence of post-normal science and post-normal governance is a focus on the need to review critically and collectively the assumptions we hold about ourselves and about the way we construct or conceive of others and the world around us. This perspective led me to the current exploration of social learning for environmental decision making and governance.

2.5.4.2 Institutional Knowledge as a Complex Responsive Process

Stacey's (2001) work applies an autopoietic perspective to understand the nature of knowledge. He describes knowledge as arising or emerging from "complex responsive processes" between humans, and defines knowledge as "participative self-organizing processes patterning themselves in coherent ways" (Stacey, 2001: 5). That is, knowledge is a complex, self-organizing process of relating; it is not a thing that resides in either the individual's mind or in the social collective but in both (Stacey 2001: 5). He points to learning as an active, ephemeral process of communication and argues that knowledge cannot be stored (*vis a vis* structure) but is perpetually created (Stacey, 2001).

Stacey oddly describes his perspective as an attempt to move beyond systems thinking, but I argue that his work embodies a systems perspective *par excellence* and that the systems thinking he wishes to move beyond is only one form or one perspective on systems thinking. In contrast to Stacey's argument that knowledge is not stored in structure, I adopt a structuration theory view of learning based on the work of Giddens (1984). In this view, knowledge is stored in repeated behaviours or rule sets of individual agents that can ultimately take the form of regimes or institutions (Francis, 2003) and is evidence of social learning.

2.5.4.3 Governance and Complex Systems Thinking

Francis (2003: 235) has developed a complex systems-based framework for analyzing the current status of governance for conservation. He moves beyond the conventional definition of governance as extending institutional arrangements beyond government to examining governance as complex rule systems under which various organizations operate. Using insights from Giddens (1984), Ostrom et al. (1999), Haas (1990) and Holling (1995, 2001), Holling et al. (2002), Francis (2003) uses concepts such as "institutions", "domains" and "regimes" to describe the complex, self-organizing processes that underlie environmental governance structures. Francis (2003: 235) describes "institutions", or perhaps more accurately the process of institutionalization, as behaviours or rule systems that are constantly created and re-created, or alternatively as the "organizational capacity to foster compliance with particular rule systems". To help describe this cyclical process of institutionalization, Francis (2003) describes the notion of a "domain" or "social space". A domain arises or is created by the actors within or who share an interest in it. The focus of a domain can be a geographic area, a social or economic sector, or a specific problem or issue. A regime "is a governance system intended to deal with a limited set of issues or a single issue area" (Francis, 2003: 236). A regime can take the form of a treaty or convention. It is a rule set or the capacity to foster compliance with a rule set.

Francis describes governance systems as consisting of a self-organizing, transient suite of domains and regimes evolving in the complex process of institutionalization, where institutionalization does not stop with an institutional structure. Instead, it is a self-organizing process that responds to but also drives changes in the human social and ecological context. While Francis (2003) does not explicitly integrate and explore the implications of social learning for environmental governance, his work does provide a broad and provocative conception of environmental decision making that integrates insights from sociology, governance theory and complex systems thinking. My work builds on Francis' view of governance systems as complex, self-organizing systems, and extends the conceptual scope to emphasize the importance of knowledge and learning on environmental planning and governance.

2.5.5 Social Learning and Environmental Management

"Social learning . . . is intended to help improve the quality and wisdom of the decisions we take when faced with complexity, uncertainty, conflict and paradox" (Röling and Wagemakers, 1998: 54). As such, the notion has begun to be applied in a variety of complex decision-making contexts, including environmental management and planning (Daniels and Walker, 2001; Sinclair and Diduck, 2001; Bouwen and Taillieu, 2004; Pahl-Wostl and Hare, 2004; Simon, 2004; Tippett et al., 2005). Environmental management and planning issues are often described as complex and highly uncertain (e.g. Funtowicz and Ravetz, 1993; Kay et al., 1999; Ravetz 2000). From this perspective, management cannot be seen as the search for an ideal or even optimal solution to a single problem but rather as an ongoing process of adaptation, learning and negotiation (e.g. Kay et al. 1999; Mitchell 2003).

Daniels and Walker (2001), in *Working Through Environmental Conflict: The Collaborative Learning Approach,* examine collaboration in environmental planning and policy-making contexts. The authors address collaboration by featuring a method, "collaborative learning," that has been designed to "create a learning atmosphere, encourage systemic thinking about complex problems, discourage strategic (competitive) behavior among stakeholders, and focus on "desirable and feasible change" rather than attempting to achieve absolute consensus on contentious land management issues" (Daniels, Walker, 2001: 248).

Tippett et al. (2005) have applied social learning to river basin management. "Social learning in river basin management refers to the capacity of different authorities, experts, interest groups and the public to manage their river basins effectively" (Tippett et al., 2005: 288). In this context, the authors note the importance of critical reflection regarding the limitations of existing institutions, to consider multi-scale, participatory forms of governance for groups involved in river basin management.

Simon (2004) takes an explicitly systems-based approach to social learning in a resource management context. Simon (2004: 473) argues that "social learning processes can improve stakeholders' awareness and participation in environmental deliberation and decision making and therefore contribute to practical change in environmental management as well as institutional change". In this sense, from a systemic view of knowledge creation across scales, social learning that results in practical change as well as broader structural or institutional change encourages more social learning – fuelling a positive feedback loop (Simon, 2004).

Pahl-Wostl and Hare (2004), Pahl-Wostl (2006) and Bouwen et al. (2004) take a similar approach to social learning, linking individual participation and learning with broader structural change or social learning. Pahl-Wostl and Hare (2004) and Pahl-Wostl (2006) view social learning as linked to individuals' participation in collaborative planning processes and how this participation and associated interactions may in turn change social structure. They define social learning as "an iterative and ongoing process that comprises several loops and enhances the flexibility of the socio-ecological system and its ability to respond to change" (Pahl-Wostle et al. 2004: 195). Bouwen et al. (2004: 141) have also developed a conceptual framework to analyze multi-party collaboration projects related to natural resource issues. They note that the technical complexity and social embeddedness of natural resource issues require the collaboration of many different groups and perspectives and the integration of many types of knowledge. Their definition of social learning includes "social organizational learning that takes place at the systemic or cultural level during joint practices and experiences when stakeholders meet in common actions and conversations on different levels of activity".

My dissertation work seeks to build upon these useful precedents applying social learning and even systems-based approaches to social learning to the field of environmental management. My work will explicitly incorporate a complex and especially critical systems-based conceptual framework and model for fostering social learning in environmental planning and policy-making contexts.

2.5.6 Social Learning and Critical Social Epistemology

2.5.6.1 Critical Pedagogy

Based on the work of Paulo Freire (1973:33), critical pedagogy "makes oppression and its causes objects of reflection by the oppressed, and from that reflection comes the necessary engagement in the struggle for their liberation". Critical pedagogy explicitly addresses power imbalances inherent in educational social structures and encourages a form of education in which teachers and students are critical co-investigators in the learning process. Freire's (1973) work highlighted the importance of critical reflection in the learning process through the process of action and critical reflection, action and critical reflection referred to as praxis. Shor (1993) provides a framework for implementing critical pedagogy that has ten descriptors of critical education. These are:

- Participatory – learners have a voice in the education process
- Situated – material reflects learners' perspective
- Democratic – teachers and learners work collaboratively to develop a learning agenda
- Dialogic – the learning process emphasizes discussion
- Desocialization – encourage inactive learners to participate in the learning process
- Multicultural – learning acknowledges cultural diversity
- Research-oriented – educators research student identities as part of the learning process and students undertake problem-oriented research
- Activists – the learning process includes active, experiential learning
- Critical – the learning process promotes self-reflection and social analysis
- Affective – feelings of learners are part of the learning, discussion process

This critical perspective on learning emphasizes that any learning or knowledge creation process is a social and political one. As such, it requires critical reflection on both the part of the educator and the learner focusing on the learning process and its associated power structures. This important conceptual precedent for critical learning has been applied to the process of environmental assessment by Fitzpatrick and Sinclair (2003) and Fitzpatrick (2006) (Section 2.5.7.1).

2.5.6.2 Transformative Theory of Adult Learning

In the psychological or pedagogical branch of social learning, the contribution of Mezirow's transformative theory of adult learning is significant. Mezirow (1994: 222-223) defines learning as "the social process of construing and appropriating a new or revised interpretation of the meaning of one's experience as a guide to action". This approach to learning, as a socially-embedded process of reinterpretation of one's perspective on experience through critical reflection and changes to frame of reference and meaning structures (Mezirow, 1994; Mezirow, 1998), resonates well with the understanding of knowledge generation described above. Mezirow (1994) describes six ideal conditions for learning, these are:

1. accurate and complete information,
2. freedom from coercion,
3. openness to alternative perspectives,
4. ability to reflect critically upon presuppositions,
5. equal opportunity to participate, and
6. ability to assess arguments in a systematic manner and accept a rational consensus as valid.

These conditions reflect the need for alternative perspectives, the need for critical reflection and the importance of acknowledging power relations within the learning process. Mezirow (1994, 1998) notes that frames of reference and meaning structures are influenced or shaped by three different types of codified knowledge: sociolinguistic (e.g., social norms, ideology, language games, theories); psychological (e.g., personality traits, repressed parental prohibitions which continue to block ways of feeling or acting); and, epistemic (e.g., learning styles, sensory learning preferences, focus on wholes or parts, or on the concrete vs. the abstract) (Mezirow, 1994: 223). These may be fruitfully linked to Flyvbjerg's (2001) Aristotelian typology of knowledge (e.g., epistemic, techne, phronesis). Mezirow's work sets the process of learning in a social or political context, and his ideal conditions for learning helped form the basis for the SEE systems conceptual framework principles (Section 3.1.2).

2.5.6.3 Triple-loop Learning

In *Diversity Management: Triple Loop Learning*, Flood and Romm (1996:xi) describe an approach to "managing the increasing diversity of issues that confront humankind in contemporary organizational and societal affairs". They describe a view of learning that includes three loops, and describe three centres of learning associated with the three loops that represent very different questions. The first centre or loop of learning asks *are we doing things right*? The second centre or loop questions the goals or assumptions of the first loop by asking *are we doing the right things*? The third centre or loop, which represents their innovative contribution to the organizational or social learning literature, asks if *power structures are acting too much in support of definitions of rightness or conversely if any presumed right way is becoming too forceful*? This triple-loop view of social or organizational learning explicitly integrates notions of power and sets learning in a social or political process. It also alludes to similar notions of repetitive actions of agents leading to the development and maintenance of structures that is the basis for Giddens' (1984) theory of structuration. Thus, Flood and Romm's (1996) triple-loop learning has formed part of the basis for the SEE systems conceptual model of social learning.

2.5.7 Social Learning, Critical Social Epistemology and Environmental Management

2.5.7.1 Critical Education Applied to Environmental Assessment

Fitzpatrick and Sinclair (2003) and Fitzpatrick (2006) have applied critical education or critical pedagogy to the process of public involvement in environmental assessment. Fitzpatrick and Sinclair (2003) applied Shor's (1993) ten indicators of critical education based on Freire's (1973) critical pedagogy (Section 2.5.6.1) to the Sable Gas Panel Review, an environmental assessment of a natural gas project situated in the Canadian Maritimes between 1996 and 1997. The results demonstrate potential opportunities for fostering critical education through an environmental assessment process. This work also provides a useful precedent for applying a critical perspective on social learning to an environmental planning and policy-making process. It also emphasizes the importance of understanding power relationships within social learning processes.

2.5.7.2 Transformative Theory Applied to the Environmental Assessment Process

Sinclair and Diduck (2001) have taken Mezirow's transformative theory of adult learning and applied it to understanding how public participation in environmental assessment processes provides opportunities for social learning. They adapt Mezirow's (1994, 1998) ideal conditions for learning to develop criteria with which to evaluate Canadian environmental assessment processes to facilitate mutual learning among participants. While Mezirow's ideal conditions were developed for use at the personal level, they note that for their purposes the conditions were adapted for use at the social or process level. My work draws on Sinclair and Diduck's (2001) innovative use of Mezirow's transformative theory and ideal conditions for learning. I argue that making links to Giddens' (1984) structuration theory, Fuller's (2001) social epistemology and aspects of complex and critical systems thinking should make Mezirow's work more directly applicable at the decision-making process and sociological governance structure scale.

Social learning emphasizes the need to focus on the *process* of learning rather than on the characteristics of the learner or on knowledge as a *thing* (Mezirow 1994, 1998; Sinclair and Diduck 2001). This perspective on social learning also highlights that learning and knowledge creation is a complex, socially embedded process requiring the learner or knower to reflect critically upon his/her perspective or frame of reference.

2.5.7.3 Feminist Scholarship, Pluralistic Civic Science and Community Forestry

Reed and McIlveen (2006) ground insights from feminist scholarship in their work applying pluralistic civic science to community forestry. This critical, feminist perspective enables them to address "the influence of power relations among ... subjects of study and in determining how scientific knowledge is defined and used". The authors focus their attention on how knowledge is produced, how participation is constrained and "to what extent community participants would benefit from critical reflection in the work". My dissertation work seeks to utilize insights from complex and critical systems thinking to develop a framework for describing and defining the complex structures and processes that enable stakeholders to critically reflect and contribute to social learning in environmental planning and policy contexts.

2.5.8 Complex Systems, Social Learning and Environmental Decision Making

Folke et al. (2005) have built on the concept of resilience of socio-ecological systems to begin to describe the social dimensions that enable adaptive, ecosystem-based management. They describe adaptive governance systems as self-organizing social networks of actor groups that draw on different knowledge systems and experiences for the development of a common understanding and policies. They describe four social sources for resilience, adaptability and transformation. These are:

- Learning to live with change and uncertainty
- Combining different types of knowledge for learning
- Creating opportunity for self-organization toward social-ecological resilience
- Nurturing sources of resilience for renewal and reorganization

(Folke et al. 2005: 452).

While the term social learning is not used, this important work explicitly links the complexity-based concept of socio-ecological system resilience with adaptive capacity and knowledge or learning in environmental management. What this approach does not highlight is the importance of critical awareness and reflection given the complexity and uncertainty of decision making within socio-ecological systems.

2.5.9 Complex Systems, Critical Social Epistemology and Environmental Decision Making

2.5.9.1 Five Strands of Social Learning

Keen et al. (2005) provide a useful precedent for integrating insights from systems thinking and critical reflection in a framework for social learning in environmental management. Keen et al. (2005: 9) describe social learning as a "process of iterative, reflection that occurs when we share our experiences, ideas and environments with others". They describe social learning as having five interrelated, orienting concepts or braided strands: reflection, systems orientation, integration, negotiation and participation.

They argue that reflection follows an iterative cycle of "diagnosing what matters, designing what could be, doing what we can and then developing a deeper understanding from reflecting on and evaluating that practical experience" (Keen et al., 2005: 9). Keen et al. (2005) utilize systems theory as a means to reflect on the links between humans and ecosystems in an integrated framework and emphasize an understanding of change processes arising from interactions. They argue that "a systems orientation allows both human and non-human elements to be included as parts of a given system, with their interaction conceived of in terms of the properties the parts possess and the constraints those properties place on each other when brought together" (Keen et al. 2005: 10). The integration strand emphasizes that the pursuit of sustainability in environmental management requires integrative frameworks from which to study the world, instead of disciplinary frameworks that divide observations into selected sets of elements. Integration and discourses on sustainability often lead to conflict and so require negotiation. They argue that conflict generates opportunities for learning. And finally, Keen et al. (2005) point to participation and engagement as the fifth strand of social learning, describing a range of possible forms of collaboration from coercion to co-learning.

Using insights from Holling and Gunderson (2002) and the four-phase, adaptive cycle of ecosystem dynamics, Keen et al. (2005) weave the five strands of learning into a learning spiral. Each phase is linked to a specific capacity. The spiral begins with *diagnosis*, requiring a capacity for accuracy. The next is the *design* phase which is linked to creative capacity. Practical skills are required in the *doing* phase, wherein new and old ideas are tested together, leading to the fourth phase of *development* or re-evaluation where a capacity for judgement is required. While Keen et al. (2005) integrate insights from systems thinking and emphasize the importance of reflection in the iterative process of social learning for management within socio-ecological systems, they do not take the next step of explicitly integrating the learning or epistemological system into the systems description.

2.5.9.2 Critical Political Ecology

Tim Forsyth (2003) has applied various aspects of complex systems thinking and critical theory to political ecology. The discourse on political ecology generally involves probing the genealogy (historical development of a concept or theory) or social and political conditions that cause environmental problems (Forsyth 2003; Sullivan and Stott 2000). Forsyth's (2003: 2-3) critical political ecology attempts to avoid the "simplistic separation of science and politics" and the use of "a priori notions of ecological causality and meaning", instead adopting a more politically aware and socially embedded understanding of the contexts in which environmental explanations emerge.

Forsyth (2003) argues that his critical political ecology can be referred to as critical for three reasons. First, critical political ecology seeks an emancipatory form of politics consistent with Critical Theory and its emphasis on knowledge and science as products of power relations and potentially oppressive regimes (Forsyth, 2003: 21). Second, his political ecology focuses on science as both a means of explanation and as a social endeavour rooted in politics. Such a critical view of science draws attention to the social context of knowledge and potential political uses of scientific knowledge (Forsyth 2003: 21). Third, Forsyth's critical political ecology adopts the onto-epistemology of critical realism. Combining a skeptical epistemology and a realist ontology allows critical political ecology to "achieve a biophysically grounded yet socially relevant form of explanation" (Forsyth, 2003: 22).

Forsyth (2003: 52) also utilizes non-equilibrium ecology or a complexity-based approach to ecology to critique traditional equilibrium or balance of nature ecological perspectives. Referencing somewhat dated and generic non-equilibrium ecology literature, Forsyth points to rapid change, flux or disturbance within ecosystems and a non-equilibrium view of ecosystems as undermining orthodox ecological science. Forsyth misses much of the recent work of Holling (1995, 2001, 2002), the work of Holling's colleagues in the Resilience Alliance, as well as Allen and Hoekstra (1992) and Allen et al. (2003),

Ulanowicz (1997) and Kay (1984), Kay, (1991), Schneider and Kay (1994), Kay et al. (1999), Kay et al. (2002), Waltner-Toews et al. (2004) to name a few. However, the use of the tools of complex systems thinking to critique conventional scientific perspectives to emphasize the need for a more critical and socially embedded view of scientific knowledge makes Forsyth's work highly salient to my research.

2.5.9.3 Human Strategies in Complexity

Christian Fuchs and his colleagues are exploring the philosophical foundations for a theory of Evolutionary Systems. In this application of aspects of complex systems thinking to human social systems and decision making, Fuchs develops a framework for understanding the roles of human agency and social structures. Using the concepts of self-organization and emergence, Fuchs describes a systemic, dialectical relationship or creative tension between the bottom-up emergence of individual human agency and the top-down emergence of social structure. Fuchs' "Dialectic Emergentist" view of social systems provides a framework for understanding the character and role of knowledge in self-organizing social systems. Fuchs (2001: 12) describes various types or levels of knowledge that can emerge (i.e., perception, interpretation and evaluation). He argues that perception combines receiving and conceiving of external data. Perception leads to interpretation that is giving these data meaning. And evaluation emerges from interpretation as the knowledge created from interpretation is set in the context of its goals (Fuchs, 2004: 12).

On the emergence of individual knowledge, Fuchs (2004: 13) concludes that "the environment can never determine cognition entirely, knowledge is however, also not wholly autonomously constructed without reference to the environment". This process is in dynamic tension with the process of creating "social" information or knowledge. Here again he describes a three-stage process or three-level characterization of the emergence of social information from acting towards resources (economy) to acting towards regularities (politics) to acting towards rules (culture) (Fuchs, 2001: 16).

Fuchs (2001: 18) concludes that "social information emerges from individual information" but that "social information constrains and enables individual consciousness and action". This dialectic relationship also involves and is influenced by asymmetric distribution of power. Fuchs concludes that competitive forms of social structure have dominated cooperative ones and that this trajectory of socio-ecological emergence must be reversed to maintain social, ecological and technological sustainability (Fuchs 2001: 22).

Fuchs (2004) has extended his perspective on knowledge which links Giddens' structuration theory and self-organization theory to an investigation of the notion of knowledge management. Viewing social systems as self-organizing entities emerging as the result of dialectic tensions between social structure and human agency, Fuchs (2004: 34) argues that knowledge management can be understood as either based on coercion and control or on cooperation and participation. Given that new structures emerge from the creative interactions of humans, Fuchs (2004: 34) concludes that any attempt to manage knowledge in a self-organizing social system should enable individuals to reach their creative potential. And so, knowledge management should be premised on principles of cooperation and participation. Fuchs (2001, 2004) integrates aspects of complex systems thinking and Giddens structuration theory into a cross-scalar view of knowledge for sustainable decision making. This dissertation extends this integrative framework to include Flyvbjerg's (2001) Aristotelian typology of knowledge (epistemic, technical and phronetic) to further explicate the knowledge requirements for fostering social learning within socio-eco-epistemological systems.

The works of Keen et al., Forsyth and Fuchs are examples of the integration of insights from complex systems thinking, critical, social epistemology and environmental decision making. They collectively highlight the complex, self-organizing, hierarchic and socially-embedded nature of knowledge for environmental decision making. These works also point to the implications of power relations embedded in knowledge for environmental decision making. Despite these integrative works, some research gaps still remain.

2.6 Some Research Gaps

This exploratory research seeks to build on the works of Holling and others (Holling, 1973; 1978; 1995; 2001; Berkes and Folke, 1998; Holling et al., 2002; Berkes and Folke, 2003) integrating understanding of social and ecological systems for environmental management. There have been some attempts to integrate elements of complex and critical systems thinking and critical social epistemology into an understanding of social learning for environmental planning (Forsyth, 2003; Fuchs, 2004). This dissertation work is intended to explore the potential of a SEE systems conceptual framework for describing and refining contributions to social learning made by environmental movement organizations.

The highly abstract, theoretical and philosophical fields of complex and critical systems thinking and critical, social epistemology can be usefully applied to the practice-based fields of planning, governance and knowledge management. Planning scholars, such as Healy (2003), Yiftachel (1998) and Innes (2004), have begun to infuse the study and practice of planning with a critical and reflective edge and have even seen the value in integrating insights from complex systems thinking. However, even these works (that bring together the fields of critical theory, complex systems theory and planning theory) have yet to integrate the social learning process into their understanding of planning within a social or ecological system.

A growing literature is highlighting the application of insights from complex systems thinking to issues surrounding environmental management. A greater appreciation of the integrated, systemic and complex nature of socio-ecological systems has emerged (White 1945, Berkes and Folke 1998, Kay et al. 1999, Holling 2001, Gunderson and Holling 2002, Mitchell 2002), and Berkes and Folke (1998, 2003) and (Waltner-Toews et al., 2004) have begun to point to the importance of the role of various knowledges and varied perspectives in understanding complex socio-ecological systems. The literature integrating complex systems thinking, critical social epistemology and environmental management (Funtowicz and Ravetz, 1992, 1993, 1994, Ravetz 1999, Fuchs 2003, Forsythe 2003 and Healy 2004) even more explicitly explores this link between the socio-ecological and the epistemological. However, none of these works provides a conceptual framework for integrating social, ecological and epistemological systems to describe the dynamics among the three, or the principles for ethical intervention within them.

Interpretations of the implications of complex systems thinking, especially manifested through critical systems thinking as well as insights from critical social epistemology, collectively point to the need to reflect critically upon how we structurally couple with the world around us and each other. That is, we should be critically aware of the influence of the social structures in which we as individual agents interact with other individuals and collectively through institutions view our systems of interest. Accordingly, complex and critical systems thinking and critical social epistemology collectively point to the need for a plurality of perspectives on any issue and to the many different types of knowledge required to comprehend the complexity of systems. And finally, they point to the need to address issues of power and inequity that become embedded in social structures, such as institutions, and how we as individual agents can intervene to ensure some measure of collective or individual improvement.

The governance literature is providing insights into the need for organizations and institutions across jurisdictions and sectors to network and collaboratively make decisions (Rosenau, 1995; Rhodes, 1996; Stoker, 1998; Pierre, 2000). Aspects of complex systems thinking have been applied in various ways to governance theory (Kooiman, 1993; Kickert, 1993; Jessop, 1998; Fuchs et al., 2001; Francis, 2003; McCarthy, 2003). These works highlight the complexity of decision making within social systems as well as the integral role of knowledge (Fuchs et al., 2001) and the ethical implications of making decisions within complex systems (McCarthy, 2003). Others, such as Francis (2003), have extended the application of complex systems thinking to governance theory and developed a conceptual framework for understanding the development and dynamics of governance systems. However, not even the work of Francis (2003) explicitly addresses the complexity of making decisions within socio-ecological, epistemological systems.

The literature on social learning engages some practical philosophical questions regarding the nature of knowledge and the process of learning. Social learning, whether on the psychological or sociological branch, does link individual learning either with the social context or to changes in social structures. Sinclair and Diduck (2001) have taken Mezirow's (1984) transformative theory of adult learning and ideal principles for learning and applied them to public participation in environmental assessment processes. Flood and Romm (1996) have developed triple-loop learning which makes an examination of power structures part of the learning process.

Other literature has brought together aspects of complex systems thinking, critical systems thinking and even critical theory and social epistemology to address the complexity and ethics of knowledge creation for decision making (Stacey 2001; Forsyth 2003; Fuchs 2001, 2004). Stacey (2001) has comprehensively applied insights from complex systems thinking to question our ability to manage something as complex as knowledge. And Fuchs (2004), using the work of Giddens (1984) and insights from complex systems thinking, has taken a critical view of social learning addressing the issue of power and the need to approach learning from a participatory and cooperative stand-point. However, little has been done to integrate these into a conceptual framework to guide research and intervention for decision making within complex socio-ecological-epistemological systems. The next chapter synthesizes this interdisciplinary literature review into a suite of principles for intervention and research in complex socio-ecological, epistemological systems. Based on these principles, an approach to planning and policy research is developed. A conceptual model of social learning has emerged based on this approach and its application to the two case studies.

Chapter 3: Socio-Ecological Epistemological Systems Conceptual Framework

3.1 Introduction

The goal of this exploratory research is to investigate the potential of a complex and critical systems-based framework for research and intervention by describing and refining the contributions of environmental movement organizations to social learning in the context of complex environmental policy making and governance systems. Approaching any issue or problem through the lens of complex systems thinking reveals inherent uncertainty, emergent structures, cross-scalar dynamics and context and perspective dependence. Approaching research and intervention from a complex systems-based perspective has led scholars (for instance, Jackson 2000; Midgley 2000) to reflect critically on perspectives and approaches to addressing uncertainty and complexity.

The intent of the broad-based, interdisciplinary literature review presented was two-fold. First, it was meant to demonstrate that insights from complex and critical systems thinking as well as critical social epistemology are pervading fields of research related to environmental planning and policy making. And secondly, it was intended to begin to synthesize some seemingly disparate perspectives or bodies of knowledge into a reflective, systems-based framework for approaching research and intervention and more specifically for describing the process of social learning.

To address objective #1 (Section 1.2) of this research, this chapter synthesizes insights from the fields of complex and critical systems thinking and critical social epistemology into a set of principles for research and intervention within complex socio-ecological, epistemological systems. These principles are then tailored, based on the literature, to the planning and policy domain through the development of a critical systems approach to planning and policy research to meet research objective #2 (Section 1.2). The conceptual framework is then applied to two instrumental case studies based on the methodological framework to address research objective #3 (Section 1.2). A model for describing and refining the contributions of environmental movement organizations to social learning in the context of complex environmental policy making and governance systems in Ontario is also presented. The development of this model meets research objective #4 (Section 1.2) and is the result of the application of the SEE systems framework retrospectively to the two empirical case studies. While this model could be refined through further empirical testing, it is presented as an example of the kind of descriptive and prescriptive conceptual tool that could result from the application of a SEE systems approach to the environmental planning context.

3.2 Conceptual Framework

3.2.1 Complex Socio-Ecological Epistemological (SEE) Systems

The following conceptual framework is meant to integrate insights from complex and critical systems thinking, Fuller's (2002a, 2002b) social epistemology, Gidden's (1984) structuration theory and Flyvbjerg's (2001) typology of knowledge to provide a theoretically grounded, but pragmatic and provocative new view of knowledge for environmental decision making. A set of principles for research and intervention has been developed based on critical, social epistemology and an understanding of complex socio-ecological, epistemological systems. This view of environmental planning and decision making may provide researchers and practitioners with a richer understanding of the nature and dynamics of knowledge creation and use for environmental decision making. It also emphasizes the complex interrelationship between the knowledge of individual agents and knowledge embedded in social structures, such as the institution of science. As well, it highlights interrelationships among epistemic or scientific knowledge, technical or local, experiential knowledge and phronetic or political or ethical knowledge. Finally, this framework and the associated principles are intended to aid environmental management researchers and practitioners in understanding the complexity of knowledge and its tight relationship with the social and ecological systems of interest.

3.2.2 Principles for fostering social learning within complex SEE systems

Two sets of SEE systems principles (descriptive and prescriptive) are provided below. First, is a set of *descriptive* principles to aid researchers and practitioners in understanding the key components and relationships within socio-ecological, epistemological systems. Second, is a *prescriptive* set of principles to help researchers and practitioners guide intervention.

3.2.2.1 SEE Systems Descriptive Principles

These descriptive principles are intended to help researchers and practitioners understand co-evolutionary, uncertain, socially-embedded and cross-scalar socio-eco-epistemological systems. Co-evolution refers to the inter-related and self-organizing nature of social, ecological and epistemological systems. Uncertainty and social-embeddedness emphasize the irreducible uncertainty that complex systems theory highlights (for instance, Kay et al. 1999), but also that we at least in part create or amplify this uncertainty as a result of the social-embeddedness of the learning process (Fuller 2002). The cross-scalar considerations principle highlights Koestler's (1967) notion of holarchy as well as Giddens' (1984) use of dialectics in understanding the complex relationship between individual agents and social structure.

3.2.2.1.1 Co-Evolution

Principle: Social, ecological and epistemological systems exhibit self-organization, emergent structures and co-evolution.

Just as Holling (1995, 2002), Berkes and Folke (1998, 2003) and Allen, Tainter and Hoekstra (2003) (Section 2.5.3) argue that social and ecological systems co-evolve and are thus usefully described as socio-ecological systems, I seek to extend this line of reasoning to epistemological or learning systems. Stacey (2001) argues that knowledge is a complex, self-organizing process of relating and therefore exhibits similar dynamics to socio-ecological systems. Fuller

(2002) argues that knowledge is created as a social process and Giddens (1984) and Fuchs (2004) argue that individual and collective knowledge embedded in emergent social structures such as regimes, organizations and institutions are tightly coupled in a dialectic relationship (Section 2.4.2). Therefore, on a conceptual level, the links between social and epistemological systems appear strong.

3.2.2.1.2 Reflexive Uncertainty

Principle: Complex SEE systems are highly uncertain and perspective-dependent.

When dealing with any complex system, the practitioner should be aware that there is inherent, irreducible uncertainty associated with complex self-organizing systems. No matter how fast the computers or sophisticated the simulation-model, fully accurate, long-term quantitative predictions are impossible within complex systems (Kay et al. 1999) (Section 2.4.1). Compounding this uncertainty in complex systems is that learning is a socially-embedded process (Fuller 2002), heavily influenced or constrained by emergent rule sets or social structures (Giddens, 1984) resulting in reflexive uncertainty (Section 2.4.2). Therefore, an understanding of complex systems and their inherent uncertainty is further "complexified" because there are many perspectives on a given system of interest manifested through a variety of possible system boundaries. Beginning any intervention within socio-eco-epistemological systems with an understanding of their complexity ensures decision makers have not only a sense of the risks and uncertainty but also a strong measure of humility in any decision taken.

3.2.2.1.3 Cross-scalar Considerations

Principle: SEE systems are holarchically nested, exhibiting both top-down and bottom-up causality.

This principle is based on Koestler's (1967) notion of a holarchy, developed in contrast to a hierarchy (Section 2.4.1). Whereas the term hierarchy implies a top-down causal relationship, because larger, slower systems constrain smaller, faster systems, in a holarchy the causal relationship is two-way (top-down and bottom-up). The activity of smaller, faster systems can concatenate up through the system, affecting the larger systems in the holarchy. Also, holarchies are nested, as systems within systems, etc. (e.g. subwatersheds, within watersheds, etc.).

Paralleling Koestler's (1967) notion of a holarchy is Giddens' (1984) understanding of the interaction between individual agents and emergent social structures. Just as Koestler's concept of a holarchy highlights mutual or bi-directional causality (top-down and bottom-up) within systems, so too does Giddens' notion of structure-agent interactions (1984) (Section 2.4.2). Social structures such as rules, laws, regimes and institutions emerge out of an individual agent's behaviour and an individual agents' behaviour is constrained by the rules and structures that emerge. Thus, intervention for change, for example in the name of sustainability, can approach such systems from the top or bottom but preferably should use both approaches iteratively.

3.2.2.2 SEE Systems Prescriptive Principles

Based primarily on the work of Jackson (2000) and Midgley (2000) on critical systems thinking, the following prescriptive principles take the understanding of complex socio-ecological, epistemological systems and translate it into principles for action or intervention.

3.2.2.2.1 Critical Awareness

Principle: Intervention within SEE systems should be undertaken with critical awareness, reflexivity and openness to different perspectives.

Practitioners should approach interventions as an adaptive process of experimentation with multiple theories and methods which result in different first- (outside the mind) and second-order (within the mind) boundaries. Throughout this process, the practitioner should keep in mind that the participants are always agents making choices among theories, methods and ultimately boundaries (the choice of not drawing a boundary should also be explored) and such choices are as a result value-laden, ethical and subject to critique. This critique should be both internal (to the individual) but also external (the result of discourse with a plurality of perspectives) (Section 2.4.1). This critique could be augmented by an understanding of boundaries and knowledge being influenced by the dynamic tension between individual agents and social structures and among technical, epistemic and phronetic boundary choices (Section 2.4.2).

3.2.2.2.2 Pluralism (Knowledge, Perspectives and Methods)

Principle: Intervention within SEE systems should incorporate a plurality of perspectives, methods and types of knowledge (e.g. epistemic, technical and phronetic).

From a complex systems perspective, absolute or exclusionary perspectives and approaches limit our options for dealing with the irreducible complexity and uncertainty of our world (Section 2.4.1). If we take seriously, for instance, the philosophical implications of autopoietic theory (that we as biological, autopoietic living systems interpret information from other systems and our environment through our structural coupling with them, both evolutionary (sensory structures) and individually - cognitively), then we cannot usefully assume a single objective reality. Thus, it is ethically sound to include a plurality of perspectives, methods and knowledges representing different dynamic tensions among scientific or other knowledge that emerges in social structures, technical or experiential knowledge of individual agents, phronetic knowledge of the power inequities embedded in dialectic between individual agents and social structures, and synthesis and reflexivity which allows for integration of multiple perspectives and critical reflection (Flyvbjerg, 2001; Fuller, 2002b) (Sections 2.4.1, 2.4.2, 2.5.3).

3.2.2.2.3 Power

Principle: Intervention within SEE systems should acknowledge power in the form of structural constraints to and opportunities for individual agents to reach their potential.

Complex systems thinking (esp. autopoietic theory), social epistemology, structuration theory and phronetic knowledge all point to the need to critically reflect upon the learning process (Sections 2.4.1, 2.4.2). From an autopoietic perspective, we are organizationally closed so intervention needs to change the way the target system thinks about itself and its capacity to change its own action (Luhmann, 1984; Teubner, 1988; Stewart and Ayres, 2001). Social epistemology and stucturation theory point to the influential role the social system and social structures can take in shaping the development of individual and structurally-embedded knowledge. Giddens' (1984) structuration theory focuses on the empowerment of individuals by illustrating the bottom-up influence that agents have over the development and emergence of social structures. Highlighting the importance of phronetic knowledge (Flyvbjerg 2001) and synthesis and reflexivity, for instance, could enhance individual agent's ability to reflect critically on the power and role of social structures and to see his or her role in intervention for change (2.4.1).

3.3 Methodological Framework: Critical Systems Planning and Policy Research

Critical systems planning and policy research is a reflective, systems-based, participatory and action-oriented approach to the study of policy development. It contrasts with more traditional problem-solving or administrative notions of policy research and builds on Shields' (1999) critical policy research, Bobrow and Dryzek's (1987) critical policy analysis, Harvey's (1990) notion of critical social research, Alvesson and Skoldberg's (1999) reflexive methodology, Flyvbjerg's (2001) phronetic social science and Fuller's (2002a) social epistemology. Policy research has been characterized as the study or analysis of social or environmental problems and provision of alternative approaches or policy options with pragmatic and action-oriented recommendations for the solution or resolution of the problem (Majchrzak, 1984).

Shields (1999) argues that traditional policy research focuses on identifying problems within organizations, and then addressing these trouble spots with the aim of making the process run more smoothly. This kind of research takes current institutional arrangements, power relations and structures of knowledge as given. Shields (1999) concludes that traditional policy research, as a result, can consciously or unconsciously justify or condone the interests of dominant actors. Critical policy research is directed at a critical appraisal of the institutional, power and knowledge framework that traditional policy research takes as given (Shields, 1999). Bobrow and Dryzek (1987) describe the task of the critical policy analyst as not simply to put forward arguments within an interactive decision-making process but to advance that process toward an open-communication ideal. In short, the critical policy analyst should work to eliminate systemically distorted policy development and implementation. Similarly, Harvey (1990) describes an approach to research that he refers to as critical social research. At the core of critical social research is the notion that knowledge is structured by social relations. The goal of Harvey's (1990) critical method for social research is to provide knowledge which addresses the prevailing social structures.

Building on these critical approaches to policy research, critical systems planning and policy research explicitly acknowledges the perspective dependence and social context of research and the associated institutional structures and power relations. Critical systems planning and policy research also seeks to incorporate tools from complex and critical systems thinking which allows for the integration of understanding about social, ecological and epistemological systems. And finally, critical systems planning and policy research aims to be participatory and action oriented. The critical systems policy researcher works collaboratively with disempowered groups to set the research agenda and provide action-oriented outcomes for exploring and critically reflecting upon existing social structures. My intent in developing critical systems planning and policy research is to:

- Describe the social, ecological and epistemological (SEE) system of interest as:
    - Self-organizing and co-evolutionary
    - Reflexively uncertain
    - Cross-scalar
- Prescribe action-oriented research and intervention using the SEE systems description based on:
    - Critical awareness
    - Pluralism
    - Power and Reflexivity

The following sections present the philosophical underpinnings and the methodological framework of critical systems policy research. This is followed in Chapter 4 by the development of case study and interviewee selection criteria and the justification of research methods.

3.3.1 Philosophical Stance: A Context for Critical Systems Planning and Policy Research

Midgley (2000: 90-91) describes three ontological paradigms or philosophical stances for research and intervention: realism, idealism and constructionism. Schwandt (2000) describes three corresponding epistemological stances for qualitative inquiry (interpretivist, hermeneutic, perspectivism). These are then contrasted with an alternative onto-epistemological perspective: critical realism (Bhaskar 1997).

Realism implies that there is a real world to which all knowledge refers (esp. Popper, 1972; Bhaskar, 1986; Mingers, 1995). While proponents of realism acknowledge that we cannot know the true or exact nature of reality (Popper's critical falliblism), realists argue for the pursuit of an ideal truth in developing knowledge (Midgley, 2000). In the context of qualitative research, an interpretivist epistemology embodies a realist ontology. An interpretivist epistemological stance for qualitative research would endeavour to find the objective meaning of a given social action (Schwandt, 2000). The quality of interpretivist research findings is judged on whether or not the understanding of an action is an accurate, correct, valid representation of that action and its meaning (Schwandt, 2000).

From an Idealist perspective (esp. Berkeley 1710, Kant 1787) one would argue that we cannot know the "real" world so we should not try to talk about the nature of "reality". A hermeneutic epistemological stance embodies an idealist ontology. Philosophical hermeneutics argues that understanding is not procedure- or rule-driven but rather is a condition of *being* (Schwandt, 2000: 194). In this sense, understanding *is* interpretation. This is a very different understanding of meaning from the interpretivists. Interpretivists see actions as having meaning determinable through a set of methods or rules. From a Hermeneutic perspective, one would argue that human action or text is not something "out there" independent of its interpretations. Meaning in the hermeneutic sense is negotiated or emerges in the act of interpretation; it is not discovered (Schwandt, 2000).

Finally, Midgley (2000) describes social constructionism. Like idealism, constructionism represents an area of strong overlap between ontology and epistemology (onto-epistemology). That is, it is difficult to distinguish between our notions of reality and how we develop knowledge of reality. This philosophical stance argues that nothing can be said about subjective individual knowledge or some notion of external reality except through social interaction. Rorty, Habermas and Foucault are among constructivism's best known advocates. Constructivists believe that knowing is not passive – a simple imprinting of sense data on the mind – but active. That is, the mind constructs abstract concepts and frameworks to interpret sensory and cognitive impressions. A type of constructionism, perspectivism argues that we do not construct our interpretations in isolation but against a backdrop of shared understandings, practices, language, and so forth (Schwandt, 2000: 197). From a perspectivist viewpoint, "the days of naïve realism and naïve positivism are over. In their place stand critical and historical realism and various versions of relativism. The criteria of evaluating research are now relative" (Denzin and Lincoln, 2000: 872).

An alternative perspective or branch of onto-epistemology that speaks directly to the issues addressed by perspectivism, or the tension between our individual construction of an external "reality" and the "reality" or the shared understanding itself, is critical realism. Critical realism is most closely associated with the work of Roy Bhaskar (1997). However, some argue that the thinking can be dated back to Kantian metaphysics (Agar,

2005) or the work of Karl Marx (Jessop, 2005). Critical realism integrates ontological realism and epistemological relativism. In this sense, it acknowledges a world of intransitive things which exist independently from human knowledge of them and also speaks to transitive things which have become saturated with human activity or knowledge and have become historico-culturally specific. In this sense, critical realism says we can have true knowledge of real objects but also recognizes that our knowledge can be time and space specific and may be outmoded in the future. Critical realism is relativistic, not in the "anything goes" sense but rather as a relativism that admits the possibility of truth or at least a limited or provisional sense of true and false (Dean et al., 2005).

My dissertation work recognizes the creative tension between constructivist, or more specifically perspectivist, and critical realist onto-epistemological viewpoints for understanding social learning in environmental policy making and governance. The autopoietic conception of knowledge creation and learning (discussed in Chapter 2) through structural coupling (physical and cognitive structures) emphasizes the tension between transitive, human knowledge and the possibility of an intransitive reality. A thorough explanation of the tension between perspectivist and critical realist onto-epistemologies for environmental policy making and governance is well beyond the scope of this dissertation. However, I argue that our knowledge of systems, such as ecological or human social systems, is complex, perspective dependent and socially embedded (for example, Funtowicz and Ravetz, 1993, 1994; Kay et al., 1999; Kay and Regier, 1999; Stacey, 2002; Fuller 2002; Francis, 2003). Thus, a critical, reflective protocol for developing knowledge (academic research, research for policy or decision making) would seem useful from either a perspectivist or critical realist perspective. This is the over-arching intent of my research and is the raison-d'etre of critical systems policy research.

A social epistemological perspective argues that the process of supporting, verifying or confirming the validity of a statement is a social process. Fuller (2002) refers to this process as granting epistemic warrant. Justifying one's research methods is an explicitly social endeavor, a process of arguing for the epistemic warrant of the research. However, at the same time granting epistemic warrant is not a completely relative process. There must be some metrics for granting epistemic warrant in policy research or we risk resorting to quoting sacred texts and relying on privately-held, individual truths (Francis, 2006).

Critical systems planning and policy research acknowledges the perspective dependence and social context of the process of granting epistemic warrant and also recognizes the need for measures of rigor in the research process. It builds specifically upon the principles or guidelines for reflexive and phronetic research provided by Alvesson and Skoldberg (2000) and Flyvbjerg (2000). Critical systems planning and policy research is also intended to be pluralistic and participatory based on precedents set by Whyte's (1991) Participatory Action Research and Ackoff's (1997) Interactive Planning. And finally, it incorporates insights from complex systems thinking and builds upon Kay et al.'s (1999) Self-Organizing, Holarchic, Open (SOHO) systems and Waltner-Toews et al. (2004) Adaptive Methodology for Ecosystem Sustainability and Health (AMESH) frameworks.

3.3.2 Building a Methodological Framework for Critical Systems Planning and Policy Research

Rigorous research methods require a level of objectivity (positivism) or at least a somewhat unbiased and accurate view (interpretivism above) to judge or test the validity of data for confirming (or denying) a hypothesis (Schwandt, 2000). That is, the researcher applying a conventional approach is expected to safeguard against the numerous potentially invalidating, or more specifically contaminating, factors which threaten interpretability of data (Harvey, 1990). Such contaminating factors can be characterized as the "reactive effects" of the researcher's presence or activities on the phenomena or individuals being observed (Harvey, 1990). As well, the researcher is generally expected to follow standardized, reproducible experiments for hypothesis testing. Rigour and claims to validity from this conventional perspective rest on an objective view of reality or a realist ontology.

The tension between critical realist and constructivist or perspectivist onto-epistemological stances, particularly as expressed though a critical systems planning and policy research perspective, requires the development of different methods and criteria for confirmation or granting of epistemic warrant. As noted in section 3.1, it draws upon critical social theory, participatory action research and systems thinking as summarized by the SEE systems conceptual framework. Critical systems planning and policy research builds upon these frameworks for describing the complex structures and dynamics that underlie socio-ecological, epistemological (SEE) systems.

3.3.2.1 Social Epistemology

Fuller (2002a: ix) defines social epistemology as "an intellectual movement of broad cross-disciplinary provenance that attempts to reconstruct the problems of epistemology once knowledge is regarded as intrinsically social". From a social epistemology perspective, learning and research are seen to be social, even political processes. As such, social epistemology challenges the view of researcher as an objective, value-neutral observer. An alternative view of the researcher and the research process is explored through this work.

3.3.2.2 Critical Systems Research

Paralleling the three main tenets or principles of critical systems thinking discussed in the previous chapter (Midgley, 2000, Jackson, 2000), Midgley (2000) notes that a methodology adequate for critical systems thinking should be explicit about three aspects. First, researchers need to reflect critically upon their choices of theories and methods and how these choices affect the research outcomes. Second, researchers should utilize a plurality of theories and methods (methodological pluralism). From a critical systems approach to research, one would advocate the incorporation of multiple perspectives or multiple boundaries to enrich the understanding of a complex system. Exploring, and critically reflecting upon, the use of multiple methods, which embody different theoretical assumptions, enriches the research process and outcomes. Third, Midgley (2000) argues that a critical systems approach should be explicit about taking action for improvement, where both action and improvement are defined in the "local" research context. This points to a participatory, action-oriented approach.

3.3.2.3 Reflexive Research

Alvesson and Skoldberg (1999) provide a useful overview of the tensions within qualitative research, highlighting the need for methods for data collection and analysis but also emphasizing the need to reflect critically upon the researcher's interpretation and perspective dependence of empirical data. To address these tensions, they outline four elements of reflective research:

> 1. *Systematics and techniques in research procedures.* Qualitative research should follow some well-reasoned logic in interacting with the empirical material, and use of rigorous techniques for processing the data.
> 2. *Clarification of the primacy of interpretation.* Research can be seen as a fundamentally interpretive activity, which in contrast to – or at least to a greater degree than – other activity, is aware of this very fact ... Thus method cannot be disengaged from theory and other elements of pre-understanding, since assumptions and notions in some sense determine interpretations and representations of the object of study.
> 3. *Awareness of the political-ideological character of research.* Social science is a social phenomenon embedded in a political and ethical context. What is explored, and how it is explored, can hardly avoid either supporting (reproducing) or challenging existing social conditions.
> 4. *Reflection in relation to the problem of representation of authority.* It has been pointed out in recent heurmeneutics that in many decisive ways the text is decoupled from the author ... the text lives its own life, as it were, and lacks any reference to anything outside itself ... the researching subject and the researched object are both called into question.
>
> (Alvesson and Skoldberg 2000: 7-8).

While the authors acknowledge that these four elements may be regarded by some as incompatible, they argue that their intent in juxtaposing them is to reflect the tensions within social science research. "The point here is not to integrate typical research from, for example, grounded theory and postmodernism, but to try abstract principles and ideas from hermeneutics, critical theory and post-modernism, with a view to endowing qualitative research with a more reflexive character, while also stressing the importance of empirical material" (Alvesson and Skoldberg 2000: 7-8).

3.3.2.4 Phronetic Research

Flyvbjerg (2001) provides a similarly critical and reflective approach to social science which he terms phronetic social science. The goal is "to carry out analyses and interpretations of the status of values and interests in society aimed at social commentary and social action, i.e. praxis" (Flyvbjerg, 2001): 60). Flyvbjerg (2001) also provides a suite of methodological guidelines. His intent is not to provide a strict protocol but instead to move towards a social science that "effectively deals with public deliberation and praxis rather than being stranded with a social science that vainly attempts to emulate natural science" (Flyvbjerg 2001: 129). Flyvbjerg's guidelines are:

1. *Focusing on values.* The phronetic researcher is forced to face the question of foundationalism versus relativism, that is, the view that central values exist that can be rationally and universally grounded, versus the view that one set of values is just as good as another.
2. *Placing power at the core of the analysis.* Phronesis also poses questions about power and outcomes: Who gains, and who loses? Through what kinds of power relations? What possibilities are available to change existing relations? And is it desirable to do so? And perhaps most importantly, of what kinds of power relations are those asking these questions themselves a part?
3. *Getting close to reality.* One gets close to the phenomenon or group whom one studies during data collection, and remains close during the phases of data analysis, feedback, and publication of results. This strategy typically creates interest by outside parties, and even outside stakeholders, in the research.
4. *Emphasizing little things.* Phronetic research is decentred in its approach, taking its point of departure in local micro-practices, searching for the Great within the Small and vice versa.
5. *Looking at practice before discourse.* Phronetic research focuses on practical activity and practical knowledge in everyday situations. Its focus is on the actual daily practices which constitute a given field of interest, regardless of whether these practices take place on the floor of a stock exchange, a grassroots organization, a hospital, or a local school board.
6. *Studying cases and contexts.* The minutiae, practices, and concrete cases which lie at the heart of phronetic research are seen in their proper contexts; both the small, local context, which gives phenomena their immediate meaning, and the larger, international and global context in which phenomena can be appreciated for their general and conceptual significance.
7. *Asking "how"? Doing narrative.* Phronetic research focuses on the dynamic question, "how?" in addition to the more structural "why?" We can only answer the question "what am I to do?" if we can answer the prior question, "of what story or stories do I find myself a part?". Narrative inquiries do not – indeed, cannot – start from explicit theoretical assumptions. Instead, they begin with an

interest in a particular phenomenon from the perspective of participants, researchers, and others.

8. *Joining agency and structure.* Phronetic research focuses on both the actor level and the structural level, as well as on the relation between the two in an attempt to transcend the dualisms of actor/structure, hermeneutics/structuralism, and volunteerism/determinism.
9. *Dialoguing with a polyphony of voices.* Phronetic research is dialogical in the sense that it includes, and, if successful, is itself included in, a polyphony of voices, with no one voice, including the researcher, claiming final authority.

Flyvbjerg (2001) highlights the need to focus research on power and values, and to get "close to reality" through the use of empirical data but directs the use of these data towards the development of narrative descriptions of cases. He also points to the need for the incorporation of multiple perspectives and multiple scales of observation (agent and social structures).

3.3.2.5 SOHO Descriptions

Kay et al. (1999) have set a useful precedent for what a SEE systems description would entail with their Self-Organizing, Holarchic, Open (SOHO) systems description. SOHO systems descriptions are a key step in understanding the emergent, cross-scalar, perspective dependent phenomena in a complex system. They are intended to highlight those structures and processes in the system that provide context for or act as constraints on policy development and implementation. They explicitly require the researcher to consider interactions and phenomena that cross jurisdictional and other hierarchic boundaries. SOHO descriptions also require the researcher to acknowledge the perspective from which the description is being developed. That is, to be critically aware of the theoretical and social context of the research. And, finally, in developing a SOHO description, the researcher should acknowledge alternative perspectives and utilize multiple methods.

A SEE systems description would begin with a review of the perspective and purpose of the research. It would describe the same types of self-organizing phenomena as a SOHO description (Section 2.5.3.4) but would highlight the integral role of learning in the creation and maintenance of decision-making "structures" and how these structures evolve and manifest themselves in power differentials. It seeks to explore the dialectic relationship between learning and the social structures we create, and how they then influence the development of new knowledge and how they influence action. Critical systems planning and policy research builds upon the notion of a SOHO description in its use of SEE systems descriptions but also seeks to be an explicitly social and political process by engaging groups as they structurally couple with existing social structures. Engaging individuals or groups through a research process has a long and fruitful history. One branch of that history stems from the field of social psychology and has resulted in participatory action research.

3.3.2.6 Participatory Action Research

In the late 1940s, Kurt Lewin, an experimental psychologist and one of the fathers of social psychology, recognized several problems with attempting to study complex social and psychological phenomena through an analytical, reductionist method. Advocating a "theory in action" approach that emphasized a holistic, humanistic and community-based perspective, Lewin highlighted the need to view the human in his or her environmental and community context. Lewin's field theory is premised on the notion that individuals are always functioning at the convergence of a set of interacting fields in which the individual and environment are interdependent parts of the whole. Therefore, in Lewin's opinion, removing the subject of study from its context artificially fractured this interdependent whole. In response, Lewin adopted an action-based research approach. Lewin's work led to several related streams of action research: Participatory Action Research (PAR) (Whyte, 1991), Action Science (Argyris and Schon, 1974; Argyris and D A. Schon, 1978; Schon, 1983), Co-operative Inquiry (Reason, 1988; Reason, 1994; Reason and Heron, 1995; Heron 1996), among many others. However, for the purposes of my research the focus is primarily on Whyte's PAR as it has been widely adopted in many fields of study.

Whyte (1991: 20) has characterized PAR in the following manner,

> in participatory action research, some of the people in the organization or community under study participate actively with the professional researcher throughout the research process from the initial design to the final presentation of results and discussion of their action implications.

Whyte (1991) notes that this type of research contrasts sharply with more conventional research approaches in that during conventional research "members of the organizations or communities are treated as passive subjects with some of them participating only to the extent of authorizing the project, being its subjects, and receiving the results" (Whyte, 1991: 20). PAR, as Whyte (1991) argues, is a "powerful process of organizational learning – a process whereby leaders of labor and management learned from each other and from the consultant/facilitator, while he learned from them" (Whyte, 1991: 30). PAR is based on sociotechnical systems thinking, and has evolved out of frustration with expert-oriented approaches. Whyte (1991: 40) describes the process of PAR as beginning with,

> the problems people who work in a firm are currently facing. Instead of beginning in the conventional fashion with a review of literature, the specification of hypotheses, and the finding of a target organization to test out our design, we start by discovering the problems existing in the organization. Only as we work with members of the organization, diagnosing those problems, do we draw upon the research literature as well as our own past experience

In this sense, the PAR process is not unlike the SOHO process, beginning with system identification and narrative description. So too, the role of the researcher in the PAR process is less as "a disciplinary expert and more as a coach in team building and in seeing to it that as much of the relevant expertise as possible from all over the organization is mobilized" (Whyte, 1991: 41). In the SOHO approach, the role of the "expert" shifts from designing futures to describing possibilities (Kay et al. 1999). Whyte's (1991) PAR provides a useful methodological precedent for engaging individuals and groups through an action-oriented, research process.

3.3.2.7 Adaptive Methodology for Ecosystem Sustainability and Health (AMESH)

Waltner-Toews et al. (2004) have developed a set of guiding principles and a five-part planning protocol for intervention, based on elements of complex and critical systems thinking and Whyte's (1991) PAR, that builds on the notion of a SOHO systems description (Section 2.5.3.8). AMESH incorporates methodological pluralism because the authors recognize "the plurality of different legitimate perspectives and the inability of one particular view to capture the whole, necessitates a variety of forms of inquiry, inclusion of, and dialogue with, persons representing different interest and different world views" (Waltner-Toews et al., 2004). They also acknowledge the importance of placing their research into a local context, recognizing that complex systems are nested and while larger systems (spatially or temporally) provide constraints on smaller ones, processes can, through self-organizing dynamics, alter their own context and so affect larger systems. This highlights the importance of their third guiding principle, self-organization. Finally, the authors stress the importance of acknowledging the uncertainty and unpredictability inherent in complex systems which have profound implications for planning and decision making. The SEE systems conceptual and methodological frameworks build upon these useful precedents but very explicitly integrate the learning process and issues of power into the research and intervention process.

3.3.3 SEE Methodological Framework for Critical Systems Planning and Policy Research

Building on critical approaches to policy research, critical social theory, participatory and action-oriented research and especially upon complex systems-based approaches, I have developed and utilized a critical systems-based approach to policy research. Critical systems planning and policy research requires the researcher to be critically aware of the purpose and implications of the choice of theories and methods; to acknowledge a plurality of perspectives and utilize multiple theories and methods; to address policy issues from a broad, systemic perspective; to be explicitly aware of power relations and encourage individuals' ability to improve their situations; to utilize empirical data to ground the inquiry; and, to engage in participatory, action-oriented research that questions existing social structures and power differentials. More specifically, the criteria for making methodological decisions in critical systems research include the following:

Critical Awareness – The researcher should be critically aware of both the social context and history of the phenomena / system of interest, as well as of the theoretical and philosophical bases for the approach to research and intervention (Jackson, 2000; Flyvbjerg, 2001; Alvesson and Skoldberg, 1999).

Complex Systems-Based – The researcher should attempt to acknowledge broad, cross-scalar, self-organizing emergent structures and processes that affect and influence the system / phenomena of interest (Kay et al., 1999; Jackson, 2000).

Pluralistic – The researcher should attempt to acknowledge multiple perspectives and utilize multiple research methods to gain understanding into the system / phenomena of interest (Jackson, 2000; Flyvbjerg, 2001). This is akin to triangulation, using information from a variety of sources to confirm or verify knowledge.

Focused on Governance Structures – The investigator should explicitly describe and acknowledge the influence of existing social/institutional/governance structures and the processes that feed into their structuration (Giddens, 1984), and how these could be altered to be more sustainability-focused, inclusive and pluralistic (Giddens, 1984; Jackson, 2000; Flyvbjerg, 2001; Alvesson and Skoldberg, 2000; Francis 2001, Gibson, Hassan, 2005).

Empirically Grounded – Critical social research in general, and critical systems research more specifically, has generally been perceived to be an abstract, theoretical exercise and therefore benefits from grounding in practical experience (Harvey, 1990; Jackson, 2000, Flyvbjerg, 2001; Alvesson and Skoldberg, 2000). The collection of empirical data through different methods and from various sources for the development of rich narrative descriptions of complex systems allows the researcher to avoid over simplifying or statistically aggregating the complexity of the system of interest (Kay et al., 1999).

Participatory / Collaborative – The general intent of critical systems planning and policy research is to explore existing social, governance structures and resulting power relations. Through a participatory and collaborative approach (Whyte, 1991), the critical systems policy researcher can work directly with groups to help them:

- improve their knowledge base (scientific, local technical, governance knowledges – Section 2.4.2.3) and continue to learn as a group
- play an effective role in governance
- explore options for making existing governance structures more sustainability focused and inclusive

3.3.3.1 Critical systems planning and policy research Protocol: A non-linear, iterative research process

Based on the above principles, the critical systems policy researcher would undertake the following activities through a non-linear and iterative research process.

- Describe the social, ecological and epistemological (SEE) system of interest as:
  - Self-organizing and co-evolutionary – social, ecological and epistemological systems self-organize and co-evolve, resulting in

emergent properties such as attractors that can only be described through an integrated SEE systems description.
    - Reflexively Uncertain – any complex system exhibits inherent uncertainty. In SEE systems, knowledge and learning about the system of interest are also treated as complex and inherently uncertain. Therefore, knowledge about the complexity and uncertainty of the system of interest results in reflexive uncertainty.
    - Cross-scalar – like other complex systems, SEE systems are holarchically nested, exhibiting cross-scalar, top-down as well as bottom-up causality
- Prescribe action-oriented research and intervention using the SEE systems description based on:
    - Critical Awareness – requires critical awareness of both the agent's personal as well as the broader structural or theoretical biases or assumptions
    - Pluralism – incorporates a variety of perspectives, methods and types of knowledge
    - Power and Reflexivity – acknowledges power imbalances imbedded in social structures which constrain and provide opportunities for learning and reflexivity among individual agents

To provide the empirical basis for the SEE systems description and facilitate application of the critical systems planning and policy research protocol described above, criteria and justification for case study selection and empirical data collection and analysis methods selection are required. The Oak Ridges Moraine and the Long Point Biosphere Reserve are used as case studies. In-depth, semi-structured, elite interviews combined with participant observation, workshops and policy analysis findings were utilized (Sections 4.2 and 4.3).

3.4 SEE Systems Conceptual Model of Social Learning

The SEE systems principles were applied throughout this research process. Two key results emerged: the methodological framework for critical systems planning and policy research (Section 3.2), and a conceptual model of social learning. Ahl and Allen (1996: 36) describe how observation and learning within complex systems "never involves access to the value-free material system ...– only cognizance of biases, if you are lucky". They illustrate this through the use of a diagram of an observer trying to view value-free, reality through a brick wall (Figure 3). My dissertation work seeks to provide a more sophisticated view of observation and learning by replacing the brick wall in Allen and Ahl's diagram with a conceptual model of social learning.

Figure 3: Observer, Observation, Material System

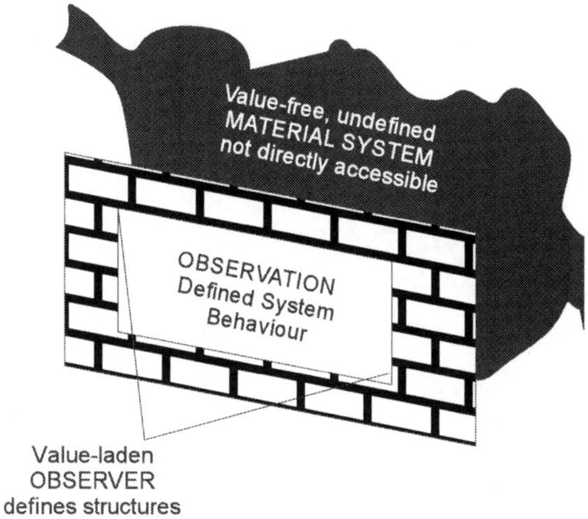

Through my research, a collaborative, participatory research relationship was forged with members of the Save the Oak Ridges Moraine (STORM) coalition and with the Long Point World Biosphere Reserve Foundation. The SEE systems conceptual model of social learning emerged out of a collaborative, participatory action research relationship forged with the STORM coalition and particularly its executive director, Debbe Crandall. It resulted from reflections on the interrelated bodies of literature explored in this chapter, Debbe Crandall's years of civil society, advocacy experience, and a preliminary analysis of the qualitative, empirical data generated through this study. The result is a conceptual tool (Figure 4) that illustrates the epistemological context for environmental governance. It describes the requirements of social learning as defined along three axes: Flyvberg's three-part Aristotelian, typology of knowledge; levels of critical reflection based on Flood and Romm's (1996) triple-loop learning; and, a scale axis from individual agent to larger social structures (Giddens, 1984).

Figure 4: SEE Systems Conceptual Model of social learning

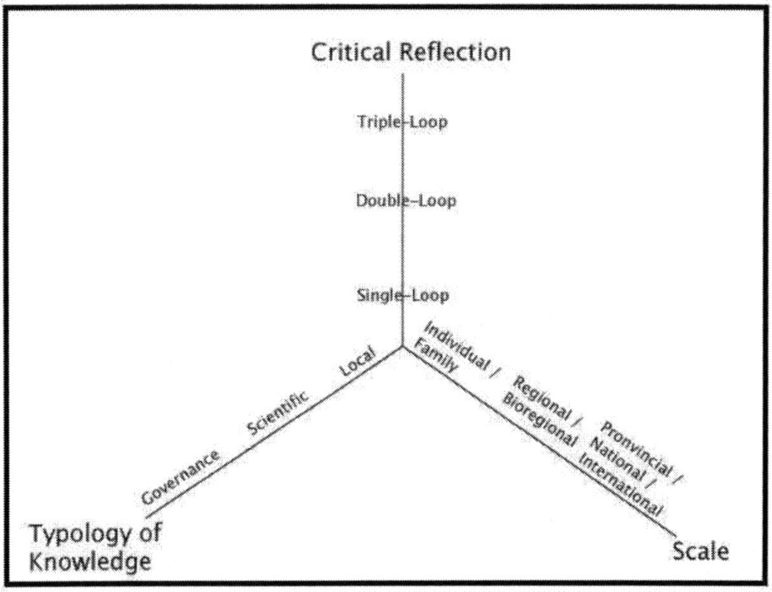

The heuristic can be used to map conceptually the epistemological and praxiological perspectives of individual agents or organizations / institutions (structures) within an environmental policy and governance context. Three archetypical, epistemological or praxiological perspectives have been mapped for illustrative purposes. A NIMBY (Not In My Back Yard) perspective can be characterized as being based primarily on local/technical knowledge, involving only single-loop learning and focused on individual interests. The discourse on ecological integrity illustrates double-loop learning and involves critical reflection on the normative goals of environmental planning and governance. Integrity is based on scientific knowledge as well as local/technical knowledge of an ecosystem and must address the pragmatic issues of conservation while also incorporating theoretical and ethical considerations. Pursuit of ecological integrity, if implemented properly, explicitly involves interaction between individual agents and environmental management structures. Where governance knowledge, scientific knowledge and local/technical knowledge are utilized and synthesized; where issues range from the very pragmatic to the deeply abstract and philosophical; and, where triple-loop learning is evoked by critical reflection on power structures, this is the realm of sustainability. The practical ideal of sustainability would require an in-depth understanding of cross-scale dynamics from individual to global institutional scales.

This conceptual model of social learning has been applied to both case studies (Sections 6.1.4 and 7.1.4) and appears to resonate strongly with the experiences of interviewees and workshop participants. It may provide planners and policy makers with a tool for designing or evaluating planning protocols or decision-making structures that foster social learning.

3.5 Conclusions

The intent of this chapter has been to develop a conceptual framework, in the form of a suite of principles for research and intervention, based on insights from complex and critical systems thinking and critical, social epistemology (Research Objective #1 – Section 1.2). These principles were then tailored to the planning and policy domain through the development of critical systems planning and policy research (Research Objective #2 – Section 1.2). Through the application of the SEE systems framework and critical systems planning and policy research to two case studies, an emerging conceptual tool or model for describing the requirements of social learning has also emerged (Research Objectives #3 and #4 – Section 1.2).

Complex and critical systems thinking and critical, social epistemology have been applied to fields relevant to the environmental decision making. However, no single work so far has integrated insights from complex and critical systems thinking, Giddens' (1984) structuration theory, Fuller's (2002a) social epistemology, and Flyvbjerg's (2001) Aristotelian typology of knowledge.

The SEE systems framework, and especially critical systems planning and policy research, are intended to help researchers and practitioners, particularly in non-governmental, environmental movement organizations, address the complex, co-evolutionary, cross-scalar, perspective-dependent and socially-embedded nature of socio-eco-epistemological systems to make decisions that enhance sustainable land and resource use. The framework provides two sets of principles, descriptive and prescriptive. The descriptive principles illustrate the components and relationships within complex, holarchic and perspective dependent SEE systems, highlighting the tensions between individual agents and social structures as well as among different types of knowledge, especially technical, epistemic and phronetic. The prescriptive principles, based primarily on critical systems thinking, emphasize the need to be critically aware, to incorporate multiple perspectives (pluralism) and to take into account power relations and individual agent's opportunities to improve their situations.

This perspective of SEE systems is one perspective, one set of boundaries from which to view the environmental planning or decision-making system of interest but not to the exclusion of more conventional approaches such as rational comprehensive planning. Within this perspective, each individual agent may view a socio-eco-epistemological system from different perspectives embodying different sets of systems boundaries. Different perspectives and knowledge emerge from the dialectic tension among individual agent and social structure (social learning), and epistemic, technical and phronetic knowledge, resulting in different understandings of a given system of interest. Commonalities as well as differences and even incommensurabilities among perspectives can occur as the result of:

- similarities or differences in individual agent's structural coupling with a system (technical knowledge)
- individual knowledge becoming embodied or rejected by social structures or institutions, such as science (scientific knowledge), should these institutions act to foster or constrain specific types of individual structural coupling
- power imbalances fostered by social institutions, such as science, that occur due to the process of knowledge structuration or, as Fuller (2002a) refers to it, the process of granting epistemic warrant (phronetic knowledge)
- extent or limitations of an individual or group's ability to reflect critically on the social and theoretical assumptions embedded in their perspective
- extent or limitations of an individual or group's understanding of cross-scalar interactions and how their knowledge and action feed into a complex, multi-scalar SEE system

An explicit commitment to sustainability provides some guidance on a normative level. And taking the view of complex socio-eco-epistemological systems as one perspective or as one set of boundaries can provide a useful and provocative view of environmental decision-making systems. Within this view, different balances among epistemic, technical and phronetic knowledges can result in different and innovative perspectives on socio-eco-epistemological systems. With questions of power and knowledge come the issues of equity and quality of knowledge.

Critical systems planning and policy research is a reflective, systems-based approach to the study of policy development. This methodological framework provides a context for the application of the SEE framework, and its descriptive and prescriptive principles, to the work of environmental movement organizations in both the Oak Ridges Moraine and Long Point Biosphere Reserve case studies. Through this illustration and initial test of the SEE systems framework and critical systems planning and policy research, a conceptual model of social learning has emerged.

The SEE systems model of social learning integrates insights from complex and critical systems thinking, Flyvbjerg's (2001) typology of knowledge, Giddens' (1984) structuration theory and Fuller's (2002) social epistemology. It describes the requirements of social learning along three axes. First, learning occurs in dynamic tension among technical, epistemic, phronetic knowledges. Second, due to the complexity and uncertainty of complex socio-ecological, epistemological systems, learning would be fostered by critical reflection upon one's assumptions (technical, theoretical and power structures – triple-look learning). Third, learning, especially social learning, requires an understanding of cross-scalar interactions and emergence. While the conceptual model requires further empirical testing, for the purposes of this exploratory research it demonstrates the practical utility of the SEE systems framework as well as its resonance with the practice of planning and policy making.

Chapter 4: Empirical Case Study Methods for Applying and Illustrating the Conceptual Framework

4.1 Introduction

Objective #4 of my research (Section 1.2) is to illustrate and begin to test the utility of the SEE systems framework (developed in Chapter 3) in the context of innovative examples of knowledge generation and social learning by environmental organizations in land use policy-making and governance. The intent of this chapter is to describe and justify the use of two instrumental case studies and qualitative data collection methods such as key informant interviews, participatory, observational research and policy document analysis for this preliminary test of the SEE systems framework and critical systems planning and policy research. Ideally, given the multi-methodological nature of critical systems planning and policy research other methods such as media analysis, focus groups, community mapping exercises, among others would be employed. However, given the exploratory nature of this research, two instrumental cases and three qualitative data sources provided an adequate empirical base to illustrate and begin to test the SEE systems framework and critical systems planning and policy research. Further testing and refinement of these conceptual tools should include more case studies, perspectives and methods.

4.2 Case Studies: The Oak Ridges Moraine and the Long Point Biosphere Reserve

4.2.1 Instrumental Case Studies

Case study research is generally the preferred strategy when the researcher has little or no control of the phenomena or system of interest, when "how" or "why" questions are being posed, and when the focus is on current issues within a "real-life" context (Yin, 2003). A case study approach is best suited for research that focuses on complex social phenomena because it allows the investigator to retain the holistic and meaningful characteristics of "real-life" events (Yin, 2003). In particular, instrumental case studies are designed to provide insight into a specific issue as well as to refine a theoretical explanation (Berg, 1998), in this case the SEE systems framework and critical systems planning and policy research. Flyvbjerg (2001) also points to the importance of studying "cases and contexts" for phronetic social science research to provide immediate meaning and to explore larger global and conceptual significance.

In my research with its focus on social learning for land-use and environmental resource policy making and governance, I had no control over the socio-ecological or policy context. Case studies are designed to provide insight into a specific issue as well as to refine a theoretical explanation (Berg, 1998), in this case phronetic, social epistemological, critical systems policy research. Two case studies were chosen: the Oak Ridges Moraine land use planning process (1988-2005), and the Long Point World Biosphere Reserve mandate evolution from conservation-focused to sustainability-focused.

4.2.2 Selection of Case Studies

Two case studies were chosen to explore and refine the SEE systems conceptual framework. The choice of the Oak Ridges Moraine as a primary case and the Long Point Biosphere reserve as a secondary case was based upon the following criteria:

1. Innovative, integrated approach to environmental policy making and governance
2. Evidence of key events or processes that have emphasized the importance of social learning in leading to structural, legislative and planning change
3. A strong role for civil society, non-government organizations but including government agencies at all levels in the structural, legislative and planning change
4. Regional in scale and bioregional or ecological boundaries to ensure cross-jurisdictional interactions
5. Sufficient documented history of the issue or environmental governance regime to develop the SEE systems description
6. A venue for action-oriented outcomes of this research, such as a periodic review process
7. Availability of funding
8. Proximity to the University of Waterloo

These criteria were chosen to maintain the scope and feasibility of the dissertation work but also to provide fertile, innovative, empirical ground to illustrate and test the SEE systems conceptual framework and critical systems planning and policy research. As indicated in the introductory chapter, the SEE systems approach is not a conventional planning or policy approach and is not meant to replace, for instance, rational comprehensive planning. As such, it may most usefully be applied in situations in which a broad, systemic, participatory, network or governance-based approach to stewardship and advocacy is being applied to initiate policy change. Thus, the first four criteria narrow the scope of the empirical base of my dissertation work to innovative, integrated, bioregional and civil society-led approaches to policy change through social learning. The remaining four criteria are meant to maintain the feasibility of the research by ensuring sufficient documentation, a constructive output for the research products and logistic and financial practicality.

Based upon these criteria, the Oak Ridges Moraine (ORM) was determined to be an excellent subject for an instrumental case study (Figure 5). After nearly two decades of public debate, advocacy and policy development, the Oak Ridges Moraine case represents an innovative, bioregional, civil-society led example of knowledge creation and social learning that has resulted in a change in environmental, land-use policy with a well-documented history. Civil society-led advocacy, particularly on the part of Save the Oak Ridges Moraine (STORM), a coalition of non-government organizations, throughout the 1990s has led to the implementation of an Oak Ridges Moraine Conservation Plan (2002) through the enactment of the Oak Ridges Moraine Conservation Act (2001).

Figure 5: Map of the Oak Ridges Moraine

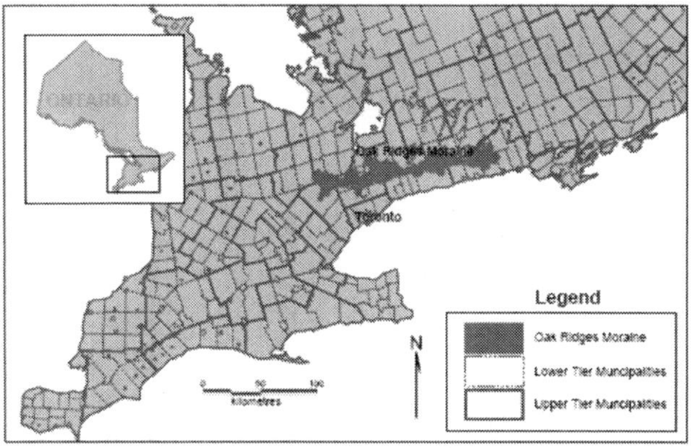

This innovative, environment-first, bioregion-specific plan and legislation reflect a remarkable change in approach to land use planning in the Province of Ontario. Prior to the Oak Ridges Moraine Plan and Act, the municipal-based approach to land use planning in Ontario was seen usually to result in "inconsistent management across municipality boundaries; lack of provincial leadership; inconsistent interpretation of policy by decision makers; no management of cumulative effects; and, ultimately compromised the ecological integrity of the Moraine" (Daphne Brasell Associates Limited , 2003: 5). "The Moraine in many respects has become symbolic of the national growth experience, and serves as an example of how Canadians are rethinking the housing and urban growth forms that have come to dominate Canada's new urban landscapes" (Hanna and Webber, 2005: 17). The resulting evolution in land use policy appears to exhibit the characteristics of learning at a broad, social scale, especially in the context of the civil society, non-government organizations that have advocated for policy change. The Oak Ridges Moraine legislation calls for a 10 year review of the plan in 2014 in conjunction with that of Ontario's Greenbelt Plan. This review will provide an action-oriented venue for intervention based upon my research. I have also engaged in a participatory research relationship with STORM, attending related meetings and engaging in cooperative research initiatives.

While the Oak Ridges Moraine represents a diverse socio-ecological system, the threats from development are most intense in the western reaches of the moraine. This rapidly urbanizing area of the moraine was chosen as the empirical focus. Three civil society, non-government organizations working on the moraine have been chosen to explore the importance of social learning in leading to structural, legislative and planning change. These groups are Save the Oak Ridges Moraine (STORM), Concerned Citizens of King Township (CCKT), and Oak Ridges Friends of the Environment (ORFE). For the purposes of triangulation and to ensure an understanding of the environmental governance system of the ORM, representatives of the relevant provincial ministries, Ministry of Natural Resources (MNR), Ministry of the Environment (MOE), Ministry of Municipal Affairs and Housing (MMAH), Conservation Authorities and municipal government were also contacted (Table 1).

STORM, as previously mentioned, is a bioregional, incorporated not-for-profit organization founded in 1989 in response to increasing development pressures on the moraine and on Ontario's Planning Act that was not addressing the environmental needs of this ecosystem. STORM's goal was to advocate for moraine-specific conservation legislation. As a coalition of groups with a variety of backgrounds, STORM quickly realized the importance of knowledge for legislative change and consequently had to build upon individual knowledge and experience and demonstrate learning at an organizational or social level. To document STORM's learning, interviews were completed with key members of its previous and current board and its executive director. Participant observation at STORM-sponsored meetings also was undertaken (Section 4.3.1.1.1 for interview details).

Part of STORM emerged as a subcommittee of a local, township-focused non-government group known as Concerned Citizens of King Township (CCKT). CCKT has been involved with various land use and environmental issues in King Township (Figure 6) for over 30 years. Throughout its long history, CCKT has informally conducted council watches, undertaken fund raising and intervened in land use decision making within the township with the goal of "keeping King green". To document the social learning associated with the evolution from a local, political jurisdiction-focused group to a bioregional coalition focused on acquiring landform-specific legislation, interviews were also conducted with key members of CCKT.

Figure 6: Map of King Township and Richmond Hill on the Oak Ridges Moraine

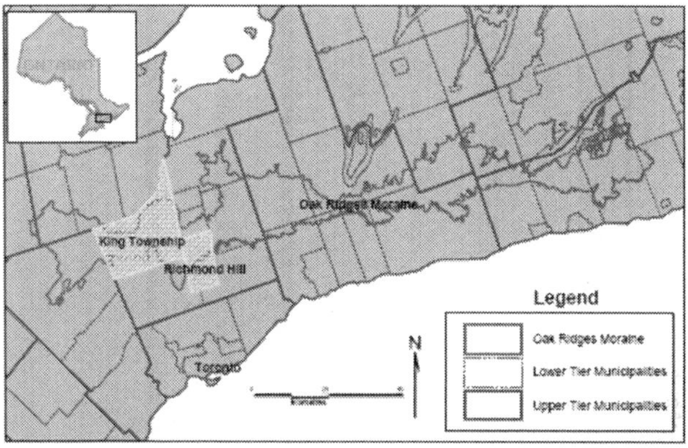

To document social learning since the ORM Conservation Act and Plan, the recently formed Oak Ridges Friends of the Environment (ORFE) group was chosen as the third volunteer, environmental movement organization. The small nucleus of ORFE is centred in the small town of Oak Ridges within the contentious area of Richmond Hill. Members of this group have been involved in several land use decision-making process, constantly referring to the ORM Conservation Act and Plan as touchstones in their advocacy work.

To triangulate the findings from the interviews with the three volunteer, environmental movement organizations, representatives from provincial, conservational authority and municipal government were interviewed. Interviewees representing three provincial ministries (MNR, MOE, MMAH) were chosen because these ministries have been instrumental in the enactment and implementation of the ORM Conservation Act and Plan. A representative of the Conservation Authorities Moraine Coalition (CAMC) was also interviewed. The CAMC is a group of nine of Ontario's 36 conservation authorities with jurisdiction on the moraine. It fosters cooperation and contributes to projects in cooperation with its provincial and municipal partners.

Table 1: Oak Ridges Moraine Interviewees

Interviewee Code	Organizational Affiliation
ORM-STORM-1	STORM Coalition
ORM-STORM-2	STORM Coalition
ORM-STORM-3	STORM Coalition
ORM-STORM-4	STORM Coalition
ORM-STORM-5	STORM Coalition
ORM-STORM-6	STORM Coalition
ORM-CCKT-1	CCKT
ORM-CCKT-2	CCKT
ORM-CCKT-3	CCKT
ORM-CCKT-4	CCKT
ORM-CCKT-5	CCKT
ORM-ORFOE-1	ORFOE
ORM-ORFOE-2	ORFOE
ORM-MNR-1	former MNR
ORM-MOE-1	former MOE
ORM-MMAH-1	MMAH
ORM-MMAH-2	MMAH
ORM-CA-1	Conservation Authority

The resulting qualitative data from these interviews were analyzed in conjunction with minutes of several STORM and Monitoring the Moraine (MTM) meetings. As part of the collaborative, participatory research design, I attended and provided meeting minutes for STORM transition team meetings, MTM monitoring advisory committee meetings, and policy monitoring brain-storming sessions. These data were analyzed based on the SEE systems conceptual framework and used to test the validity of the SEE systems conceptual model of social learning.

The research is also intended to provide a conceptual framework for a related research project which is exploring the potential of the Oak Ridges Moraine and its governance system to be designated as one of UNESCO's World Biosphere Reserves. As a comparative counter point, a long-standing biosphere reserve was chosen as a secondary case study. The Long Point World Biosphere Reserve (Figure 7) and its recent efforts to broaden its mandate from a conservation to a sustainability focus were chosen as they meet the above criteria as an innovative, bioregional, civil-society led example of social learning that has resulted in a change in environmental, land-use policy with a well-documented history.

Figure 7: Map of Long Point

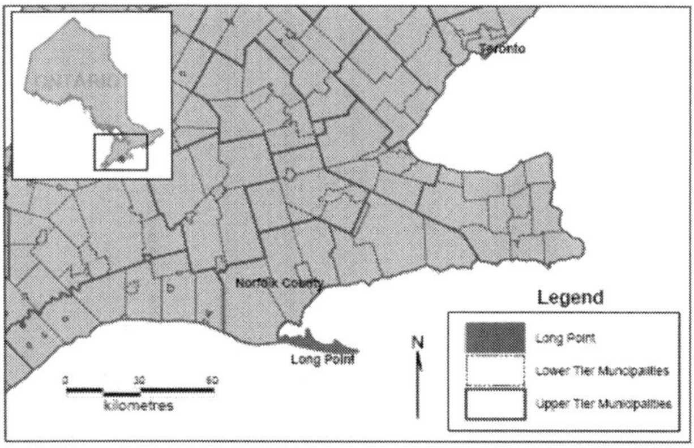

Nominated in 1985 (Francis, 1985a, 1985b), Long Point received its UNESCO World Biosphere Reserve designation in 1986. However, the Long Point area land use planning and governance system has often been described as fragmented and uncoordinated due to the complex overlay of public and private ownership, multi-scalar jurisdictional and bioregional planning and management institutions with varying mandates and management philosophies (Skibicki, 1996). In spite of this, "the biosphere reserve concept has provided an opportunity to integrate a wide range of government conservation initiatives, private stewardship practices, and economic activities into a more coherent planning vision for the Long Point area" (Skibicki, 1996: 1).

In the twentieth year of Long Point as a biosphere reserve, the Long Point World Biosphere Reserve Foundation (LPWBRF), a charitable, not for profit, volunteer organization, decided to expand its activities from a primarily environmental focus (Craig et al., 2003; Francis and Whitelaw, 2001) to one that encompasses a broader notion of sustainability. To this end, the LPWBRF hosted a series of four community sustainability workshops during December 2005 designed to engage the local biosphere reserve community with the objective of identifying possible sustainable development projects that the Board might facilitate to help improve planning and management in the Long Point area. The four workshops targeted stakeholders from four key groups in the

Long Point community: business and industry, the service sector, agriculture and conservation. The workshop process is more fully described in Section 4.2.2.1.2.1 and the number of attendees for each workshop are listed below in Table 2. The business and industry workshop had 6 participants, the service sector workshop 6, the conservation workshop 25, and the agriculture workshop 19.

Table 2: Long Point Sustainability Workshop Series Attendees

Workshop	Number of Attendees
Business and Industry	6
Service Sector	6
Agriculture	19
Conservation	25

This process has been documented in conjunction with the LPWBRF and researchers at the University of Waterloo, including the author (Whitelaw and McCarthy, 2006; McCarthy et al., In Press). It has been argued that this process highlights the value of the community sustainability workshops for improved biosphere reserve logistics activities and provides an example of social learning (McCarthy et al., In Press). To triangulate the findings of these workshops and to provide a richer longitudinal perspective of the LPWBRF, past and current board members and advisors were interviewed (Section 4.6.1.1.1 for interview details) (Table 3).

Table 3: Long Point World Biosphere Reserve Interviewees

Interviewee Code	Organizational Affiliation
LP-1	Current LPWBRF Board Member
LP-2	Current LPWBRF Board Member
LP-3	Former / LPWBRF Board Member
LP-4	Board Advisory / Former MOE

4.3 Empirical Data Collection and Analysis

4.3.1 Data Collection and Analysis for the Oak Ridges Moraine Case Study

4.3.1.1 Selection of Methods: Key Informant Interviews, Participatory, Observational Research and Policy Document Analysis

Midgley (2000) identifies three interrelated problems associated with the use of only one method, or a very narrow set of methods. These are that the intervener is likely to be unresponsive to diverse understandings of issues; that the intervener is unlikely to address change or learning as people's understanding evolves; and, that the intervener may see all issues and perspectives through the same lens. Thus, for the purposes of critical systems policy research, combining multiple methods and acknowledging a plurality of perspectives are crucial.

4.3.1.1.1 Interviews

Interviewing allows the researcher to gain an in-depth, detailed account of the socio-ecological and policy context of the respondents and their individual perspectives on it (Fontana and Frey, 2000; Lewis, 2003). For the development of SEE systems descriptions of both case studies, a synthesis of various, relevant perspectives is key. In total, 20 interviews were conducted for the Oak Ridges Moraine case study and 4 for the Long Point case study between March and August 2006.

4.3.1.1.1.1 In-depth, Semi-Structured, Elite Interviews

Complex processes or structures are best captured using in-depth interviews, as they provide a depth of focus and the opportunity for detailed explanation and clarification. Specifically, to gain an understanding of the complex process of knowledge creation and use for policy making requires the detailed personal focus that in-depth interviews allow. In-depth interviews provide researchers with a depth of focus not possible with focus groups or other fora (Lewis, 2003).

A standard set of questions provided some systematic and consistent aspects to the qualitative database (Appendix A). This type of interview involved use of a number of predetermined questions and / or special topics. These questions were generally asked of each interviewee in a systematic and consistent order, but the interviewees were allowed freedom to digress. That is, the interviewers are permitted (in fact expected) to probe far beyond the answers to their prepared and standardized questions (Berg, 1998). This style of interview allows the researcher to probe a consistent set of issues from a variety of perspectives (Berg, 1998; Hughes, 2002).

4.3.1.1.1.3 Interview Transcription

There are two main ways to collect qualitative data from an interview: note taking and verbatim tape recorded transcription (Hughes, 2002). Note taking with digital recording for verification purposes was chosen. Note taking allows the researcher to capture commentary outside the context of the interview (e.g. document references, contextual notes) (Arthur and Nazroo, 2003). Digital recording allows for verification of notes taken from the interview and could be transcribed at a later date but were not directly transcribed as verbatim transcription is time consuming and costly (Hughes, 2002).

4.3.1.1.1.4 Protocol for Interview Data Collection

Interviewees were chosen based on their experience with the Oak Ridges Moraine planning and policy process from 1988-2005 as identified through an initial screening with long-standing members of the STORM coalition. Snowball sampling was also used in the context of the interviews to identify other potential interviewees.

Snowball sampling generally refers to the identification of potential interviewees based on the recommendation of previous informants (Berg, 1998; Ritchie et al., 2003). It is particularly useful as a sampling technique for groups that are small and connected only by a particular interest such as professional expertise (i.e. civil society, non-government environmental advocacy groups) (Ritchie et al., 2003). Each interviewee was asked who else the researcher should talk to regarding the Oak Ridges Moraine land use process from 1988-2005. If a name was identified more than twice, an interview was requested with the identified individual.

4.3.1.1.1.5 Interview Protocol

4.3.1.1.1.5.1 Initial Contact

An attempt was made to implement a consistent approach to communicating with and interacting with interviewees to foster a respectful research relationship. Potential interviewees identified either through initial screening or through snowball sampling were contacted either by telephone or e-mail. This initial contact identified the research team and its affiliations (Debbe Crandall, Department of Environmental and Resource Studies, University of Waterloo and Dan McCarthy, School of Planning, University of Waterloo), outlined the nature of the research, and the nature of their involvement should they choose to participate (90 minute interview). A copy of the interview questions and a statement of the University of Waterloo ethics approval were also provided (usually by e-mail). The University of Waterloo ethics review requires all faculty, staff, undergraduate and graduate students conducting research with humans on or off campus to ensure that their projects undergo prior ethics review and clearance through the Office of Research Ethics (ORE). The intent of the ethics review process is to ensure that all research involving human participants is consistent with UW's Guidelines and the Tri-Council Policy Statement: Ethical Conduct for Research Involving Humans (1998), as well as ethics guidelines of professional associations. This process offers a level of assurance to the research participants, the researchers and the University that the procedures proposed are consistent with these research ethics guidelines, that the rights and welfare of the participants will be protected, and that the participants will be involved in a consent process which is fully informed and voluntary (Office of Research Ethics, 2005).

4.3.1.1.1.5.2 Interview

In the context of the individual interviews, respondents were asked if the interview questions as provided were an appropriate way to proceed or if they preferred an alternative approach to addressing the relevant issues. If the interviewee was comfortable with the questions, the proposed questions were used. At the beginning of each interview, the interviewee was asked to review, and if he or she chose, sign the consent form approved by University of Waterloo Research Ethics Office. Interviewees were also asked verbally if he or she was comfortable with the interview being digitally recorded. For each interview, there were at least two members of the research team present, the interviewer and a designated or lead scribe. If a third member of the research team was available, this person acted as a secondary scribe. The lead scribe took notes on a laptop computer; these notes would eventually become the interview transcript. After each interview, the members of the team would take time to review their notes to ensure completeness and accuracy.

4.3.1.1.1.5.3 Follow-up E-mail

Following the interview, an e-mail was sent extending the thanks of the researchers, requesting any documents offered, and responding to any interviewee questions, concerns or requests.

4.3.1.1.1.6 Handling of Transcripts

Each transcript, a digital word processing file, was manually reviewed and then reviewed against the digital recording of the interview to ensure readability, accuracy and completeness.

4.3.1.1.1.7 Transcript Analysis

The transcripts were analyzed manually based upon the interview questions. Due to the semi-structured nature of the interview, the interviewee had the option of deviating from the preset questions and simply recounting the narrative, from their perspective, of the development of the Oak Ridges Moraine planning and policy-development process. Despite this option, critical elements relevant to the themes of this research could still be pulled out of such narrative descriptions. In both cases, key events, key individuals / groups/ organizations / agencies, the role of knowledge and learning and resulting shifts in policy or mandate could be identified. In particular, evidence of the three descriptive and three prescriptive SEE systems conceptual framework principles (Section 3.2.2) was extracted from the transcripts. Emphasis on certain themes (such as scale, types of knowledge and critical reflection) resulted in further analysis and eventually resulted in the conceptual model for social learning. If the interview transcript lacked clarity or the transcriber missed information, the researcher referenced the associated digital audio recording, if the interviewee agreed to be recorded. All interviewees agreed to be recorded.

4.3.1.1.2 Participant Observation

Participant observation refers to "research that involves social interaction between researcher and informants in the milieu of the latter, during which data are systematically and unobtrusively collected" (Taylor et al., 1984: 15). Participant observation can serve as a useful method or complement to other methods for producing empirical material on non-trivial phenomena in a "natural context" (Alvesson and Skoldberg, 1999). This interpretation of participatory observation "assumes that knowledge develops from experience, particularly the experience of social-political action" (Neuman, 1997: 24). Participant observers generally gather data through several means, including,casual conversations, in-depth, informal, and unstructured interviews, as well as formally structured interviews (Jorgensen, 1989). Aside from interviews, I gathered qualitative data for both case studies by attending and participating in meetings and workshops and through casual conversations with meeting attendees. In both cases I kept detailed notes on the content and context (e.g. group dynamics, non-verbal responses) of meetings.

I actively engaged members of the STORM coalition in collaborative research initiatives, including fundamental aspects of the conceptual and empirical basis for this research. I have been involved with the development of a policy monitoring framework for the STORM Monitoring the Moraine (MTM) project and have participated in the documentation of the MTM's Monitoring Advisory Committee meetings. In consultation with Debbe Crandall, STORM's executive director, my research has embraced the concept of social learning as a key factor in citizen-led, land use policy change. And I have also begun to explore the potential of an Oak Ridges Moraine World Biosphere Reserve. Together, a team of researchers and practitioners from the University of

Waterloo and STORM have sought and received funding to undertake the exploratory research and documentation review as a basis for recognizing the Oak Ridges Moraine as a unique landscape and model for sustainability worthy of the World Biosphere Reserve designation. Throughout the participant observation process I kept detailed notes capturing not only the content of discussions but also contextual information such as organizational affiliations of individuals, group dynamics and non-verbal responses. This research is meant to provide STORM with a framework for knowledge and social learning in its pursuit of the UNESCO Biosphere Reserve designation.

4.3.1.1.3 Policy Document Analysis

In the context of the interviews, each respondent was asked to identify the key documents for understanding the issues and events associated with the Oak Ridges Moraine land-use planning process between 1988 and 2005. In the follow-up e-mail, a request was made to respondents for documents that they had offered to acquire on our behalf. Many of the background policy documents were acquired in this way. Documents that could be acquired through the internet or through the University Library were collected. If the document could not be acquired through these means, the referring interviewee was contacted to inquire about its availability.

Once all the documents were acquired, they were systematically reviewed as a means of triangulation and to enrich the SEE systems descriptions. For each policy document, its purpose, content and significance for the research were described. The policy document analysis was used to verify details regarding key events, key individuals / groups / organizations / agencies, the role of knowledge and learning and resulting shifts in policy identified in the context of the interviewees' narrative descriptions of the ORM policy development process. A newspaper or media analysis could be undertaken in the context of a broader participatory, socio-ecological systems description as described in Section 4.3.

4.3.2 Data Collection and Analysis for the Long Point Biosphere Reserve Case Study

4.3.2.1 Selection of Methods: Key Informant Interviews, Participatory, Observational Research and Policy Document Analysis

4.3.2.1.1 Participant Observation – Community Sustainability Workshops

I have forged a collaborative, participatory research relationship with members of the LPWBRF similar to the collaborative relationship with members of STORM. I became involved in the facilitation and documentation of the community sustainability workshop series held in December of 2005. As a participant observer I attended all of the workshops and participated directly in the documentation for the small group or open space sessions as well as in the follow-up analysis, and co-authored the final workshop synthesis report for the LPWBRF Board. All of the flip charts and notes from the facilitated sessions as well as detailed notes regarding workshop attendee organizational affiliations, group dynamics and non-verbal responses provided a rich qualitative database for analysis.

4.3.2.1.2.1 Workshop Facilitation and Documentation

The LPWBRF Board made the decision to host four workshops organized around four community sectors in December of 2005. These included business and industry, service, conservation and agriculture. Extensive efforts were made to contact representatives from each of these sectors and invite them to the workshops. The workshops were held in or near the Town of Simcoe. Attendance varied with each workshop. The business and industry workshop had 6 participants, the service sector workshop 6, the conservation workshop 25, and the agriculture workshop 19.

Each workshop consisted of three main phases.

1. An introductory presentation on biosphere reserves and the work of the LPWBRF since the reserve was established in 1986.

2. A presentation by the Norfolk County Planning Department on the County's 2026 Sustainability Vision (Norfolk County, 2003), developed as part of the County's latest Official Plan review process.
3. A facilitated session to allow participants to express their views on the topic of sustainability.

The type of facilitated session was determined by the number of workshop attendees. The smaller workshops involved roundtable discussions, while the larger sessions involved the facilitated technique known as "Open Spaces". Open Spaces has been described as a systems-based "self organizing practice that releases the inherent creativity and leadership in people" (Tartaglia and Ramnath, 2005). Open Spaces consists of four phases: introductory presentations; a plenary discussion where attendees identify discussion topics; one or two rounds of small group discussions where attendees vote with their feet on topics of discussion; and, a final summary plenary discussion. The initial plenary discussion was meant to identify the topics that the group of participants wanted to discuss after hearing the purpose of the workshops and the two presentations. These topics were listed on one or two flip charts. Each topic was numbered on each chart from one through ten. The participants were then asked to choose the topic they were most interested in on the first flip chart. Participants then moved to a pre-determined station numbered one through ten where they discussed the topic with others who also chose that topic. A note taker and reporter were assigned for each group. Once discussions finished, the group returned to a plenary session to present and discuss their results. This procedure was repeated for the second flip chart themes, time permitting. The technique provided valuable information about what the group was actually interested in because they determined the topics and then voted with their feet in terms of what topics were discussed.

For both the Open Spaces sessions and the small group discussions, the following points were used to stimulate discussion.

1. Trends
2. Issues
3. Barriers
4. Existing Resources
5. Ideas that may work in the Long Point context

Graduate students from the University of Waterloo, Faculty of Environmental Studies assisted with note taking and transcription. Furthermore, team members involved with the Biosphere Sustainability Project (www.fes.uwaterloo/research/biosphere), led by Dr. Robert Gibson and Dr. George Francis of the Environment and Resource Studies Department, also contributed to analysis of the workshop results.

4.3.2.1.2 Interviews

To ensure some measure of comparability between the Long Point case and the primary Oak Ridges Moraine case study, four in-depth, semi-structured, elite interviews were conducted using the same data collection methods described above. The questions used in the Oak Ridges case study (Appendix A) were adapted for use in the Long Point case (Appendix B). These interviews were meant to triangulate and augment the findings derived from the Community Sustainability Workshop Series. Evidence of the three descriptive and three prescriptive SEE systems conceptual framework principles (Section 3.2.2) was extracted from the transcripts. Further analysis sought evidence of the themes of scale, types of knowledge and critical reflection relating to the resonance of the SEE systems model for social learning with the Long Point case study.

4.3.2.1.3 Policy Document Analysis

Relevant policy documents were identified and collected in a similar manner to that undertaken in the primary case study. As above, the purpose, content and significance of each policy document for the research were described. The policy document analysis was utilized to verify details regarding key events, key individuals / groups/ organizations / agencies, the role of knowledge and learning and resulting shifts in policy identified in the context of the interviewees' narrative descriptions of the Long Point World Biosphere Reserve's evolution from a conservation-focus to address a broader notion of sustainability.

4.4 Development of the SEE Systems Descriptions

A SEE systems description differs from more traditional abiotic, biotic, cultural (ABC) descriptions of integrated resource and environmental systems (Nelson and Wilcox, 1996). ABC descriptions represent a significant step toward integrating social and ecological systems descriptions. SEE systems descriptions build on this precedent and focus on the interaction among social, ecological and epistemological systems.

The SEE systems description is most usefully viewed in the context of a long-term, collaborative, systems-based description of an environmental policy issue such as those documented in such seminal works as *Barriers and Bridges* (Gunderson et al., 1995), *Linking Social and Ecological Systems* (Berkes and Folke, 1998), *Panarchy* (Gunderson and Holling, 2002) and *Navigating Social-Ecological Systems* (Berkes and Folke, 2003). Such socio-ecological systems descriptions do not view humans systems as embedded in an ecological system or ecosystems as embedded in human systems but rather as a different type of system altogether (Walker et al., 2006). Walker et al. (2006) document the development of the theoretical tools including resilience, adaptability and panarchy (Section 2.5.3) that have emerged inductively from long-term case studies of abrupt change and paradoxes in resource management. Kay et al. (1999) and Waltner-Toews et al. (2004) (Section 2.5.3) have also developed protocols for describing integrated socio-ecological systems. Folke et al. (2005) have even highlighted the importance of knowledge and learning and social sources of the resilience and adaptability in socio-ecological systems. All of these approaches to socio-ecological systems descriptions require collaborative, participatory relationships with stakeholders and a long-term case study and monitoring approach. Each of these participatory approaches requires several general, non-linear, iterative phases:

- Document the system context (spatial and temporal) - document the history of the system and the scales of the socio-ecological system
- Describe and analyze social, economic, political, biological, ecological, geological (etc.) systems
- Synthesize knowledge into a systems description / narrative – describing self-organizing phenomena, attractors, thresholds, cross-scalar dynamics (etc.)
- Develop a vision or goal for the system of interest based upon a democratic, participatory process

- Monitor for change
- Adapt management and governance structures

While this type of participatory, interdisciplinary process is beyond the scope of this research, the intent here is to incorporate epistemology and learning explicitly into this type of systemic description and planning process. A SEE systems description therefore would require such a process to be critcally reflective, that is, to describe how it is describing the system. Or, put differently, to describe the knowledge and learning that contribute to the system description thus making it a more transparent process.

Interview and workshop transcripts, policy document analysis and secondary sources were all utilized to develop the SEE systems descriptions of both the primary and secondary case studies. Throughout the collection and analysis of the qualitative data for both cases, I focused attention on emerging evidence of the interconnections among the social (especially political and economic), ecological and epistemological systems. In particular, I looked for evidence supporting the three-part typology of knowledge (scientific, local technical, governance).

Interview and workshop transcripts were manually analyzed, utilizing digital audio recordings (where available) for clarification purposes only. Themes such as the interactions and interconnections among social, ecological and epistemological systems and the three types of knowledge as described by the interviewee or workshop attendee were highlighted. I also looked for emergent themes such as the evolution of civil society organizations on the ORM coming to understand the need to "scale-up" their focus from local to regional to bioregional and beyond; and, the lack of recognition and understanding of the World Biosphere Reserve concept in the Long Point area community. These themes were then integrated and analyzed in the context of the socio-ecological, epistemological systems description.

4.5 Conclusions

This chapter was intended to justify the selection and use of multiple methods and two case studies in the context of a critical systems planning and policy research methodological framework. Critical systems planning and policy research is a reflective, systems-based and action-oriented approach to the study of policy and policy development. The intent of critical systems planning and policy research is to explore the implications of a complex and critical systems-based approach to policy research; describe the structures and dynamics of complex SEE systems; explain the interactions, interconnections among social, ecological and epistemological systems; and, provide action-oriented research outcomes.

Two case studies, one primary (Oak Ridges Moraine) and one secondary (Long Point World Biosphere Reserve), were chosen. The case studies were selected based upon their innovative, integrated approach to environmental policy making; evidence of social learning leading to legislative change; a strong role for civil society organizations; regional in scale with bioregional boundaries; a well-documented history; a venue for action-oriented outcomes; an opportunity to examine social learning in both a potential and existing World Biosphere Reserve; and, the availability of funding and proximity to the University of Waterloo.

The next chapter provides general background on the history and context of integrated land use planning in Ontario and on the concept and implementation of UNESCO's World Biosphere Reserves in Ontario. More specific background on the two case studies, including the integrated land use SEE system from 1988-2005 and the shifting of the mandate of the Long Point World Biosphere Reserve Board from conservation-focused to a broader notion of sustainability, is presented in chapters six and seven.

Chapter 5: Background for the Empirical Case Studies

5.1 Introduction

The goal of this chapter is to provide the background for the SEE systems descriptions of both the Oak Ridges Moraine and the Long Point World Biosphere Reserve in the next two chapters. This chapter provides a preliminary sketch of the kind of governance knowledge require for systems-based, holarchic, multi-perspective descriptions of the interrelated social, ecological and epistemological issues associated with environmental policy development (as described in Section 4.3).

As noted in Section 4.5.1, the Oak Ridges Moraine land use planning and policy development process from 1988-2005 and the Long Point World Biosphere sustainability workshop process provide excellent case studies for exploring the SEE systems framework. Both exemplify the need to understand the complex, systemic interconnections among social, ecological and epistemological systems; individual agents and social structures; scientific, local technical and governance knowledges; and, the plurality of perspectives involved in environmental governance. The Oak Ridges Moraine, as the primary case study, is described first. The Long Point case follows to reinforce the findings of the ORM case through cross-case comparison of the application of the SEE framework and conceptual model of social learning.

As described in Section 4.3, a SEE systems description is most usefully developed in the context of a broader, long-term, participatory, systems-based planning process. As such, the systems descriptions developed in this chapter, to the extent possible, follow the general phases of the socio-ecological systems description outlined in section 4.3. Thus, the chapter provides a brief history of conservation and the environmental and conservation planning in Canada. This is followed by an overview of the current, environmental planning and policy context in the province of Ontario. This provides a context for chapters six and seven that provide narrative descriptions and analyses of both case studies based upon the SEE systems conceptual model of social learning. These descriptions and analyses are based on relevant policy documents, grey literature, workshops and in-depth, semi-structured interviews. Insights are drawn from the empirical grounding of the SEE systems framework in the two case studies, setting the stage for Chapter eight which examines the implications of this work and provides recommendations and conclusions.

5.2 A Brief History of Environmental Planning and Policy in Canada

This section provides a brief summary of the evolution of environmental policy in Canada. The intent is to provide general historical context for both case studies and illustrate the type of governance information required for a SEE system description. This is followed by a description of the current policy context for the two empirical case studies.

In *Canadian Natural Resource and Environmental Policy: Political Economy and Public Policy*, Hessing et al. (2005) describe four stages of environmental policy evolution in Canada. The four stages include the era of government inaction (pre-1800); a concern with resource rents (1800-1880); a concern with resource conservation (1880-1950); and, the current "management" era (1950-Present).

Before 1800 the governments of colonies of Great Britain in North America took little action to protect the region's natural resources. While some resources, such as gold and timber suitable for ship building were reserved for the Crown, most resources were available for use by individual colonists. Eventually, colonial governments began to secure different forms of property rights to ensure mining and forestry operations had exclusive right to extract the relevant resources. Resource use on private lands experienced little regulation. However, the area of privately held lands during this era was vastly out-stripped by the area of Crown lands. To take advantage of the vast potential of resource extraction on Crown lands, commissions were established to survey, title and lease these lands (Hessing et al., 2005).

This led to what Hessing et al. (2005) describe as the Era of Revenue Generation (1800-1880). During this era, annual rents were collected for mineral and timber claims.

Royalty and stumpage charges were levied and early forms of corporate taxation schemes were developed. To administer these programs, the first government departments were formed. Confederation in 1867 brought about a new, provincially-based land use regime. Confederation allowed most lands and resources to be retained and sold by the provinces, allowing for the generation of provincial government revenues. By 1880 the negative results of this land use and environmental policy regime were evident on the deforested central and eastern Ontario landscape.

Hessing et al. (2005) characterize the period from 1880 to 1950 as one of conservation. Technological advances in resource extraction and processing in the pulp and paper and oil industries required governments to intervene and moderate resource extraction. Constitutional arrangements distributing federal and provincial responsibilities established the early environmental policy framework for Canada and its provinces. However, most of these pre-WWII environmental policies were fragmented and primarily aimed at protecting human health. In spite of this, the "conservation era" did see the establishment of Canada's system of national parks and reserves as well as the Commission of Conservation Canada (more details below) which was meant to guide resource conservation through comprehensive resource inventories. The 1930s and 1940s also saw the establishment of two regionally-significant and integrative conservation programs: the Prairie Farm Rehabilitation Administration and Ontario's Conservation Authorities. Non-government, environmental movement organizations such as the Federation of Ontario Naturalists (FON) and the Ontario Conservation and Reforestation Association (OCRA) also emerged to address environmental degradation issues.

The post-war era began with the passing of the Canada Forestry Act (1949) and provincial-level initiatives to ensure long-term resource conservation, such as Ontario's Conservation Authorities Act (1946). This fourth and final era Hessing et al. (2005) describe as the Management Era (1950-Present). "Over this period, the consolidation and force of environmental activity, in both legislative and administrative character, accelerated dramatically" (Hessing et al., 2005: 57). In 1960, the Diefenbaker government attempted to develop national-level structures for natural resources management by establishing federal departments of forests, energy and resources. Despite some resistance by provincial governments, this period saw environmental protection shift from self-regulation by industry to government regulation. As such, both provincial and federal governments developed structures to regulate, especially regarding industrial pollution. However, environmental management was largely fragmented and narrowly focused. In 1971, the Trudeau government restructured existing resource departments to formally recognize the breadth of the environmental agenda, including pollution protection and the preservation of air, water and soil quality, with the establishment of Environment Canada. The 1970s and 1980s saw the development of environmental departments at the provincial level, and environmental impact assessment was introduced to anticipate and mitigate environmental degradation associated with major resource projects. In spite of these attempts to integrate and defragment the environmental agenda in Canada, disciplinary and jurisdictional "silos" continued. As a result, "policy approaches tend to focus on resolving political disputes over resources, rather than on fostering an effective strategy for long-term sustainability" (Hessing et al., 2005: 59).

Howlett (2002) also has traced the evolution of environmental policy in Canada. He describes three main phases of environmental policy development in Canada: pre-regulatory, private, common-law era; public-law era; and, the contemporary era of market-based and multi-stakeholder environmental governance approaches. These three phases loosely correlate with Hessing et al.'s (2005) four phases but focus more directly on the history of Canada's environmental policy as it has led to a Canadian environmental implementation style (Howlett, 2002).

Overlapping Hessing et al.'s (2005) conservation and management eras, Howlett (2002) describes the pre-1960s as the common-law or pre-regulatory era of Canadian environmental policy. During this era, a variety of common-law policy instruments was available to individuals to deal with nuisance pollution and other damages to private property as a result of industrialization. This approach proved inadequate in dealing with non-point source pollution where liability was difficult if not impossible to determine. Howlett (2002) indicates that, nearing the end of this period, courts in the United States allowed for notions of public trust to be considered regarding common resources such as air and the coast line. Canadian courts refused to acknowledge such concerns. Class action suits and criminal charges could also be used in an effort to protect the public good from the impacts of pollution and habitat loss.

With the failure of private, common-law to address the broad and complex impacts of environmental degradation, a public-law and thus, a more regulatory approach to environmental policy developed between the 1960s and the 1990s (Howlett, 2002). This public-law or regulatory period witnessed the formation of Canada's distinct environmental policy implementation style. "In the 1960-1990 period Canada developed all the elements of a compliance system of environmental policy implementation in which recourse to penalties and coercion exists only as a very infrequently used last resort of administrators" (Howlett, 2002: 34). As a result of the historical importance of resource-based industry in Canada, and especially single-industry reliance in many areas of the country, this implementation style was characterized by close bargaining between corporate interests and government agencies. The role of citizens within this environmental governance regime was formally limited, even after the enactment of the 1982 Canadian Charter of Rights and Freedoms, by Canadian legal precedent. This style of environmental policy implementation was, ironically, not focused on environmental protection but rather on the modification of business activities (Howlett, 2002).

The contemporary era (1990s-present) of Canadian environmental policy, according to Howlett (2002), has been characterized by market-based, cooperative, multi-stakeholder and comprehensive environmental policy instruments. These recent environmental governance trends are driven both by a greater appreciation of the complexity of environmental issues and neo-conservative political-economic pressure for governments at all levels to do "more with less" as a result of economic globalization. Tax-based incentive and voluntary cooperative programs emerged as part of Canada's response to international treaties such as Kyoto, including the Canadian Industry Packaging Stewardship Initiative and the Voluntary Challenge and Registry program. However, these programs as well as many of the initiatives of the 1990 Canadian Green Plan failed to have a significant impact (Howlett, 2002). Cooperative, multi-party initiatives meant to bring together representatives from government, industry and environmental non-government organizations such as the provincial Round Tables in the Environment and Economy also emerged during this era. The Round Tables, despite having been abandoned, as well as the legacy of environmental assessment in Canada (described below), now ensure that environmental decision making incorporates some kind of public consultation process.

Gibson et al. (2005) also describe four stages in the development from environmental regulations to advanced environmental assessment (EA), and twelve trends in the growth of EA. The first stage corresponds to Howlett's public law or regulatory phase of environmental policy development. The second phase speaks less to a shift in policy and more to a shift in thinking around environmental policy. Phases three and four correspond to, but move beyond, Howlett's contemporary era of integrated, cooperative, multi-stakeholder policy to address explicitly sustainability in environmental governance. Gibson et al.'s (2005) major trends document the evolution of Canadian environmental policy from fragmented, expert-oriented, law-based regulation to more open and participatory, comprehensive, integrative approaches that acknowledge different kinds of knowledge and move beyond formal regulatory processes:

> Stage 1: reactive pollution control through measures responding to identified local problems (usually air, water or soil pollution), with solutions considered technical matters to be addressed through closed negotiation of abatement requirements between government officials and the polluters.
>
> Stage 2: proactive impact identification and mitigation through impact assessment and project approval/licensing, still focused on biophysical concerns (although now integrating consideration of various receptors) and still treated as a largely technical issue with no serious public role (but perhaps expert review).
>
> Stage 3: integration of broader environmental considerations in project selection and planning through environmental assessment processes with:
>
> - Consideration of socio-economic as well as biophysical effects;
> - Obligatory examination of alternatives, aiming to identify the best options environmentally as well as economically; and,
> - Public reviews (that reveal expert conflicts and uncertainties, and consequently the significance of public choice).
>
> Stage 4: integrated planning and decision making for sustainability, addressing policies and programs as well as projects, cumulative and global effects with review and decision processes:
>
> - Devoted to empowering the public;

- Recognizing uncertainties and favouring precaution, diversity, reversibility, adaptability; and,
- Expecting positive steps towards sustainability.

(Gibson et al., 2005: 22).

Collectively, these studies highlight an evolution in Canadian environmental policy from colonial resource extraction, to a realization of a need for conservation, to active, expert-oriented management and regulation, and finally to the contemporary era of integrated, multi-stakeholder environmental policy. Given this context, the next section provides an overview of the current structures and processes that underlie the current environmental policy system for the two case studies.

5.3 A Brief History of Environmental Stewardship in Ontario

As early as 1870, foresters began calling for extensive reforestation projects in response to the environmental degradation that followed European settlement (Fisher and Alexander, 1993). The new conservation-oriented SEE system self-organized around civil-society groups such as the Federation of Ontario Naturalists (FON) and Ontario Conservation and Reforestation Association (OCRA) with links to key government bureaucrats and academics.

The provincial government's response of establishing key resource protection agencies, such as the Department of Planning and Development and the conservation authorities, was the culmination of many years of concerted effort by groups of dedicated Ontarians concerned with preserving the Province's natural resources (Richardson, 1974). Many of these concerned individuals, amateurs and professionals alike, had come together to form naturalist or conservation groups due to their concern over the degradation of natural resources in Ontario. Richardson (1974) cites the influence of two groups, FON and OCRA, in the conservation movement.

The FON was an amalgamation of naturalist clubs from across the province, drawn together formally in May 1931 to have more influence on legislation affecting wildlife (Richardson, 1974: 1). In 1938, among its other achievements, the FON completed the

Natural Resources of King Township report. This report summarized a survey of the deterioration of the natural resources of King Township (on the ORM) and presented a basis for a plan of rehabilitation (Richardson, 1974: 2). Although the rehabilitation effort was not carried out as the report recommended, a key contribution was the profound realization that "conservation cannot be attained by piecemeal methods, but rather that it must be accomplished with a multi-purpose programme for the renewal of all natural resources in an area" (Richardson, 1974: 3). The report and the FON garnered many accolades and soon began to receive support from a like-minded organization, the Ontario Conservation and Reforestation Association (OCRA). OCRA was formed in 1936. It was an informal organization made up of elected county officials invited by the farming community, in particular Watson H. Porter, managing editor of the *Farmer's Advocate* (London, Ontario). The association was initiated to respond collectively to the impacts of the 1936 drought (Richardson, 1974: 2). OCRA's unique strength was its rural base and the direct involvement of local elected officials. As Watson H. Porter indicated in a 1936 *Farmer's Advocate* article, "if the farm people and the officers of rural municipalities would not put their shoulders to the wheel, then it would not be worthwhile going any further" (Richardson, 1974: 4).

In February 1941 at its annual meeting, the members of OCRA passed the following resolution meant to address conservation and restoration in Ontario and another potentially pressing issue for the province and the nation as the Second World War progressed:

- Realizing the vital necessity of conserving our natural resources and appreciating the fact that Canada will be confronted with a vital problem of rehabilitation following the present war,
- Therefore be it resolved that this association appoint a committee to study the establishment of a Canadian conservation corps or other plans related to conservation and reforestation.
- And be it resolved that such a committee be appointed by the chair today with power to act, and that this committee proceed to secure the support and active cooperation of all other interested bodies.

As this committee began to seek out the support of other interested parties, it discovered that the FON at its annual meeting two weeks prior to the OCRA meeting had appointed a committee with the same intent (Richardson, 1974: 9). Acting together, the two committees organized a conference at the Ontario Agricultural College in Guelph for late April 1941, inviting representatives from all organizations active in conservation and restoration in Ontario. This influential group, to become known as the Guelph Conference, comprised a "who's who" of conservation at the time. The Conference's members were representatives of the following organizations: Ontario Conservation and Reforestation Association (ORCA), Canadian Society of Forest Engineers (later the Canadian Institute of Forestry), Federation of Ontario Naturalists, Royal Canadian Institute, Canadian Society of Technical Agriculturalists, Canadian Conservation Association, Ontario Federation of Anglers and Hunters, Royal Canadian Legion, and Men of the Trees (Richardson, 1974: 10). The Guelph Conference established the following four main objectives:

1) To give coherence and coordination to a program of conservation
2) To make available to government or municipal bodies the advice and guidance of its members who are recognized as specialists in their respective fields.
3) To give impetus in every possible way to implementing recommendations regarding conservation measures.
4) To disseminate information relating to the present status of our renewable natural resources and the need for undertaking adequate measures for their restoration. (Richardson, 1974: 10).

To achieve these objectives, the members of the Conference set out an agenda to describe and assess the present conditions of the province's natural resources (e.g. desiccation, floods, forest cover, soil management), the necessary actions to address the degradation of the resources, and the anticipated difficulties associated with these actions (Richardson, 1974: 13). The necessary actions were meant to address the degradation of natural resources that had resulted from "the unplanned individualistic exploitation of the past hundred years" through "planned management based on knowledge and recognizing public as well as private interest" (Richardson, 1974: 13). It was recognized that

> Natural resources form a delicate balanced system in which all parts are interdependent and they cannot be successfully handled, piecemeal. The present situation requires the coordination of existing relevant knowledge and its amplification where necessary, and then the development of a comprehensive plan for treating the natural resources on a wide public basis. To this end a body of technically trained men should be appointed, with powers to use pertinent information, wherever available, to initiate field work where needed to complete the knowledge and to draw upon a

> working plan of conservation, carrying on their task at all times in close co-operation with the administrative authorities
> (Richardson, 1974: 13).

Of the two main difficulties identified by the Guelph Conference, one was a function of the global political context of the time and the other due to a difficulty still facing conservationists today. First, it was made clear that such a conservation agenda would require trained people to carry it out. It was realized that during the war there would be a shortage of such people and that training programs would be required. Second, the members of the Guelph Conference astutely recognized the innovative nature of their approach to natural resources and that it would "cut across traditional lines, both of opinion and administrative practice" (Richardson, 1974: 13). Aside from recognizing the ideological and institutional barriers to their approach, they also wisely identified a potential opportunity to tie conservation to the political economic climate of the day. "The future welfare of the province depends on the maintenance of its natural resources; and Canada will be faced with the problem of re-establishing many men in civil life. A well-planned programme of conservation meets these demands to a high degree" (Richardson, 1974:13).

In August 1941, the Guelph Conference convened again to discuss a demonstration survey to act as a model for conservation efforts. It was to be a seminal piece of conservation research meant to have general application across the country. The chairman of the Guelph Conference discussed several proposals with the then premier of Ontario, Mitchell Hepburn, in December 1941. With the support of the Ontario government, the Ganaraska Watershed Study subsequently was initiated and jointly financed by both levels of senior government. The Ganaraska Study was a profound achievement. It was heralded as "a classic" (Honorable Dana Porter – Richardson, 1974:18) and as "a landmark in Ontario conservation literature" (Prof. J.R. Dymond – Richardson, 1974:17). It included surveys of climate, soils, vegetation, forestry, physical and economic aspects of agriculture, plant diseases, entomology, wildlife, waterflow and utilization (Richardson, 1974: 17). Despite the breadth and complexity of the study, it was designed not just for the specialist but for public consumption. The report provided practical recommendations for the implementation of a watershed-based conservation and restoration program that would include woodlot improvement, tree planting, erosion control, dam construction, the organization of recreational centres and farm improvement (Richardson, 1974: 17).

This new conservation-oriented SEE system emergent structure self-organized as the system reorganized after the ecological collapse (i.e. deforestation and desertification) caused by the previous exploitation-oriented SEE system, environmental policy structure or regime. The collapse can be seen as the result of the exploitationist, frontier mentality characteristic of the time. Others, including Gunderson et al. (1995) and Berkes and Folke (2002), have documented similar institutional dynamics or social learning in response to environmental crises, perceived or otherwise, using complex systems-based heuristics.

This type of SEE system emergent structure could also be seen in the work of the Canadian Commission of Conservation (CCC) (1909-1921). Emerging in response to what was seen as "the squandering of the Dominion's natural resources", the commission was established by the Minister of the Interior, Clifford Sifton. For its era, the CCC was an impressive environmental (in all but name) program in the extent of its documentation and policy advocacy (Francis, 2006). The commission demonstrated an integrated approach to resource management, noting the linkages between the squandering of natural resources and problems associated with urbanization, water resources, erosion, habitat destruction and demands for hydro-electricity. "Anticipating the Brundtland Report by over seventy years, the commission proclaimed that 'each generation is entitled to the interest on the natural capital, but the principal should be handed on unimpaired'" (Canadian Institute of Planners, 2000). The commission was buttressed by some of the most innovative conservation/preservation thinking of the day, as well as an explicit awareness of the political-economic context (i.e., the end of the frontier in the U.S. and the opportunity to learn from American mistakes by Canada's western provinces) (Francis, 2006).

It can be argued that this kind of dynamic, the emergence of new SEE system structures, was notable several times in southern Ontario in the mid- to late-1800s in the Long Point area; in the early part of the century with the CCC; in the 1930s and 1940s with the

Guelph conference; in the mid-1950s and again in the 1980s. A conservation-oriented SEE system emergent structure self-organized in response to 1954's Hurricane Hazel through the work of the Metro Toronto Region Conservation Authority (Fisher and Alexander, 1993; Bocking, 2005). Of particular relevance to this dissertation, the 1980s saw the emergence of the phenomena again through the advocacy work of the Save the Oak Ridges Moraine coalition and through efforts to designate Long Point as a UNESCO World Biosphere Reserve.

5.4 Current Environmental Planning and Policy Context in Ontario

In Canada, land use policy and planning authority at the regional and local level flow from laws enacted by the provincial government. In Ontario, the provincial government has traditionally been directly involved in regional and local municipal governance, providing funding for local infrastructure and administration. However, in the early 1990s Ontario began a local/provincial "Disentanglement Process". Beginning under the Bob Rae, New Democratic Party government and rapidly accelerating under the 1995 Progressive Conservative Party government of Mike Harris, the disentanglement process resulted in the amalgamation of municipalities and the transfer or downloading of provincial responsibilities and services to the municipal level. This transfer of responsibility usually did not come with an adequate increase in provincial budgetary transfers to municipal governments (Hanna and Webber, 2005).

In broad political-economic terms, the Harris government's approach was a manifestation of a global trend towards Thatcherian, and Reaganite neo-conservative politics and economic policy (Jessop, 1993; Cerny, 1997). In terms of environmental and land use policy, the result was what Kathleen Cooper of the Canadian Environmental Law Association referred to as Ontario's Four-Step Strategy to Trashing Environmental Protection (Cooper, 1998: 1). The four steps were dismantling environmental laws; weakening the role of government; shutting out the public; and, privatizing natural resources (Cooper, 1998: 1). Within this context, the influence of several key components of the Ontario land use and environmental policy structure for the Oak Ridges Moraine and Long Point case studies should be clarified.

5.4.1 The Planning Act

The Ontario Planning Act (Ontario 2002) defines land use planning roles through delegation of specific responsibilities to the municipal level. The Planning Act is meant to protect the public interest by ensuring that land use decisions are consistent with provincial policies.

Section 2 of the act identifies 17 provincial interests that municipal planners "shall have regard to" when developing municipal official plans. However, the phrase "shall have regard to" does not legally oblige institutions to adhere to these principles. In the early 1990s, the Rae NDP government initiated the Commission on Planning and Development Reform in Ontario and replaced "shall have regard to" with "shall conform with", resulting in a much stronger land use planning legislative framework. With the change in provincial government in 1995, however, the Harris conservative government reversed this decision, returning Section 2 to its less rigorous "shall have regard to" form and thus allowing for a more flexible development process (Hanna and Webber, 2005). Section 3 of the Planning Act outlines a series of Provincial Policy Statements (PPS) meant to define or operationalize the provincial interests described in Section 2. Other key sections of the act require municipal governments to adopt Official Plans to guide future land use decisions and mandate local municipal government land use decisions to conform with regional-scale government growth and settlement plans (Hanna and Webber, 2005).

5.4.1.1 Provincial Policy Statement

A Provincial Policy Statement is issued under Section 3 of the Planning Act. "It provides direction on matters of provincial interest related to land use planning and development, and promotes the provincial "policy-led" planning system" (Ontario Ministry of Municipal Affairs and Housing, 2005b). The most recent Provincial Policy Statement came into effect on March 1, 2005, the same day the Strong Communities (Planning

Amendment) Act, 2004 came into effect. This act requires that planning decisions subject to the new PPS "shall be consistent with" the new policies.

The Provincial Policy Statement recognizes "the complex inter-relationships among economic, environmental and social factors in planning and embodies good planning principles" (Ontario Ministry of Municipal Affairs and Housing, 2005b). It includes more stringent policies relating to issues that affect communities, such as the efficient use and management of land and infrastructure; protection of the environment and resources; and, ensuring appropriate opportunities for employment and residential development, including support for a mix of uses (Ontario Ministry of Municipal Affairs and Housing, 2005b).

5.4.2 Regional Government

While several amalgamations were initiated under the Harris government, the development of regional governments has generally resulted in a two-tier municipal government structure in Ontario. The upper tier, regional government, has responsibility for regional-scale planning and the provision of infrastructure. The lower tier is responsible for land use decisions through development approval and zoning. Despite the intention for regional governments to provide a balance of interests at a regional scale, lower-tier zoning and development approvals are often made in relative isolation and can, as a result, have little regard for cumulative land use impacts (Hanna and Webber, 2005).

5.4.3 The Ontario Municipal Board

The Ontario Municipal Board (OMB) is a unique quasi-judicial, independent tribunal charged with adjudicating land use planning related appeals in a public forum. Under the Planning Act, parties involved in a land use or planning dispute can appeal local and regional planning decisions to the OMB regarding, for instance, changes to official plans, zoning by-laws, or plans of subdivision. Consisting of provincially appointed adjudicators, the OMB bases its decisions on planning principles as expressed in municipal plans and especially the Planning Act. The Board also decides, in the context of a pre-hearing, what parties are designated as "parties with standing" which allows them to present evidence, cross-examine and offer final arguments (Hanna and Webber, 2005). The OMB has played significant role in the evolution of planning, land use and urban development in Ontario but because the members are provincial appointees, the Board's credibility, non-partisan objectivity and accountability have at times been called into question (Hanna and Webber, 2005).

5.4.4 Ontario's Conservation Authorities

Ontario's conservation authorities (CAs) are provincially-created agencies with a broad mandate to manage, protect and restore Ontario's water and related resources on a watershed basis (Shrubsole, 1996; Ivey et al., 2002). They have been internationally recognized as leaders in innovative, science-based, locally responsive watershed management (Krause et al., 2001; Mitchell and Shrubsole, 2001). CAs are a key node in Ontario's water resources governance network. They are at a nexus between the provincial government, upper and lower tier municipal governments, non-governmental organizations and private sector stakeholder groups. Under the 1946 Conservation Authorities Act, CAs could be formed at the request of the majority of municipalities in a given watershed (Ivey et al., 2002). The CA's mandate was "to ensure the conservation, restoration and responsible management of Ontario's water, land and natural habitats through programs that balance human, environmental and economic needs" (Conservation Ontario, 2000). To implement this mandate, they were authorized to "undertake research, acquire land, raise municipal levies, construct works, control surface water flows, create regulations, and prescribe fees and permits" (Ivey et al., 2002: 314). In 2006, there are 36 conservation authorities whose jurisdictions (mainly in Southern Ontario) include approximately 90% of Ontario's population.

5.4.5 UNESCO World Biosphere Reserves

World Biosphere Reserves are designated by the United Nations Educational, Scientific and Cultural Organization (UNESCO) for sites which innovate and demonstrate approaches to conservation and sustainable development. The UNESCO biosphere reserve program was established in 1971 and is centred on non-regulatory designation of special areas to promote the ideals of conservation within a landscape context supported by interdisciplinary research, monitoring and educational initiatives. Biosphere reserves serve three main functions: conservation; promotion of sustainability for local or regional economies; and, logistic functions such as research, monitoring and education. Additionally, biosphere reserves have experimented widely with means of building long-term viability through decision-making approaches, programs and research initiatives (governance) that integrate attention to stewardship, livelihoods and learning. As such, biosphere reserves are much more than protected areas. They are a means for people who live and work within and around them to attain an integrated relationship with the natural world and they contribute to the needs of society more broadly, by providing a model of ecological and economic sustainability. As of 2006, there are over 482 biosphere reserves in 102 countries; 13 are in Canada, and four are in Ontario (Francis, 2004).

These are some of the key environmental policies, legislation and institutions that provide context for the two case studies. This is not a comprehensive list, but rather a brief overview of the key governance structures that have influenced both the Oak Ridges Moraine integrated land use decision-making process and the evolution of the Long Point World Biosphere Reserve. The next two chapters provide more specific background to the two case studies and apply the SEE systems conceptual framework and model of social learning.

Chapter 6: Oak Ridges Moraine Case Study

6.1 The Oak Ridges Moraine System Description

6.1.1 Historical SEE System Context

The Oak Ridges Moraine, as a system, can be described as a "major glacial moraine landform that serves as an important "green space" corridor for the rapidly expanding urban region centred on the Greater Toronto Area" (Francis, 2005: 2). Its legislative boundary "is based on a number of topographical, geomorphological and geological attributes, including the 245 metre (above sea level) contour along the southern boundary of the Moraine from the Town of Richmond Hill to the eastern boundary of the Municipality of Clarington" (Ontario Ministry of Municipal Affairs and Housing, 2002: 6).

The Oak Ridges Moraine is located to the north of the City of Toronto and extends from the Niagara Escarpment in the west to the Trent River system in the east. The moraine is approximately 195,000 hectares in size, 160 km in length and between 3 and 24 km wide. It rises some 229 meters above Lake Ontario (Figure 5). The landform itself is the result of multiple advances and retreats of Pleistocene glaciers. The final glacial advance, the Wisconsin stage, began about 100 thousand years before present and the later series of advances and retreats occurred approximately 10 to 15 thousand years before present. It is an inter-lobate moraine formed between glacial lobes (Whitelaw, 2005; Oak Ridges Moraine Technical Working Committee, 1994; Chapman and Putnam, 1984). As the two lobes melted, they left a glacial till moraine between them composed mainly of sand, clay, silt and gravel. The resulting landscape can be described as kame and kettle. Kames are small rounded glacial till hills with V-shaped valleys and sharp ridges, and kettles are deep, round depressions that are the result of large blocks of buried glacial ice melting out to form kettle lakes or spring-fed wetlands. There are 32 such kettle lakes across the moraine, ranging in size from 2 to 49 ha (Whitelaw, 2005; Francis, 2005). This unique landform with its variable topography, moderate climate, and mixed land use, as well as being located in the transition area between two forest regions (Great

Lakes-St. Lawrence and the Carolinian Forest Regions), results in an area of high biodiversity (Francis, 2005).

The moraine has been heavily influenced by human intervention through deforestation, agricultural uses, aggregate resource extraction, urban development pressures and, of course, conservation efforts. These interventions have been based on an evolving understanding (knowledge) of the social and ecological system. It is this interaction among the social, ecological and epistemological that is the focus of this dissertation. The intent in this section is to describe the Oak Ridges Moraine land use planning system as a complex socio-ecological, epistemological system (SEE) and to trace its evolution as a learning system.

Archeological evidence indicates that the moraine was generally used as a hunting and gathering ground for several different cultures before European settlement (Fisher and Alexander, 1991). Due to inter-tribal conflicts, which were intensified by European settlement and the fur trade, the moraine was often devoid of any human settlement for long periods. The Cayuga tribe established a village at the mouth of the Ganaraska River in approximately 1666, only to be later forced out of the area by the Mississauga tribe about 1700 (Fisher and Alexander, 1993). Despite this lack of permanent settlement, evidence of several major trail systems across and along the crest of the moraine indicates some ongoing human use (Fisher and Alexander, 1993).

European settlement brought the importation of new technologies and ideologies to the moraine. Early settlers referred to the moraine area, characterized by wooded, rolling hills, as the oak ridges or pine ridges (Whitelaw, 2005; Francis, 2005). The oak and the pine did not last long after European settlement. Based on a pioneer, Christian "subdue the land" ethos as well as a European myth that forest cover equated with good potential farm land, much of southern Ontario, including the Oak Ridges Moraine, was rapidly deforested. The oaks were harvested for ship building and the pine for local construction purposes. Logging continued in earnest until approximately 1850 (Whitelaw, 2005; Francis, 2005). The result was mass deforestation and near desertification on parts of the sensitive geomorphology of the moraine (Fisher and Alexander 1991). The ideology and praxis of exploitation pushed the socio-ecological system beyond a critical threshold and caused it to collapse (Gunderson and Holling, 2002).

The process of urbanization has long been a focus of environmental discourse (Bocking, 2005). Its implications for the landscape of southern Ontario, as elsewhere, have included the loss of agricultural land, countryside amenities and natural habitats; increased energy use and air pollution, especially in low-density, car-dependent suburbs; the expense of providing services, from sewers to highways; and, social exclusion from and unequal access to urban opportunities and amenities (Bocking, 2005). Fisher and Alexander (1991: 102) have described the most recent human "invasion" of the Oak Ridges Moraine as being technologically driven, spawned by the automobile. Even as early as the 1920s, the *Toronto Star* documented motorists visiting the moraine for its "tumbled oak ridges" and "wooded knobs and kettle lakes" (Coleman 1924/5/2 in Fisher and Alexander 1991).

With reforestation and the abandonment of many farms due to poor soils and erosion, the moraine became a quiet, scenic and rolling countryside that was very attractive to those seeking refuge from the rapidly urbanizing GTA. The moraine countryside not only drew motorists but also a select group of ex-urbanites became a new kind of moraine resident. They purchased farms as an escape from the rapidly expanding urban areas to the south. Most occupied existing farm houses while some built new dwellings. Generally, however, these new residents were aware of and respected the sensitivity of the moraine, and even contributed to reforestation efforts (Fisher and Alexander, 1993; Whitelaw, 2005).

King Township has been a focal point of environmental research and advocacy on several occasions since the late 1930s, beginning with the FON's Natural Resources of King Township report in 1938 (section 5.3). As ex-urbanites came to reside on the moraine, citizen's groups began to emerge to protect the moraine countryside and their rural lifestyle. One such citizen group formed in an area of King Township known as King Hills. The King Hills Residents Association formed to contest the development of a seniors' home in the area, raising concerns over ambulance access (ORM-EMO-2B). In the 1970s, this very local group merged with a newly-formed, Township-wide Concerned

Citizens of King Township (CCKT) to dispute the placement of a hydro corridor. Members of CCKT realized that to engage effectively in an issue at the scale of altering the route of a hydro corridor a Township-wide perspective would be required (ORM-CCKT-1; ORM-CCKT-4). This evidence of learning on a group level can be seen to be based on knowledge of the relevant governance system and results from an understanding of importance of scale and some measure of critical reflection.

Estate housing developments began in the 1970s, but development pressures did not begin to affect the moraine until the mid-1980s (Hanna and Webber, 2005). The province of Ontario grew from about 7.8 million in 1971 to almost 12 million people in 2001 and may reach 13.5 million by 2011 (Statistics Canada and Ontario Ministry of Finance, 2004). Immigration has contributed greatly to this growth and particularly that of urban centres such as the GTA. Canadian annual immigration rates ranged from 12,000 to 30,000 between 1977 and 1987 but increased from approximately 40,000 in 1987 to 90,000 in 1993 (Ley and Tutchener, 2001). Much of the growth affecting the moraine has occurred in York Region. The number of York Region residents living on moraine lands in 1991 was nearly 55,000 but this number grew to over 85,000 by 1998 and is projected to grow to over 120,000 by 2011 (Oak Ridges Moraine Technical Working Committee, 1994; Blais, 2002). One of the key centres of growth and conflict on the moraine has been the town of Richmond Hill in the Region of York. Richmond Hill's population grew from approximately 32,000 in 1971 to over 80,000 in 1991 and was over 130,000 in 2001 (Hanna and Webber, 2005).

The need for aggregate resources to support this rapid urban growth has compounded development pressures on the moraine. It has been estimated that over 75 per cent of the GTA's aggregate has come from two of the most accessible sources of aggregate resources in southern Ontario: the Niagara Escarpment and the Oak Ridges Moraine (Winfield and Taylor, 2005). As a result, these two significant land forms have been the focus of aggregate resource extraction controversies over the past several decades (Whitelaw, 2005; Whitfield and Taylor 2005). And, in spite of rehabilitation efforts, "the evidence indicates that land is being degraded at a faster rate than pit and quarry sites are being rehabilitated, with the result that the total impact of aggregate extraction operations continues to grow" (Winfield and Taylor, 2005: 9).

These combined threats to the ORM resulted in a land use planning process initiated in the late 1980s by a coalition of environmental movement, non-government organizations, culminating in the Oak Ridges Moraine Conservation Act and Plan in 2001 and 2002, respectively. The following section describes the emergence of the civil-society-led, conservation-focused SEE system emergent structure between 1988 and 2005, similar to that which self-organized as the result of degradation on the moraine in the 1930s (described in Section 5.3).

6.1.2 Current SEE System Context 1988-Present

In response to development pressures across the moraine, various local environmental groups emerged. Whitelaw (2005) illustrates how these groups formed, initially based on a Not In My Backyard (NIMBY) perspective, but then learned and evolved to embody a broader conceptual and geographical perspective in their advocacy work on the moraine. This evolution can be interpreted as evidence of social learning. That is, evidence of critical reflection on the groups' goals (NIMBY to bioregional conservation) and an understanding of the importance of scale in environmental policy issues.

In mid-1989, two of these groups emerged, in two different parts of the moraine (King Township and Peterborough), calling themselves Save the Oak Ridges Moraine (STORM). Representatives of the Concerned Citizens of King Township (CCKT) and an Ontario Environment Network Land Use Caucus from Peterborough first realized that there were two STORMs when they attended an Environmental Assessment Advisory Committee Hearing (EAAC) in 1989. The EAAC hearing had been requested by another influential environmental movement organization, Save the Ganaraska Again (SAGA) to assess the efficacy of the current land use planning process' ability to address cumulative environmental effects resulting from multiple subdivision proposals in the Ganaraska River watershed (Whitelaw, 2005). In October 1989 these two groups, among others, met again in King Township and formed the STORM coalition. The STORM coalition would go on to be one of the most influential stakeholders advocating for moraine-specific legislation.

The STORM coalition not only represented the geographic integration of environmental movement organizations across the moraine but also brought together the political savvy, local knowledge and scientific expertise of the environmental movement organizations, government bureaucrats, and academic researchers from Trent University. This environmental movement organization formation, combined with several key government interventions (described below), represented the self-organization of a new SEE emergent structure similar to that which emerged in the 1930s, both resulting from perceived environmental degradation.

The provincial government was also reacting to perceived impacts of development on the moraine through two key initiatives: the *Royal Commission on the Future of the Toronto Waterfront* and the *Greater Toronto Area Greenlands Study*. The *Royal Commission on the Future of the Toronto Waterfront*, headed by former City of Toronto Mayor David Crombie, operated from 1989 to 1992 and helped to define the GTA as a bioregion which included the ORM (Bocking, 2005; Whitelaw, 2005; Hanna and Webber, 2005). The Crombie Commission, as it came to be called, published two key reports, *Watersheds* and *Regeneration*, whose insights were influenced by the work of the STORM coalition which highlighted the connection between the waterfront and the headwaters of the area's rivers and streams located on the moraine (Whitelaw, 2005). Crombie's reports explicitly recommended the protection of the ORM as part of an ecosystem-based planning approach for the GTA (Royal Commission on the Future of the Toronto Waterfront, 1992; Bocking, 2005; Hanna and Webber, 2005).

The government also examined the impacts of growth on the greenfield areas of the GTA through a study released in 1990 entitled, *Space for All: Options for a Greater Toronto Area Greenlands Study* (Kanter, 1990). The objective of this study was to define a greenlands system for the GTA. Headed by Ron Kanter, Liberal MPP, the report, later known as the "Kanter Report", explicitly recognized the ORM as a sensitive and significant component of a GTA Greenlands system. Particularly, the report cited the hydrogeological importance of the moraine as a groundwater discharge and recharge zone and as the head waters for many of the region's rivers and streams. Kanter's report noted that, due to the inconsistency in planning approaches and the lack of any reference to the moraine in municipal official plans, the greatest threat to the ORM was from "small-scale, short-term planning decisions" (Kanter, 1990: 2). As a result, Kanter recommended that the province intervene in order to protect the ecological, aesthetic and recreational significance of the moraine.

The Kanter report resulted in three interrelated responses from the Province. First, it recognized the moraine through an "expression of interest". Second, the province initiated the development of a set of *Implementation Guidelines for the Oak Ridges Moraine area of the GTA* (Whitelaw, 2005; Hanna and Webber, 2005). And third, the government formed the Oak Ridges Moraine Technical Working Committee.

During this time and throughout the next decade, key members of the provincial bureaucracy in the MNR, MOE and MMAH either became directly involved in moraine issues or in undertaking moraine-specific research (ORM-MNR-1; ORM-MOE-1; ORM-MMAH-2; ORM-STORM-5; ORM-STORM-2). As interest in the moraine began to increase and even as it waxed and waned over the coming years, these civil servants would continue to provide non-governmental, environmental movement organizations with advice to build a strong science-based case for moraine conservation. For instance, Fred Johnson, formerly of the MNR, who later would be a key contributor to the writing of Oak Ridges Moraine legislation, prepared a conservation biology-based argument for moraine protection as early as 1991 (Ontario Ministry of Natural Resources, 1991). As one interviewee indicated, timing would be a key to the success of achieving moraine-specific conservation policy and having the right information prepared for when the governance system was ready for it would be critical.

Perhaps due to the impending fall 1990 election, the Liberal government opted for an expression of provincial interest in the moraine through the development of a set of implementation guidelines as opposed to the adoption of a more stringent Provincial Policy Statement under Section 3 of the Planning Act. In June of 1991, the newly elected New Democratic government issued the Interim Implementation Guidelines (Whitelaw, 2005). The guidelines were to be used by municipalities in their official plan and development approvals processes as well as in identifying the types of background environmental studies required for making planning decisions on the moraine (Hanna and Webber, 2005). The provincial guidelines were intended to address the threat of small-scale, cumulative planning decisions on the moraine. Unfortunately, due to the project-specific and legally ambiguous nature of the guidelines, planning decisions based upon them were vulnerable to challenges before the Ontario Municipal Board. Because the OMB utilizes the Planning Act as the legislative basis for its decisions, the moraine remained legally unprotected (Hanna and Webber, 2005).

In August 1991, the Minister of Natural Resources, Howard Hampton, launched a comprehensive study on the protection of the ORM and at the same time the province formed the ORM Technical Working Committee (TWC) (Whitelaw, 2005). With representation from the STORM Coalition, municipalities, conservation authorities, provincial ministries, developers and the aggregate industry, the TWC oversaw the development of 15 technical reports examining moraine-related issues including natural heritage protection, water, land use, cumulative effects and monitoring (Whitelaw 2005; Hanna and Webber 2005). The information and knowledge developed through three years of work by the TWC led to the May 1994 release of the *Oak Ridges Moraine Strategy – Draft for Public Discussion.* After incorporation of input from seven public meetings, the final *ORM Strategy for the Greater Toronto Area* was released in December 1994. The strategy identified and highlighted three key natural systems to guide planning decisions:

- Natural Heritage System – divided into core (essential to ecological processes) and corridor areas (areas of connection)
- Water Resources System – included those areas of significant surface and groundwater sources
- Landform Conservation System – involved areas and landforms of aesthetic importance

Only months after the release of the strategy, in June 1995, Mike Harris' Progressive Conservatives swept to power riding a Thatcherian and Reaganite neo-conservative political, economic wave. Harris' immediately accelerated the NDP-initiated local-provincial, Disentanglement Process, setting in motion the amalgamation of municipalities and the downloading of provincial responsibilities to municipal governments. As part of the Conservative effort to demonstrate its pro-business credentials and create a smaller provincial government with less intervention in local governance, the ORM strategy was immediately shelved (Parliamentary Commissioner for the Environment, 2003; Bocking, 2005; Hanna and Webber, 2005; Whitelaw, 2005). This lack of provincial interest and enforceable policy had a two-fold impact. First, development pressures on the moraine would continue virtually unchecked, setting the stage for pivotal conflicts in such areas as Richmond Hill. And second, due to the politically unreceptive climate, the campaign for a moraine-specific conservation framework would go dormant until 1999 (ORM-STORM-1; ORM-STORM-5; ORM-MNR-1; ORM-MOE-1; ORM-MMAH-1; ORM-MMAH-2).

In September 1999, in response to continued development threats to the moraine, the regions of York, Durham and Peel issued a state of the moraine report recommending renewed provincial interest in the protection of the moraine (Regional Municipalities of York, 1999; Whitelaw, 2005). One month later in October 1999, political controversy helped rekindle the campaign as the Minister of Municipal Affairs, Stephen Gilchrist, resigned over allegations of wrongdoing by moraine developers (Whitelaw, 2005). In the wake of these events as well as the June 1999 reelection of the Harris conservatives, advocates for the moraine protection led by the STORM coalition had little to lose but to reinvigorate the campaign. In November 1999, in conjunction with the Federation of Ontario Naturalists, STORM released an action plan to protect the moraine. The action plan recommended tough new land use planning controls, a moratorium on all public spending on projects that might affect the moraine, dedication of 5% of Ontario's $20 billion SuperBuild Growth Fund to acquire lands in southern Ontario including the ORM, and a provincial development surcharge on each new residential lot, golf course and extraction operation (Whitelaw, 2005).

Only months later in January and February 2000, with a renewed focus and sense of purpose, the campaign to protect the moraine took on a very public face when thousands of citizens packed two Town of Richmond Hill Council meetings to protest several applications for sub-division on moraine lands (ORM-STORM-1; ORM-STORM-3; ORM-MNR-1; ORM-MOE-1; ORM-MMAH-2). The Town of Richmond Hill had adopted a planning approach that attempted to balance rapid urban expansion and environmental protection through two secondary plans (OPA 129 and 138) in the late 1990s. However, elements of this land use balancing act began to threaten the east/west connectivity of the ORM (Hanna and Webber, 2005). The town attempted to address these threats through OPA 200 – *Official Plan Amendment to Implement New Urban Boundary and Environmental Corridor Study*. The intent of this amendment was to expand the existing urban boundary while protecting or buffering sensitive ORM lands with a natural corridor. The result would be an increase in the amount of developable land accompanied by strict conservation measures on moraine lands, representing the town's attempt at formally incorporating the Implementation Guidelines introduced nine years previously (Hanna and Webber, 2005). Despite council initially voting to continue the OPA 200 process in January 2000, due to overwhelming public pressure the Town chose to defer its decision on the amendment until the Province provided a better legislative framework for moraine protection. The developers responded by appealing to the Ontario Municipal Board. The resulting hearing represented a critical threshold or tipping point in the campaign to protect the ORM.

The Richmond Hill OMB hearing began in May 2000. With no appropriate land use policy in place due to the failure to pass OPA 200, the Town of Richmond Hill resorted to a science-based argument, using the concepts of landscape ecology and conservation biology embodied in the connectivity and corridor principles presented in OPA 200. At the same time, members of the STORM coalition approached the City of Toronto seeking its support in the OMB hearing based on the fact that the moraine was the headwaters of many of Toronto's streams and rivers. The OMB rejected the City of Toronto's application for status as a party to the hearings and thereby, failed to adopt a regional or bioregional view of the moraine as a significant landform, providing ecological connectivity and valuable hydrogeological functions (Bocking, 2005; Hanna and Webber, 2005).

The Richmond Hill OMB hearing was originally scheduled to be completed in 12 weeks. After a year of contentious testimony, the province intervened, halting the hearings due to the high cost and fears over the public reaction to what appeared to be an impending victory for the developers (Hanna and Webber, 2005). The province passed the Oak

Ridges Moraine Protection Act in May 2001 which imposed a six-month development moratorium on the moraine and created the ORM Advisory Committee consisting of members of environmental movement organizations such as STORM and FON as well as developers and other parties with interests on the moraine (Whitelaw, 2005; Bocking, 2005). This multi-stakeholder committee was charged with developing an ORM conservation plan in six months. The resulting plan, released in fall 2001, became the framework for the Oak Ridges Moraine Conservation Act passed in December 2001. The Oak Ridges Moraine Conservation Plan was approved by the government of Ontario in April 2002 (Ontario Ministry of Municipal Affairs and Housing, 2002).

As intended by the Advisory Committee and as embodied in the plan, the Province's vision for the moraine was "a continuous band of green rolling hills that provide form and structure to south-central Ontario, while protecting the ecological and hydrological features that support the health and well-being of the region's residents and ecosystems" (Ontario Ministry of Municipal Affairs and Housing, 2002). The objectives of the ORM Act and Plan were:

1. Protecting the ecological and hydrological integrity of the Oak Ridges Moraine Area;
2. Ensuring that only land and resource uses that maintain, improve or restore the ecological and hydrological functions of the Oak Ridges moraine Area are permitted;
3. Maintaining, improving or restoring all the elements that contribute to the ecological and hydrological functions of the Oak Ridges Moraine Area, including the quality and quantity of its water and its other resources;
4. Ensuring that the Oak Ridges Moraine is maintained as a continuous natural landform and environment for the benefit of present and future generations;
5. Providing for land and resource uses and development compatible with the other objectives of the Plan;
6. Providing for continued development within existing urban settlement areas and recognizing existing rural settlements;
7. Providing for a continuous recreational trail through the Oak Ridges Moraine Area that is accessible to all including persons with disabilities;
8. Providing for other public recreational access to the Oak Ridges Moraine Area; and,
9. Any other prescribed objectives

(Ontario Ministry of Municipal Affairs and Housing, 2002)

The Act and Plan defined the boundary of the moraine based on several topographic, geomorphological and geological attributes and identified land-use designations meant to override all existing local and regional policies. Regional and local municipal official plans were required to conform to the new designations. Regional governments were given 12 months to ensure conformity to the plan, while local municipalities were given 18 months. There were four key land-use designations defined in the ORMCP. These include:

- **Natural Core Areas** – (38% of the moraine) - protect those lands with the greatest natural heritage features which are critical to maintaining the Moraine as a whole. Only existing uses and very restricted new resource management, agricultural, low intensity recreational, transportation and utility uses are allowed in these areas.
- **Natural Linkage Areas** - (24% of the moraine) - protect critical natural and open space linkages between the Natural Core Areas and along rivers and streams. The only uses allowed are those allowed in Natural Core Areas, plus some aggregate resource operations.
- **Countryside Areas** - (30% of the moraine) - provide an agricultural and rural transition and buffer between the Natural Core Areas and Natural Linkage Areas and the urbanized Settlement Areas. Prime agricultural areas as well as natural features are protected. Most of the uses typically allowed in agricultural and other rural areas are allowed here. Within the Countryside Areas, the Oak Ridges Moraine Land Use Designation Map also identifies and delineates Rural Settlements. These are existing hamlets or similar small, generally long-established communities identified in official plans.
- **Settlement Areas** – (8% of the moraine) - reflect a range of existing communities planned by municipalities to reflect community needs and values. Urban uses and development as set out in municipal official plans are allowed.

(Ontario Ministry of Municipal Affairs and Housing, 2002)

Several key policies in the ORMCP prohibited new aggregate extraction in Natural Core areas and placed strict new standards on new aggregate pits in Natural Linkage Areas; limited golf courses to Countryside areas; and, prevented the placement of transportation and utility corridors in Natural Core and Linkage areas unless need and no viable alternative could be demonstrated (Ontario Ministry of Municipal Affairs and Housing, 2002; Whitelaw, 2005).

Building on Fred Johnson's work (Ontario Ministry of Natural Resources, 1991) and Richmond Hill's use of conservation biology and landscape ecology principles (connectivity and corridors), the ORM conservation plan embodies a process-oriented view of the moraine as a complex ecological system based on the concept of ecological integrity. The plan calls for the prevention of development that will "adversely affect the ecological integrity of the Plan area" (Ontario Ministry of Municipal Affairs and Housing, 2002). The plan defines ecological integrity as follows:

> ecological integrity, which includes hydrological integrity, means the condition of ecosystems in which,
> (a) the structure, composition and function of the ecosystems are unimpaired by stresses from human activity,
> (b) natural ecological processes are intact and self-sustaining, and
> (c) the ecosystems evolve naturally;

This definition bears a remarkable resemblance to the concept of integrity defined by Kay et al. (1999) in the context of the development of monitoring indicators in conjunction with the Province of Ontario. Similar to conservation biology and landscape ecology approaches, the plan calls for the preservation of ecological structure and the processes that support them. However, from a systems perspective, the use of ecological integrity represents a conceptually sophisticated normative goal for conservation in that it also calls for the preservation of the system's ability to evolve naturally, or, in systems terms, continues the process of self-organization (Kay et al., 1999).

Even the broad concept of sustainability was included in the plan with reference to the development of municipal water budgets and conservation plans for maintaining sustainable water supply. While a more comprehensive view of the concept of sustainability has yet to be formally implemented through policy on the moraine, the notion of considering human well-being as part of monitoring has been discussed (MAC meeting, January 2006)

A 10-year review mechanism was built into the Plan to ensure stability and flexibility. The review could not remove land from Natural Core or Linkage areas but would allow for changes to the plan if the requisite public consultation and incorporation of input from stakeholders such as local governments, interest groups and the general public could be demonstrated (Ontario Ministry of Municipal Affairs and Housing, 2002).

In May 2002, the provincial government created the Oak Ridges Moraine Foundation to fund moraine-specific projects and research, and appointed the North Pickering Land Exchange Review Panel to explore "land swaps" to further protect moraine lands (Parliamentary Commissioner for the Environment, 2003).

In February 2005, the Greenbelt Plan was introduced (Ontario Ministry of Municipal Affairs and Housing , 2005a). The Greenbelt Plan is intended to define where urbanization can occur in one of North America's fastest growing regions, Ontario's Greater Golden Horseshoe. The Plan area includes the Oak Ridges Moraine, the Niagara Escarpment and approximately 400,000 hectares of natural areas and agricultural lands in what is termed Protected Countryside. Like the ORMCP, the Greenbelt Plan is to be implemented through incorporation within municipal official plans and zoning by-laws (Ontario Ministry of Municipal Affairs and Housing, 2005a; Monitoring the Moraine, 2006). Critics of the plan question the consistency of implementation across the over 60 municipalities; the lack of sufficient provincial oversight; inadequate harmonization with existing ORMCP and Niagara Escarpment Plans; and, finally, partisan politics creating tensions between the Conservative created ORMCP and the Liberal Greenbelt Plan (Monitoring the Moraine, 2006; Whitelaw, 2005; ORM-STORM-2; ORM-MNR-1; ORM-MOE-1; ORM-MMAH-2).

Also in early 2005 the STORM coalition, in conjunction with Citizen's Environment Watch and the Centre for Community Mapping, initiated the Monitoring the Moraine (MTM) project. "It is designed to engage and sustain community volunteers in science, stewardship, monitoring and decision-making on the Oak Ridges Moraine" (Monitoring the Moraine, 2006). The MTM project has filled a policy gap by leading the development of a framework for both environmental and policy monitoring on the moraine. In conjunction with provincial, regional, academic and EMO partners, the MTM project is intended to ensure adequate monitoring data, information and knowledge are available for making informed decisions in the context of the 2014, ten-year plan review. In June 2006, MTM marked the four-year anniversary of the enactment of the ORMCP by publishing its *Status Report on the Implementation of the Oak Ridges Moraine Conservation Plan.*

The status report provides several key observations regarding the municipal uptake of the Act and Plan, and the effectiveness of the provincial role in their implementation. The report notes that 63% of lower-tier municipalities met the deadline for official plan conformity to the Plan. However, only 38% have met the deadline for zoning by-law conformity (Monitoring the Moraine, 2006). At the provincial scale, the status report indicates a distinct lack of accountability. The MTM report highlights the province's failure to provide municipalities with essential tools for policy delivery (including, mapping, technical papers and provincial resources and staff time) and its failure to set time frames for implementation. The MTM status report questions the provincial commitment to the effective implementation of the ORMCP, observing that the government may have underestimated the complexity of integrating the ORMCP into 32 municipal planning structures (Monitoring the Moraine, 2006).

This section summarizes some of the key events, stakeholders and policies that have contributed to the current environmental policy context for the Oak Ridges Moraine. The current environmental protection policy system can be usefully interpreted as a complex SEE system emergent structure similar to that which self-organized in response to environmental degradation in the 1930s. Such a systems-based perspective could provide environmental movement organizations, bureaucrats and researchers with an understanding of how to foster the social learning required to intervene effectively in complex SEE systems. Based on this dissertation research, such insights include the identification of the types of knowledge required for effective intervention, an understanding of the dynamics across scales from individual agents to large institutional social structures, and, the need for various levels of critical reflection (Section 2.5.6.3). The next section recasts the development of the Oak Ridges Moraine policy context explicitly in terms of the development and use of knowledge as it is embedded in social structures through the process of social learning.

6.1.3 Discussion – The Oak Ridges Moraine as a Complex SEE System

The intent of this section is to apply the SEE systems framework to the Oak Ridges Moraine case study and demonstrate how the application of these principles has led to the development the SEE systems conceptual model of social learning. Given the complexity and uncertainty associated with the Oak Ridges Moraine ecological and social (planning and governance) system and the high decision stakes associated with protecting the moraine landscape and associated hydrological resources (Section 1.1.1) the application of a critical systems approach to research and intervention is highly appropriate. As indicated in section 4.3, the SEE systems conceptual framework and model would be most usefully applied in the context of a broader research and planning protocol for describing and intervening in complex socio-ecological systems (Gunderson et al., 1995; Berkes and Folke, 1998; Kay and et al., 1999; Gunderson and Holling, 2002; Berkes and Folke, 2003; Waltner-Toews et al., 2004; Folke et al., 2005). Here the goal is to describe the Oak Ridges Moraine as a complex SEE system by providing empirical evidence from the ORM case study of the six principles of the SEE systems framework (Section 3.1.2). The application of this framework to the ORM case has led to the development of the conceptual model of social learning previously described in Section 3.2.

6.1.3.1 Co-Evolution

While interviewees did not use the complex systems terminology (e.g. self-organization, attractors, co-evolution of socio-ecological systems), they did describe the tight and complex interconnections between social and ecological systems. In telling the story of their involvement in Oak Ridges Moraine conservation, interviewees from environmental movement organizations, government agencies and academic institutions alike described the interactions among the ecological and hydrological, as well as social, economic and political aspects of the ORM planning process. Interviewees demonstrated a rich understanding of the ecological and hydrological importance and sensitivity of the moraine, and readily linked its sustainability to threats from human development pressures and flaws in the environmental planning policy-making process. One interviewee noted that she had learned a great deal through her experience in moraine conservation, such as the "importance of cold water streams, what happens when land gets paved over" and "the deeper you get in there is increased complexity, you have to know players, how decisions are made, the rules, how government works, how they can be affected politically" (ORM-STORM-3). Another interviewee emphasized the importance of understanding "ecosystems and the importance of water and how cities can be sustained by their surroundings. Raising consciousness of the Oak Ridges Moraine and the Niagara Escarpment - made people realize that they live in a region instead of just a city" (ORM-CCKT-5). Whether the issue was around a development application for a nursing home, a gas station, or a plan for subdivision, interviewees demonstrated an understanding of the connections between social, ecological and knowledge systems that resonates well with the concept of co-evolution.

6.1.3.2 Reflexive Uncertainty

Uncertainty around the sensitivity of the moraine as an ecological and hydrological system was a key driver in its protection. Preventing development on the moraine to protect the surface and ground waters of the Greater Toronto Area from the potential adverse impacts demonstrates an acknowledgement of the complexity of the moraine and the inherent uncertainty surrounding the impacts of development. However, another level of uncertainty that results from the co-evolutionary nature of socio-ecological, epistemological systems became evident through the analysis of empirical findings. That is, uncertainty surrounding differences among perspectives and power imbalances within associated decision-making structures. For instance, several interviewees described decision-making bodies such as councils or OMB hearings as inherently biased towards a given perspective. One interviewee noted that the local council was "strongly pro-development" (ORM-CCKT-2). Another described how the process of an OMB hearing may have biased the results "There were many breaks in the hearings so the evidence wasn't heard in the most logical fashion" (ORM-MMAH-2). When asked to describe the ORM planning process, one respondent colourfully noted that the "first thing that came to mind was Alice in Wonderland – it seemed to reflect how planning takes place. The Queen sentences first, and provides the verdict afterwards - they'd approve a planning project and then justify it later or mitigate it" (ORM-STORM-3). Despite strong scientific evidence against development on the moraine due to uncertainty, biases in decision-making structures compound uncertainty within complex SEE systems. This level of decision-making uncertainty is often not explicitly acknowledged by conventional planning approaches or structures but was an important facet of the environmental planning processes described by interviewees.

6.1.3.3 Cross-Scalar Considerations

The importance of scale and an understanding of cross-scalar interactions within SEE systems was one of the strongest themes raised over the course of my dissertation work. Several interviewees described the importance of responding to issues on the right scale. A member of a very local group recalls the merger of several smaller groups for a particular issue in the 1960s, "a group fighting hydro lines decided that they needed a township-wide association" (ORM-CCKT-4). And then in the late 1980s, in order to address the "scope of the moraine" and "the number of municipalities and regions involved", several groups came together to form STORM (ORM-CCKT-1). STORM provided these smaller, local groups with a moraine-wide perspective and the knowledge and tools to fight locally to protect the moraine and to engage in formal processes such as the OMB (ORM-STORM-1; ORM-CCKT-1; ORM-CCKT-4; ORM-CCKT-3; ORM-STORM-5; ORM-STORM-1; ORM-MNR-1; ORM-MOE-1). A provincial bureaucrat described the scale of his perspective on the moraine issue "working here, my mental map is really big. Ontarians are starting to see that the broader scale needs to be seen and not just local issues" (ORM-MMAH-2). The importance of scale and in particular the importance of creating organizations or governance structures appropriate to the scale of the system or issue of interest was a theme raised by all of the interviewees. Further discussion of the role of scale is provided in Section 6.1.4.1.

6.1.3.4 Critical Awareness

Through the process of engaging in the ORM planning process, respondents came to recognize a need to reflect critically upon their own positions and assumptions. Interviewees reported that through interaction with other stakeholders and exposure to new information interviewees, they were led into several types or levels of critical reflection. Many interviewees said they began to re-examine their initially quite local goals after they had been exposed to information such as a map showing the extent of the moraine or a report on the hydrological importance of the moraine as the headwaters of many of the key rivers that flow through the GTA (ORM-STORM-1; ORM-STORM-3; ORM-STORM-4; ORM-STORM-5; ORM-CCKT-2; ORM-CCKT-3; ORM-CCKT-4;

ORM-ORFOE-1; ORM-ORFOE-2). Several respondents also decribed having experiences with formal decision-making structures such as the municipal council meetings or OMB hearings, which caused them to reflect on power relations that influenced policy making (ORM-STORM-3; ORM-STORM-5; ORM-CCKT-1; ORM-CCKT-2). Critical reflection emerged from the qualitative data as a key component of many of the respondents' narratives of the ORM planning and policy-change process. Further discussion of the importance and role of critical reflection in the ORM case is provided in Section 6.1.4.3.

6.1.3.5 Pluralism

The ORM case provided evidence of various perspectives and the importance of incorporating a variety of knowledges in an environmental planning and policy-making process. Again, all the respondents acknowledged the diverse perspectives involved in the ORM planning process, including those of developers, politicians, bureaucrats, and environmental advocates. Each of these groups expressed a variety of perspectives across a number of scales. One interviewee noted that there were "different types of groups on the moraine – STORM was centrist, Federation of Ontario Naturalists and the Nature Conservancy were institutional and groups like Earth Roots and Save the Rouge were protest-oriented" (ORM-MOE-1). The interviewee concluded that "there couldn't have been change without all three - they made each other look good" (ORM-MOE-1). So too, all levels of government agencies as well as non-government groups played key roles in the fight for moraine-specific legislation. "The environmental groups picked up the ball and lead the charge and then the municipalities started thinking more progressively ... the geological study by the Feds that made the municipalities more aware of their water" (ORM-MMAH-1) and provincial civil servants provided scientific background and intelligence to environmental groups (ORM-MMAH-2; ORM-MOE-1; ORM-MNR-1).

6.1.3.6 Power

References to power, power imbalances and even feelings of powerlessness were widespread through the Oak Ridges Moraine case study work. Several respondents highlighted the advantage of drawing the City of Toronto into the moraine planning process. That is, advocates realized they had a better chance of achieving moraine-specific conservation legislation if they could "get Toronto involved since they have the money, power, and ear of the province" (ORM-CCKT-3). Another example of the importance of power relations in the ORM planning process highlighted by several interviewees was, as a result of the 1995 election of the Harris Conservatives, "STORM laid low so that the (Oak Ridges Moraine) strategy wouldn't get shredded" (ORM-STORM-1). Powerlessness was also a theme that several interviewees described. One respondent noted that she had "learned a lot about politics and power ... lost all faith ... saw that power corrupts. And seeing that money is more important than the environment" (ORM-CCKT-2). While describing having had their knowledge of the planning process dismissed by a so-called expert, one interviewee remarked "don't tell us that we don't understand planning, we understand planning – we just hope that we're wrong" (ORM-STORM-3). The intent of bringing power imbalances to the fore in describing and prescribing interventions within SEE systems is to promote any individuals' and groups' ability to reflect on their position and improve it. One thing the ORM case points to is the power of collective action through volunteer environmental movement organizations such as the STORM coalition.

These principles are most usefully considered in the context of a broad collaborative, systems-based planning protocol as described in Section 4.3 (Gunderson et al., 1995; Berkes and Folke, 1998; Kay et al., 1999; Gunderson and Holling, 2002; Berkes and Folke, 2003; Waltner-Toews et al., 2004; Walker et al., 2006). Through the application of the SEE systems principles to the ORM case study, several key findings have emerged that provide insights into planning and policy making in complex socio-ecological systems. These findings are the importance of scale, the need for multiple knowledges and the value of critical reflection in environmental planning and policy making. These findings, discussed in detail in the next section, have led to the development of the SEE systems conceptual model of social learning.

6.1.4 Findings – Social Learning and the Complex Oak Ridges Moraine SEE System

Through the application of the SEE systems principles to the Oak Ridges Moraine instrumental case study, several key findings emerged. When one adopts a view of individual and social learning as socially-embedded processes within a complex socio-ecological, epistemological system, effective intervention within such systems appears to be heavily influenced by three factors:

1. An understanding of the importance of **Scale**
2. The development and use of **Three Types of Knowledge**
3. Multiple levels of **Critical Reflection**

Each of these findings is described in turn with reference to the empirical results of the ORM case study.

6.1.4.1 Scale

The importance of understanding the multi-scalar, holarchic structure and cross-scalar dynamics of complex SEE systems became evident in the Oak Ridges Moraine case study. Several interviewees described the necessity of creating new groups or social structures at progressively broader conceptual and spatial scales to address increasingly complex policy issues. For instance, the evolution of the environmental movement organizations in King Township from the 1960s to the present illustrates this important facet of collective or social learning. Several interviewees described how the Concerned Citizens of King Township (CCKT) created an Oak Ridges Moraine sub-committee which eventually, in conjunction with other groups across the moraine, formed the STORM coalition (ORM-STORM-1; ORM-CCKT-1; ORM-CCKT-2; ORM-STORM-2). The intent was to create a new structure that could more effectively address the complex inter-jurisdictional, hydrological and spatially-large issues associated with the entire moraine.

As described in a previous section, another interviewee who had lived in King Township since the mid-1960s indicated that this was not the first time this kind of organizational "scaling-up" had occurred. The interviewee indicated that a local group calling itself the

King Hill Resident's Association emerged in response to a very local concern over the placement of a retirement home (ORM-CCKT-4). However, when faced with the broader-scale issue of protesting the route of a hydro corridor, this group merged with the Concerned Citizens of King Township (CCKT) as they "decided that they needed a township-wide association" (ORM-CCKT-4).

Throughout the interviews, it was emphasized how rhetorically important it was in the relevant planning or policy-making process to be able to present as a group with an appropriate scale of interest (ORM-CCKT-4; ORM-STORM-1; ORM-STORM-5; ORM-CCKT-1; ORM-CCKT-3). If a group's focus was too single-issue focused or too geographically-specific, it could be dismissed by decision makers as special-interest or NIMBY. Interviewees have indicated that one of the reasons the STORM coalition has been given so much legitimacy or epistemic warrant is because it is focused on broadly-based ORM conservation issues and because it represents over 30 member groups from across the moraine. At the same time, STORM's interest in protecting the moraine through the implementation of the ORMCA sometimes requires member groups to consciously focus on a smaller area. For instance, one interviewee noted that for a recent infrastructure issue CCKT "didn't link STORM into this - this was a conscious decision ... the mandate of CCKT is to maintain rural life of King Township and (we didn't) see this as conflicting with the ORMCA" (ORM-CCKT-1).

6.1.4.2 Types of Knowledge

Another key finding is the importance of the development and use of three generic types of knowledge (local technical, scientific, governance) in environmental policy-making processes. One respondent described how three key members of their organization possessed three different types of knowledge. One "had a good political nose", another had a background in science, and the third "was like the lawyer of the group" with an understanding of local logistics of the planning process (ORM-STORM-3).

These are not discrete categories. Each type is in dialectic tension with the others, but in many ways is also dependent on the other types (Section 2.4.2.3). When asked about the role and types of knowledge and learning related to the key events in the development and enactment of the ORM Act and Plan, interviewees described the importance of scientific knowledge within planning and policy-making processes such as OMB hearings (ORM-STORM-1; ORM-STORM-2; ORM-STORM-3; ORM-CCKT-1; ORM-CCKT-2; ORM-CCKT-3; ORM-CCKT-4; ORM-ORFOE-1; ORM-ORFOE-2; ORM-MNR-1; ORM-MOE-1; ORM-MMAH-2). For instance, one interviewee noted that "at the OMB ... your word won't carry any weight if you're not an expert" (ORM-CCKT-3). Given the legalistic framework of the OMB process, professional credentials and hard scientific evidence were granted legitimacy or epistemic warrant (Fuller, 2002b; Bocking, 2005).

The seasoned provincial bureaucrats, the Town of Richmond Hill and the STORM coalition have all recognized the importance of a strong scientific basis for arguments within a planning or policy-making process (ORM-MNR-1; ORM-MOE-1; ORM-MMAH-2). Several interviewees noted how critical it was that key provincial bureaucrats had continuously and diligently worked on moraine-related research using conservation biology principles and developing important hydrological data. "This was one of the ways that bureaucrats keep things going under the radar - trying to highlight the issue to get it into the government's mind ... even if the government puts the lid on it they (the bureaucrats) continue working on it on the edges" (ORM-MMAH-2).

Conservation biology and landscape ecology were also used by the Town of Richmond Hill. When the town had no appropriate land use policy in place due to the failure to pass OPA 200 in the context of the OMB hearing, town staff resorted to an explicitly science-based argument. The STORM coalition also has long recognized the importance of a strong scientific-basis for its advocacy work. It is this appreciation for the importance of scientific knowledge that has contributed to its legitimacy and to its interest in developing a strong monitoring program through the Monitoring the Moraine project to ensure sufficient and reliable data for the ten-year review of the ORMCA.

Interviewees also described the importance of the local knowledge of one's property, neighbourhood or municipality (ORM-STORM-1; ORM-STORM-1; ORM-CCKT-2; ORM-CCKT-4; ORM-CCKT-5). Several respondents cited the importance of experiential knowledge of local ecology and hydrology as well as informal social and decision-making structures of one's locale. One interviewee noted that her group, CCKT, needed to "keep their eye on what is happening both locally and the wider picture. And if you don't then you lose the contacts" (ORM-CCKT-2). Through her experience with her local planning department, she also pointed to the need to "watch the Committee of Adjustment and not just Council (as) ... a lot of land use decisions happen behind those closed doors" (ORM-CCKT-2). Such knowledge is often context-specific and is frequently undervalued in formal decision or policy-making processes. However, this kind of knowledge of the local hydrology (e.g. a well drying up) or an understanding of local planning or decision-making processes (e.g. a good working relationship with a local planner or town councilor or government bureaucrat) can be invaluable for influencing decision making within a complex SEE system, especially through informal processes.

Related to this, interviewees also identified the need for a third type of knowledge: understanding the structures and dynamics of the relevant planning, decision-making or governance system. This type of knowledge is also often under-valued or excluded from so-called objective decision-making fora such as the OMB. However, most interviewees indicated that, in the context of the campaign to protect the moraine, power relations (either for or against) played a key role in processes leading to the passage of the Oak Ridges Moraine Conservation Act and Plan. One interviewee asserted that, "the contribution of the grassroots to the moraine fight can't be overemphasized. If not for the grassroots public pounding on the government's door - it wouldn't matter what studies the bureaucrats had undertaken" (ORM-MOE-1). Whether it was an understanding of the need to scale-up the conceptual or geographic focus of a group (KHRA to CCKT to STORM) or the value in allowing the ORM conservation campaign to go dormant due to the election of a politically hostile provincial government, these demonstrate the importance of governance knowledge (ORM-STORM-1; ORM-STORM-2; ORM-CCKT-1; ORM-CCKT-2; ORM-CCKT-3; ORM-CCKT-4; ORM-MNR-1; ORM-MOE-1; ORM-MMAH-1; ORM-MMAH-2).

6.1.4.3 Critical Reflection

The third major finding is the importance of critical reflection in effective intervention in complex SEE systems. Evidence of critical reflection was pervasive throughout the interviews. Flood and Romm (1996) provide a useful categorization of levels of critical reflection in their work on triple-loop learning. They identify three centres or levels of reflection that lead to learning (Section 2.5.6.3). Evidence of the first level can be found in NIMBY arguments for preserving the moraine. At this level of reflection, the question of "are we doing things right?" is relevant. Put differently, interest in moraine protection from this perspective might involve asking, "what will increased development do to my property value?" or "how will development on the moraine affect my privacy?". Here little concern is given to questioning whether development should occur but instead only focuses on its immediate implications, usually for an individual.

Several respondents described their interest in the moraine beginning with NIMBYism or watching other members of their respective groups become involved because of NIMBY-type concerns, and even leaving in frustration if these concerns were not being addressed. However, these interviewees described a learning process whereby they eventually saw past NIMBYism and were able to see the broader benefits of moraine conservation, for instance, the protection of head waters of rivers and streams or ground water protection (ORM-STORM-1; ORM-STORM-3; ORM-STORM-4; ORM-STORM-5; ORM-CCKT-2; ORM-CCKT-3; ORM-CCKT-4; ORM-ORFOE-1; ORM-ORFOE-2). One respondent noted that she'd been "living here since 1969 – didn't even know I lived on the moraine – not sure what an aquifer was". She later came up with the name STORM, became one of its first co-chairs and helped initiate the campaign for moraine-specific legislation. This represents another centre of learning or level of reflection that Flood and Romm (1996) describe as double-loop learning.

In double-loop learning, individuals and groups begin to reflect on their assumptions and question their goals. "Are we doing the right things?" becomes the more relevant question. Interviewees described key events that caused them to reflect on their reasons for becoming involved in moraine conservation, such as seeing a map of the entire moraine for the first time or attending a meeting where representatives from groups from all across the moraine came together to discuss similar concerns or making the link between conservation and groundwater protection (ORM-STORM-1; ORM-STORM-2; ORM-STORM-5; ORM-CCKT-2; ORM-CCKT-2; ORM-ORFOE-1). This represents a level of reflection and learning that took the individual or group beyond questioning the immediate implications of development on their property to questioning the broader ecological or hydrological implications of development and questioning the need for development. These experiences can be somewhat jarring (Mezirow, 1994, 1998) but at the same time quite profound. Interviewees that chose to speak about these experiences referred to them as almost spiritual or life altering (ORM-STORM-2).

A few interviewees who described such a shift from single to double-loop learning, that is from asking "are we doing things right?" to "are we doing the right things?", also described instances where they realized or reflected upon the implications of power relations (ORM-STORM-3; ORM-STORM-5; ORM-CCKT-1; ORM-CCKT-2). Described as triple-loop learning or a third centre of learning, these few respondents described coming to an understanding whereby they could see that certain social or institutionally-structured notions of right were reinforced or continuously selected due to power imbalances. These respondents described development interests encroaching on moraine lands because of the financial clout of large developers and connections to local and provincial politicians, or certain municipal councils simply being "pro-development". "Our council is pro-development so that is a problem for them to be responsible. Having required public meetings are a way of managing people that fulfills their mandate and ignores the people. This discourages the people, but you haven't got a choice of attending" (ORM-CCKT-2). Others described OMB chairs, with what they perceived to be pro-development interests, dismissing out of hand the testimony of certain expert witnesses or citizen scientists due to their conservationist agendas. And finally, respondents cited the election and re-election of the Harris Conservative government as shifting the power balance toward pro-development interests. Again, respondents indicated that this new level of reflection on the implications of power relations for notions of "rightness" or "truth" was jarring, if not disheartening. However, without this kind of reflection, the need to become involved in shifting power imbalances would not be evident. As a result of this triple-loop learning, respondents utilized governance knowledge to put the moraine campaign on hiatus as the result of the re-election of the Harris Conservatives.

6.1.4.4 SEE Systems Model of Social Learning

To conceptually map the learning described by interviewees, we can use the three-axis, SEE systems conceptual model described in Chapter 3 (Section 3.2 – Figure 4). This conceptual model for understanding social learning in the context of environmental policy systems (Figure 8) was developed through a participatory action research approach in conjunction with STORM executive director, Debbe Crandall. It brings together insights and conceptual tools from the literature with the three major findings from the case study research, and resonates strongly with the experience of Ms. Crandall. The three axes in the diagram are set in dynamic or dialectic tension. That is, they are not completely independent from one another. Moving along one axis can result in a shift along one or both of the other axes.

Three generic perspectives can be described using this model of social learning to illustrate its utility. These are not meant to be a comprehensive list of the possible perspectives that could be described by this conceptual model. Instead, they demonstrate the linkages between the empirical data and the conceptual model. The darkest circle on the diagram represents an individual or group whose perspective can be characterized by NIMBYism. For instance, in the context of the ORM case study, individuals or groups concerned primarily with the immediate implications of development for their property value or privacy do not explicitly reflect on the broader impacts of development or question the need for development. This perspective is quite often based on local knowledge and is generally focused on a very local scale of influence (i.e., one's property or tax structure of a local municipality).

A second illustrative perspective can be related to the use of conservation biology and landscape ecology principles or the concept of ecological integrity as a normative conservation goal (the medium-sized, lighter circle). This perspective is one in which an individual or group has critically reflected upon its assumptions and questioned its goals.

As described above, interviewees described shifting from a NIMBY perspective to coming to an understanding of the broader ecological and hydrological implications of moraine development. In this case, the need for a strong scientific basis for preservation replaces the self-serving NIMBY arguments and the scale of influence expands beyond the individual property or municipality to the entire moraine, the watersheds flowing off of it and the aquifers beneath.

A third descriptive perspective that can be mapped onto the SEE system social learning model is that of a broad-based sustainability viewpoint (the largest, lightest coloured circle). A few respondents described moving beyond an understanding of the need for a change in normative goals to reflecting on the ethics of decision making and the power relations that reinforce certain normative policy goals. This triple-loop learning can be linked to or can be the result of an understanding of the governance system (that is, an understanding of the role of power in complex policy issues). And generally a sustainability perspective would have to address scales from the individual to the global.

Movement down any of the three axes does not necessarily imply or force movement down another. For instance, several members of the long standing King City environmental group CCKT have demonstrated the use of all three types of knowledge and some measure of each level of critical reflection (single, double and triple-loop learning) but explicitly maintain their focus on King Township. Their governance knowledge and reflection on power structures is centred within the boundaries of the township.

This conceptual model of social learning could be used in the context of a socio-ecological systems description as described in Section 4.3. It would explicitly integrate knowledge and learning into the systems description and synthesize knowledge for environmental planning and policy making within complex socio-ecological systems.

Figure 8: SEE Systems Conceptual Model of Social Learning Applied to the ORM Case

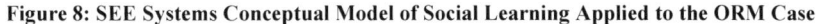

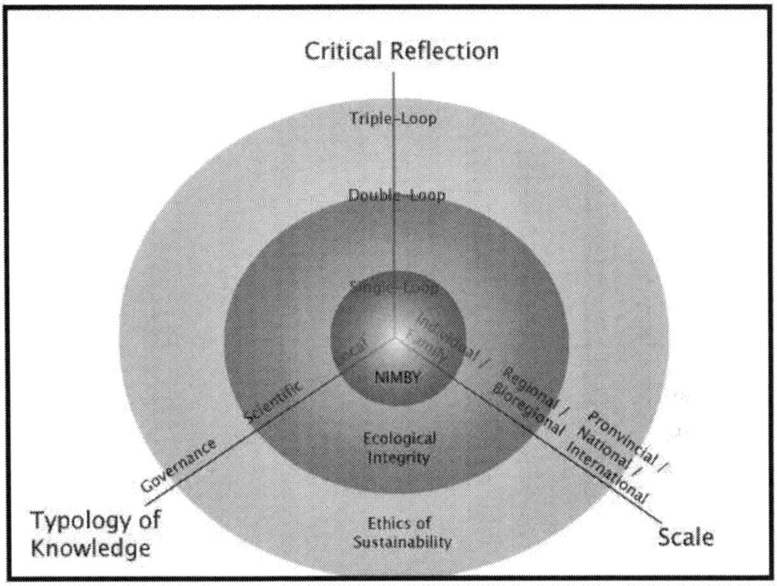

In beginning to consider the implications of this conceptual model of social learning in complex SEE systems, several other generic insights can be derived. Some groups, depending on their history and the way they have interacted with the policy and decision-making structures of a given SEE system of interest (structural coupling), may evolve to be more adept at the development and use of different kinds of knowledge. Government agencies or groups that have become involved in adversarial or judicial fora such as the OMB process may have evolved to rely on or value scientific evidence. Or, depending on their experience, they may have come to reflect on the power relations within such decision-making processes and relied more heavily on knowledge of the relevant governance system and/or the local informal decision-making structures.

In any case, the SEE conceptual model of social learning may provide environmental movement organizations, government agencies or academic researchers with a provocative tool to explore or conceptually map the requirements of effective intervention within complex SEE systems. The next chapter applies the SEE conceptual model of social learning to a less adversarial case within the same Southern Ontario environmental policy context: the evolution of the Long Point World Biosphere Reserve.

Chapter 7: Long Point World Biosphere Reserve Case Study

7.1 The Long Point World Biosphere Reserve as a Complex SEE System

7.1.1 Historical SEE System Context

The Long Point World Biosphere Reserve is an internationally recognized geomorphological and ecological system, historically protected as a sports fishery and game reserve surrounded by rural agricultural lands. The Point itself is the largest erosion deposit sand spit formation in the Laurentian Great Lakes. It extends 32 km into Lake Erie from its north shore (Figure 7). It has long been a focal point for hunting, fishing and birding enthusiasts as well as academic researchers, due to its diverse terrestrial and aquatic habitats. The area has supported a vibrant sports fishery and is an internationally recognized waterfowl migration staging area. Terrestrially, the area is characterized by Carolinian deciduous forest supporting species found nowhere else in Canada. It has been actively protected by various conservation and preservation organizations and agencies since 1866. In 1982 it was recognized as a RAMSAR site, and in 1986 was designated as a UNESCO World Biosphere Reserve (Nelson and Kerrie Wilcox, 1996; Francis and Whitelaw, 2001).

Geologically, the area is underlain by sedimentary Paleozoic bedrock of the Silurian and Devonian eras over which the Norfolk sandplains had been deposited by glacial Lake Whittlesey approximately 13,000 years ago. The actual Long Point sand spit formation began to form approximately 7,600 years before present at the location of a cross-lake glacial moraine. Approximately 4000 years ago, the formation was reworked again when the present configuration of Lake Erie emerged. The Point as we know it today was created by sediments carried eastward and deposited in a series of sand waves along the underwater moraine. Formations such as the Long Point sand spit are dynamic physical features, often eroding at times of high water or storm surges and then reforming with subsequent long shore deposition (Nelson and Wilcox, 1996; Francis and Whitelaw, 2001). As a result, Long Point was more often an island or set of islands than a peninsula throughout its history, with the gap between the island and the mainland growing to nearly 0.8 km in 1865 (Laidler 1944 in Nelson and Wilcox, 1996).

Long before European settlement began in the 1790s, aboriginal peoples used the Long Point area for seasonal hunting, fishing and gathering. However, evidence of an agricultural village settlement dates from approximately 900-1300 AD, and at least two key archeological sites in the area date from 2900-2400 and 1100 to 700 BC (Francis and Whitelaw 2001). From about 1400 to 1650, the Long Point area was home to Neutral Iroquoian people, so named as they avoided warfare among aboriginal groups to the north and south (Francis and Whitelaw, 2001). By the early 1650s, the dispersal of the Neutral peoples of the area meant that the Long Point and much of the north shore of the Lake area was devoid of permanent settlement, with the exception of Iroquois and Algonquin hunting or war parties portaging across from the point while traveling along the Erie shoreline (Nelson and Wilcox, 1996).

The 1780s witnessed the end of the American Revolution and the subsequent influx of United Empire Loyalists to Canada from the newly independent United States. This led to a rapid settlement of the Long Point area as the Lieutenant Governor of Upper Canada actively encouraged the Loyalists to settle in "Long Point Country" (Department of Lands and Forests 1963 in Nelson and Wilcox, 1996). The land surrounding the point in what is today Norfolk County was ideal for settlement, "owing to the large proportion of plains which is found to be easily brought into a state of cultivation, and other parts ... with excellent timber for fencing, building etc."(land surveyor Thomas Welch 1797, in Nelson and Wilcox, 1996). Due to its attractiveness to settlers and its accessibility from the lake, the area was settled quickly even before it was properly surveyed (Department of Lands and Forests 1963 in Nelson and Wilcox, 1996).

Settlers in the Long Point / Norfolk area mainly grew wheat throughout the 1800s until the 1880s when competition from the prairies led to barley, oats and corn becoming the predominant crops of Norfolk County (Wilcox, 1993; Nelson and Wilcox, 1996). In the

1860s, fruit farming, including vineyards and peach orchards, also scattered the landscape and livestock were also raised until about 1870. Despite agriculture being the primary economic activity of Norfolk County, an iron ore industry, pine and oak lumber industry and a commercial fishery all existed in the area throughout the 19th century (Barrett, 1979; Nelson and Wilcox, 1996).

By 1860 the impacts of European settlement began to leave their mark on the natural resources and landscape of the Long Point area. As forests on the mainland were depleted, the Point itself began to be cleared, resulting in large blowouts and the loss of kilometres of shoreline (Nelson and Wilcox, 1996). Aside from direct impacts on the landscape through, for instance, deforestation, European settlement brought with it a strong market for fresh bird meat. Soon entrepreneurial local hunters began to exploit the vast numbers of wild turkey, ruffed grouse, as well as ducks and other waterfowl in the Long Point bay (Nelson and Wilcox, 1996). At the same time, the Point began to develop a colourful reputation due to "wild but all too accurate tales … (of) drunkenness, murder and debauchery of every kind" (Barrett, 1979: 143).

In response to the multi-faceted threat to the rich natural resources and public perception of Long Point, a group of sportsmen and businessmen chartered the Long Point Company and in 1866 purchased 6044 hectares of land on the Point from the provincial government. By 1871 the Company owned the entire point, with the exception of two parcels of land, one owned by the government for lighthouse purposes and another owned by a local lumberman, Walter Anderson (Barrett, 1979). Of the eighteen clauses in the company's charter, the following is of particular interest to this work:

> The Company may carry on the business of pursuing, protecting, and granting licenses to take game, muskrats, mink, otter, beaver, and fish, upon the said lands and property or the water covering the same; and generally the doing of such other acts or things with the said land or with any mineral substance or thing, grown, or to be grown, found or being in or upon the same, as may promote the interest of the Company, and not being contrary to the laws of this Province, or the terms of the Patent from the Crown. (Barrett, 1979: 146)

In accordance with its charter, the Long Point Company began private policing and preservation of the Point's natural resources. Barrett (1979: 148), a local historian, argued that, "it was fortunate that the Company was made up of well-educated, tough, hard-headed businessmen who ruled with an iron hand, tempered with a spirit of fair play and respect for anyone with similar ideals, be he a corporation president or a local punter guide". In contrast, the Company has also been accused of "being a monopoly by which rich men have deprived others of access to the bounty of nature" (Barrett, 1979: 143). In either case, it can be argued that, without the Company's strict, self-serving preservation, the fragile ecosystem would not be as healthy and diverse and enjoy the international distinction it has today (Barrett, 1979; Skibicki, 1993; Nelson and Wilcox, 1996; Francis and Whitelaw, 2001).

In 1979 the Long Point Company arranged for large blocks of its land holdings to be transferred to the Canadian Wildlife Service to ensure the continued protection and sustainable use of waterfowl habitat and of the fragile Long Point ecosystem more generally. This transfer was indicative of a shift that had slowly occurred for decades from private to public resource management in the area (Skibicki, 1996). Government land ownership in the area has taken the form of National Wildlife Areas (federal), a Provincial Park (provincial) and Conservation Areas (regional). This private to public land management shift continued until the 1980s when government agencies began to feel political and economic pressure to downsize, reducing their operational budgets and ultimately their capacity (Skibicki, 1996).

7.1.2 Current Context 1986-Present

7.1.2.1 The Long Point World Biosphere Reserve

In response to the growing threat to the environmental governance of Long Point, the idea of a UNESCO World Biosphere Reserve was first raised in 1981 (Nelson and Wilcox, 1996; Francis and Whitelaw, 2001). The notion of nominating Long Point for the prestigious international designation was informally raised by an inter-university research group looking at Great Lakes Ecosystem Rehabilitation at a meeting with local staff from several government agencies (Francis and Whitelaw, 2001). A series of meetings and correspondence followed between the Canada/MAB Working Group on Biosphere Reserves, officials in agencies with jurisdiction over Long Point lands, and representatives of private sector, property owners in the area. Over the next three years the process continued until sufficient support was obtained for the nomination and until the Canadian Wildlife Service and the Ontario Ministry of Natural Resources were satisfied. In 1985, after an often contentious process, the nomination for a Long Point World Biosphere Reserve was submitted to UNESCO and approved in April 1986 (Francis and Whitelaw, 2001).

The Long Point World Biosphere Reserve consists of a core protected area (Long Point National Wildlife Area), a buffer area (defined by the 10 meter depth contour offshore and the regulatory 1:100 year flood line onshore) and an undefined "zone of cooperation" (Canadian Man and Biosphere Committee, 1990). Inventories of the area which include the biosphere reserve include 1384 species of plants, 370 species of birds (187 of which breed in the area), 102 species of fish, 46 species of mammals, 34 species of amphibians and reptiles, and 91 species of butterflies. Altogether, 172 species of biota found in the Long Point area are considered rare in Ontario (Francis and Whitelaw, 2001).

The governance arrangements for the biosphere reserve were initially going to take the form of inter-agency cooperation among various federal, provincial, regional and local government agencies. However, through a series of public meetings it became apparent that as many as 30 local community groups also were very interested in becoming involved. This interest was actively supported by the governments at all levels. From 1985 to 1990 there were several efforts to operationalize a multi-stakeholder governance structure. Finally, in 1989, after a contentious and even confrontational process, a non-profit corporation was established with open membership and a 15 member executive committee elected for three-year terms, once renewable. In 1993 the Long Point World Biosphere Reserve Foundation (LPWBRF) was formally incorporated and received charitable status (Francis and Whitelaw, 2001).

Despite receiving in kind support from its partners and being formally acknowledged in the Norfolk County Official Plan (Norfolk County, 2006), the Long Point Biosphere Reserve, as with all Canadian biosphere reserves, does not receive any core funding and so is volunteer-based. As a result, since the designation and formation, the LPWBRF's priorities have been a function of its fund-raising efforts which have included the annual "Groundhog Day Dinner and Dance", co-sponsorship of community events or special-project fund raising (Francis and Whitelaw, 2001). On average the volunteers of the LPWBRF raised approximately $50,000 per year between 2000 and 2005. However, funding levels have varied greatly from around $6000 to approximately $130,000, depending on the time and efforts of the volunteers (Francis and Whitelaw, 2001).

7.1.2.2 Sustainability and the Evolving Mandate of the Long Point World Biosphere Reserve

The activities of the Long Point Biosphere Reserve over its first nearly two decades can be characterized as environmental conservation or preservation-focused. The foundation has engaged in community-oriented and multi-disciplinary activities such as the 1993-94 public process to develop a "Community Action Plan" promoting conservation and sustainable resource use and the "Environmental Folio for the Long Point World Biosphere Reserve and Area" in conjunction with researchers at the University of Waterloo between 1992 and 1994. Much of the time and resources of the LPWBRF have gone into explicitly environmental conservation or preservation-focused activities and research, including:

- environmental monitoring workshops and the establishment of Ecological Monitoring and Assessment Network (EMAN) biodiversity monitoring plots
- studies on the impact of deer populations on the regeneration of vegetation on Long Point, before and after a major reduction of the deer herd in 1989 and 1990
- study of the ecology of Lyme disease, which is carried by infected "ticks" (an arthropod, Ixodes sp.) through small mammals and deer to humans at Long Point (one of only a few places where it has been confirmed in Canada)
- study of population trends of migrating landbirds at field stations maintained by the Long Point Bird Observatory since 1960
- various studies on waterfowl staging at Long Point, including numbers, food habits and food sources
- studies of the longshore transfer of sediments and onshore movements of these into fore-dunes and dune areas at Long Point
- monitoring of sports fish stocks in Long Point Bay by index trawls, creel surveys, and angler diary programs
- water quality sampling in Long Point Bay for major ions, nutrients, metals and organochlorine pesticides
- changes in breeding bird populations between 1979 and 1989 on managed and natural coastal marshes in the Big Creek National Wildlife Area

(Francis and Whitelaw, 2001: 20-21).

Two related major LPWBRF programs have focused on forest fragmentation and restoration. The foundation's 1995-1998 Forest Corridor Project was intended to help landowners assess and enhance the quality of remnant forests, reduce the forest fragmentation, and increase the connectivity among patches in ways that could benefit both agriculture and wildlife. Through this project, approximately 1800 ha were surveyed and 57 ha have been restored, involving over 100 community volunteers (Francis and Whitelaw, 2001). The other related initiative, "Project CARE - Carolinian Action, Restoration and Education", involved local high school students collecting and propagating seeds from native trees and grasses for use in restoration work. Ontario Power Generation has helped to continue this program with funding since 2001, and in so doing they are linking reforestation to emissions-trading credits (Francis and Whitelaw, 2001).

The LPWBRF in 2005 decided to expand its activities from what can be argued to be a primarily environmental focus (Craig et al., 2003; Francis and Whitelaw, 2001) to one that encompasses a broader notion of sustainability. The notion of sustainability explicitly links environmental, economic and social concerns, and views these integrated issues over a multi-generational time-scale. In the context of Long Point, the sensitive ecosystems have been protected through the efforts of concerned citizens, government bureaucrats, academics and others through social structures such as the Long Point Company, the National Wildlife Area, the Provincial Park and by the Long Point World Biosphere designation. However, the economy of the surrounding county has suffered numerous recessions, often linked to declines in the agricultural sector. During the last two decades of the 19th century and into the 20th, the Long Point area faced an economic recession due to a myriad of factors including the large-scale removal of forest cover, continuously declining soil fertility, international competition and decreasing subsidies for Canadian agriculture (Nelson and Wilcox, 1996).

During the 1920s and 1930s, however, the economic decline was temporarily reversed with the introduction of tobacco farming to the area. The aboriginal peoples of the area had grown tobacco in the Long Point area, and in 1920 the first experimental crop of

Burley tobacco was grown. The tobacco growing industry flourished throughout the next several decades. By 1930 approximately 7000 hectares were planted and by 1950 tobacco was being grown on over 21000 hectares (Nelson and Wilcox, 1996). The tobacco growing industry has become the main economic driver of the Norfolk and Long Point area, producing nearly 60% of Ontario's tobacco and contributing $158 million and over 2500 full-time equivalent jobs to Norfolk County (Gowan, 2004).

Despite the initial success of tobacco farming throughout the last 40 years, agriculture in the Norfolk/Long Point area has faced a continuous decline as the total number of farms, total farm population and number of persons per farm decreased and the average size of farms increased (Nelson and Wilcox, 1996). In 2001 just over 13000 hectares of tobacco were in production, down nearly 30% since 1950 (Norfolk County, 2003). As the tobacco growing industry continues its decline, the Long Point area is once again facing economic crisis (Gowan, 2004).

In part to address the region's economic decline, the LPWRBF initiated a series of sustainability workshops designed to engage the local biosphere reserve community in identifying potential sustainable development projects that the Foundation might facilitate to improve planning and management in the Long Point area. The LPWBRF decided to host four workshops organized around four community sectors. These included business and industry, service, conservation, and agriculture. Extensive efforts were made to contact representatives from each of these sectors and invite them to participate. The workshops were held during the month of November 2005 in or near the Town of Simcoe, Ontario. Attendance varied with each workshop. The business and industry workshop had 6 participants, the service sector workshop 6, the conservation workshop 25, and the agriculture workshop 19.

Each workshop had three main phases.

1. An introductory presentation on biosphere reserves and the work of the LPWBRF since the reserve was established in 1986.
2. A presentation by the Norfolk County Planning Department on the County's 2026 Sustainability Vision (Norfolk County, 2003), developed as part of the County's latest Official Plan review process.

3. A facilitated session designed to allow the participants to express their views on the topic of sustainability.

The type of facilitated session depended on the number of workshop attendees. The smaller workshops involved roundtable discussions. The larger sessions involved a plenary discussion in which attendees identified potential discussion topics; small group discussions on topics further refined by the participants; and, a final plenary discussion. A note taker and presenter were assigned within each small group. Both techniques provided valuable information on the interests of workshop participants and generated ongoing discussion as participants were able to respond to each other throughout the process.

For both the roundtable discussions and small group discussions, the following subjects were used to stimulate discussion.

1. Trends affecting the community,
2. Issues currently of interest,
3. Barriers to achieving sustainable livelihoods,
4. Existing resources available to the community, and
5. Ideas for future sustainability projects that might work in the Long Point context

Graduate students from the University of Waterloo, Faculty of Environmental Studies assisted with note-taking and transcription. In conjunction with other researchers from the University of Waterloo, I forged a collaborative, participatory research arrangement with the LPWBRF board. Through this relationship, researchers at the University of Waterloo helped facilitate, synthesize and analyze the results of these workshops for use by the board. Furthermore, team members involved with the Biosphere Sustainability Project (www.fes.uwaterloo/research/biosphere), led by Dr. Robert Gibson and Dr. George Francis of the Environment and Resource Studies Department in the Faculty of Environmental Studies, contributed to analysis of the workshop results. In conjunction with interviews with key members of the LPWBRF (past and present), the results of these workshops were used as an empirical basis to explore the SEE systems conceptual model of social learning and further test the results from the ORM case study. The trends and themes that emerged from the four workshops highlight opportunities for social learning across these four diverse groups and for the board to continue to evolve and learn as a group.

7.1.2.2.1 Workshop Trends

Both global and regional trends were identified by workshop participants as having influence on the Long Point area. A negative trend involving globalization and the loss of agricultural markets was identified by participants in both the agriculture and conservation workshops. Negative impacts on the local economy from agricultural decline were linked to this global trend. Solutions presented by participants included communicating, marketing and demonstrating the Long Point biosphere reserves' exemplary agricultural practices through branding, the marketing of locally grown agricultural products, and fostering land use stewardship and conservation through the Alternative Land Use Services (ALUS) Program (Bailey, 2005).

A second negative trend identified in all four workshops was the loss of young people from the Long Point area. There was general agreement that sustainable development projects involving ecotourism and education/interpretation might help counter this trend. A third trend identified by participants in the business and industry, service and conservation workshops was the increasing number of people choosing the Long Point area as a retirement destination. This was identified as positive and one that the biosphere reserve might consider tapping in terms of resources both for money and volunteers.

7.1.2.2.2 Workshop Themes

Several major themes emerged from the four workshops and are summarized in a recent publication (McCarthy et al., In Press). Workshop attendees demonstrated critical awareness of complex and multifaceted themes such as rural poverty, community pride, education, ecotourism and the need for a strong biosphere reserve communications strategy.

The sense of pride in the Long Point community by all participants was notable. Of interest is the fact that the UNESCO biosphere reserve designation is given to areas in recognition of the progressive work being carried out. However, the community appears to have minimal knowledge of this prestigious designation, although participants believe the Long Point area is special and that the area has the potential to address the sustainability challenge by building on existing strengths. Communication, marketing and networking were identified as critical activities for the biosphere reserve. One participant in the business and industry workshop indicated that after deciding to attend the workshop, he went online to find out about biosphere reserves and specifically the LPWBR. He indicated that he found out that biosphere reserves were everything he thought they were not, and suggested that the LPWBRF improve its communication and marketing activities. Participants in the business and industry, service and conservation workshops indicated that many sustainable development initiatives are taking place in the Long Point area (e.g. ecotourism, farm gate sales), and that these should be inventoried and then marketed by the LPWBRF (McCarthy et al., In Press).

The theme of education was discussed extensively in three of the four workshops – business and industry, service and conservation. Participants believed public education was critical to the success of the biosphere reserve and achieving sustainability. Extensive discussions revolved around the idea of developing an international interpretive centre in Port Rowan with new environmental recreation facilities (e.g. board-walks in the marsh area of Long Point to act as an anchor for environmental education and tourist destination) (McCarthy et al., In Press).

Ecotourism was also a focus of discussion in the business and industry, service and conservation workshops. Many participants indicated that the Long Point core, currently off limits to people, should have limited, controlled and managed access to promote ecotourism. Other ideas included the development and promotion of the Long Point area as an ecotourism cycling destination. Many existing activities and services in the Long Point area were also identified including boating, hiking and birding. Inventorying and better coordinating and marketing these ecotourism activities were suggested (McCarthy et al., In Press).

Rural poverty and associated depression were identified as an important issue in need of further attention by the service and agriculture workshops. This rural issue was directly linked to the decline of tobacco and other constraints on agriculture resulting from globalization. Urban issues were also raised in the business and industry workshop. The focus was on the need to address urban homelessness and urban renewal (McCarthy et al., In Press).

In general, the participants of the workshops raised a broad and rich mix of trends and themes in relation to the sustainability of the Long Point community. Trends from the local to the global, including youth emigration and the impacts of economic globalization on the agricultural community, were highlighted by the workshop participants. The complexity of the notion of sustainability was reflected in themes raised by the attendees. Themes as varied and multifaceted as rural poverty, community pride, education, ecotourism and the need for a strong biosphere reserve communications strategy spoke to a well-informed and reflective group of workshop participants (McCarthy et al., In Press).

7.1.3 Discussion – The Long Point Biosphere Reserve as a Complex SEE System

This section is meant to apply the SEE systems framework and conceptual model of social learning to the Long Point World Biosphere Reserve case study. Section 4.3 contextualizes the SEE systems conceptual framework and model within a broader research and planning protocol for describing and intervening in complex socio-ecological systems (Gunderson et al., 1995; Berkes and Folke, 1998; Kay et al., 1999; Gunderson and Holling, 2002; Berkes and Folke, 2003; Waltner-Toews et al., 2004; Folke et al., 2005). Here the goal is to describe the Long Point World Biosphere Reserve as a complex SEE system by providing empirical evidence from the sustainability workshops and interviews regarding the six principles of the SEE systems framework (Section 3.1.2).

7.1.3.1 Co-Evolution

As with the Oak Ridges Moraine case study, respondents in both the workshops and the interviews did not use complex systems terms but did demonstrate a rich understanding of the complex relationships among social, ecological and knowledge systems. Workshop participants were able to draw strong connections between global economic systems and their local agricultural economy as well as opportunities for augmenting their floundering local economy with eco-tourism based on the Long Point World Biosphere Reserve. Long Point interviewees also described how the LPWBRF board is "waking up to the fact that we don't have an environmental problem, it is a social problem that we have on planet Earth" (LP-2). Another noted that "the issue between the economy and the environment has always been important, yet not often emphasized, addressed, and labeled ... it's not just the environment and the economy, it's the environment and people and their day to day lives" (LP-1). Respondents also made reference to the significance of University of Waterloo, Faculty of Environmental Studies, *Long Point Environmental Folio* (Nelson and Wilcox, 1996). The Folio synthesized abiotic, biotic and cultural aspects of the Long Point landscape. One respondent noted that "one of the biggest projects was initiated back in 1995, and it was the Forest Corridor Restoration Project, evolved out of Nelson's Long Point Folio" (LP-2). The recognition of needs for more explicit integration of social, economic and ecological concerns, expressed by interviewees as well as by the authors of reports from the Long Point Folio study, reflects at least some understanding of the co-evolutionary nature of social, ecological systems.

7.1.3.2 Reflexive Uncertainty

Long Point case study workshop participants and interviewees described uncertainty around the sensitivity of the Long Point landform to the impacts of tourism, around what a Biosphere Reserve was or was not, and around the decline of the local agricultural economy and youth emigration in Norfolk County. Respondents also described another level of uncertainty associated with decision making and governance structures. One former LPWBRF board member noted that "according to UNESCO you get every shade of a group, every opinion, and put them together and then discuss, compromise and work things out … it is very difficult to get a group together of such diversity and cooperate" (LP-3). Others noted times of extreme tension and conflict on the board. This kind of uncertainty associated with different perspectives coming together in decision-making structures compounds the inherent uncertainty associated with the social and ecological systems such structures are meant to manage.

7.1.3.3 Cross-Scalar Considerations

The importance of scale and cross-scalar interactions in the Long Point case study was a strong theme highlighted by both the workshop participants and interviewees. Workshop respondents, especially in the agricultural session, readily connected the impacts of their local land, economy and livelihoods to international agricultural quota systems and the impacts of economic globalization. One LPWBRF board member who attended the workshop sessions noted "the process made me realize how much there is I don't know regarding global markets and impacts on farmers, quotas, etc. … it was intimidating to realize that some of these connections exist (global influences, beyond local control)" (LP-1). As in the ORM case, catalyzing cross-scale interactions and understanding is a critical factor in learning and intervening in complex socio-ecological, epistemological systems. Further discussion of the importance of scale is provided in Section 7.1.4.1.

7.1.3.4 Critical Awareness

Critical reflection and awareness was demonstrated through the LPWBRF board decision to shift its mandate from a conservation-oriented to a broader notion of sustainability that was the catalyst for the sustainability workshop series. The board has at times also reflected upon its general make-up. A former board member noted that "there was a tendency for older people to be involved" (LP-3) which resulted in an effort by the board to attract younger members. Reflecting on the role of knowledge and power in board activities, an interviewee noted that "we had a number of people that knew what was going on, but the politics got in the way so that knowledge was not always tapped, or utilized" (LP-3). As with scale, critical reflection and awareness was raised as a key component of learning in environmental planning and policy making in the Long Point case study. The importance of critical reflection for social learning is discussed further in Section 7.1.4.3.

7.1.3.5 Pluralism

Respondents also described the importance of acknowledging different perspectives as well as the power relationships and conflicts that can result when they are brought together in a decision-making process. However, in the case of the Biosphere Reserve many of the conflicts were the result of misunderstandings related to the objectives / purpose / function of the biosphere reserve *vis a vis* "telling people what they could or couldn't do ... especially in relation to real-estate and farming interests (private property rights)" (LP-1). The importance of bringing together a plurality of perspectives on an issue as complex as sustainability was the main driver behind the LPWBRF board's sustainability workshop series. This is the result of a "more well-rounded board from different sectors, resulting in a broadened social network" (LP-2) and therefore "the mandate is now evolving because of the people, and different interests and skills that have been brought to the table ... health care background, insurance agents, and coinciding learning process, learning from each other" (LP-2).

7.1.3.6 Power

Power and power imbalances were more of an issue in the Oak Ridges Moraine case; they were not as prevalent in the less confrontational Long Point case. However, as noted above, due to the politics around conservation and private land use the knowledge-base was often under utilized (Section 7.1.3.4), and misunderstandings around the purpose of the biosphere reserve have caused tensions within the Long Point community (Section 7.1.3.5). Both of these examples point to the importance of explicitly considering power relationships in environmental decision making. A current board member pointed to the importance of having "a new official plan with restricted development that is much more forward thinking than before and that recognizes the biosphere reserve" and having "key planners in the County that believe strongly in maintaining sustainability, and ecological integrity" (LP-2).

The application of the SEE systems principles to the Long Point case also points to three key elements of social learning in environmental planning and policy making: scale, types of knowledge and critical reflection. The next section describes how these findings have led to the development of the SEE systems model of social learning.

7.1.4 Findings – Social Learning and the Complex Long Point World Biosphere Reserve SEE System

The mid 1980s convergence of academic researchers, public sector bureaucrats and civil society groups through their collective interest in a biosphere reserve designation for Long Point could be interpreted in systems terms as the self-organization or reemergence of a SEE system emergent structure. Similarly to the environmental regime formation seen on the Oak Ridges Moraine (Whitelaw, 2005 and Section 6.1.4.4), this new emergent structure also self-organized in response to perceived threats to the Long Point socio-ecological system. Even the Long Point Company, given the historical context, with its interest in conservation and active preservation in the Long Point area, could be viewed as a similar phenomenon with its actions emerging in response to perceived degradation of the socio-ecological system of interest. Despite the reasonable allegations of elitism and self-serving motivations for preservation, the Long Point Company may also have represented the convergence of well-informed, influential individuals with a broad view of the importance of conservation and an openness to multiple perspectives (Barrett, 1979). However, such an interpretation of the Long Point Company's perspective would require further research. The intent here is to apply the SEE systems conceptual model of social learning to a reinterpretation of the evolution of the Long Point World Biosphere Reserve Foundation's mandate since designation, particularly focusing on the shift from environmental conservation to a broader notion of sustainability.

As previously mentioned, since the designation of the Biosphere Reserve in 1986 the activities of the LPWBRF have focused primarily on environmental conservation with projects such as the establishment of EMAN biodiversity monitoring plots, studies of waterfowl staging and migrating landbirds, water quality sampling, and the Forest

Corridor and Project CARE programs (Francis and Whitelaw, 2001). The focus has since evolved, primarily as a result of renewal of the LPWBRF board. Recent board members include individuals from the health care sector and insurance industry in contrast to previous board members who were largely from local conservation groups and government agencies. The most recent board has learned as a group, building on an understanding of the strong links between the environment and the economy and collectively coming to realize that environmental problems are human "social" problems. They also have built on the experience of previous boards, emphasizing the importance of partnerships but explicitly attempting to broaden support for the biosphere reserve with the understanding that all of the Long Point and Norfolk County community members are part of the biosphere reserve. As a result, recent biosphere reserve activities have represented an attempt to address a broader suite of socio-ecological of issues with a more inclusive approach to partnerships.

The biosphere reserve board's decision to host four sectoral sustainability workshops represents an excellent example of the LPWBRF's attempt to reflect on and refocus its efforts through the broad lens of sustainable development. The evolution of the LPWBRF's mandate and especially its sustainability workshop series can be interpreted as a social learning process. The rest of this section is intended to further the empirical exploration of the SEE systems conceptual model of social learning. It will build on the insights from the development of the socio-ecological, epistemological systems model of social learning as it emerged from the SEE systems conceptual framework applied to the ORM case study. As with the Oak Ridges Moraine case, the importance of scale, the development and use of three types of knowledge, and the need for multiple levels of critical reflection provide a context for social learning in the Long Point SEE system.

7.1.4.1 Scale

In the context of the sustainability workshop series, when asked about the trends, issues, resources and barriers to sustainability in their area, community members did not simply cite regulatory- or policy-related issues or even issues related to the policy-making process itself. Instead, much of the discussion focused on much broader institutional perspectives such as the impacts of economic globalization on the local agricultural economy and the social implications of this economic decline. The agricultural group easily made connections across these scales, linking global markets and international quota systems to their livelihoods and the implications for their land and their community. Sharing this knowledge in the context of the workshop provided a learning opportunity for the LPWBR board. One board member noted, "the process made me realize how much there is I don't know, for example, global market and impacts on farmers, quotas, etc.". In the context of generating potential sustainable development-focused projects and policies, this broad, sophisticated level of reflection is necessary to address such complex, interrelated and controversial issues as the collapse of the tobacco industry, rural poverty and the impacts of economic globalization on the agricultural sector (Schon and Rein, 1994).

Throughout the workshop series, it became evident that many of the community members already possessed a sophisticated understanding of the trends, issues, resources and barriers to sustainability in the Long Point area. Attendees pointed to previous learning experiences in such sustainability-related community engagement processes as the recent County of Norfolk Official Plan Review process, the Norfolk Tobacco Community Action Plan process and the Alternative Land Use Services program. By raising issues such as rural poverty, the influx of retirees, youth emigration and describing the influence of trends such as the collapse of the tobacco growing industry and the impacts of globalization, community members demonstrated an understanding of the importance of scale and cross-scalar interactions.

7.1.4.2 Types of Knowledge

The Long Point World Biosphere Reserve case has demonstrated the development and use of three generic types of knowledge (local technical, scientific, governance). The activities of the LPWBRF confirm a strong understanding of the local social and ecological system. Since its inception, the LPWBRF has sought to develop a rich understanding of the ecological and human historical systems of the area. In partnership with local government agencies and researchers, especially at the University of Waterloo, the biosphere reserve board has undertaken projects and programs such as the EMAN biodiversity monitoring plots, the Forest Corridor Project and the Long Point Environmental Folio to monitor and study key species, habitats, threats to biodiversity and ecological integrity in the Long Point area. The LPWBR board hosted "a dinner at the community hall – many people came out to identify projects, and talk about what needed to be done" (LP-2). They also undertook "consultations with members of the community as part of the Long Point Country Community Action Plan which brought all diverse groups together to discuss how we could address energy issues, recycling, etc." (LP-2).

The board's decision to engage the local community in the December 2005 sustainability workshop series on the broad and complex issue of sustainability demonstrated its interest in the continuous development of knowledge of its local socio-ecological system. The workshop series has helped the LPWBRF and members of the local community develop knowledge around the local linkages among economic, social and environmental issues such as rural poverty and opportunities for ecotourism.

The importance of the development and use of scientific knowledge by the biosphere reserve has been demonstrated over and over through its various environmental studies and programs. The LPWBRF has been a partner (as previously noted) in studies on waterfowl staging, landbird migration, impacts of vegetation regeneration on the local deer herd, and water quality sampling for major ions, nutrients metals and organochloride pesticides (Francis and Whitelaw, 2001). Despite the fact that the Biosphere Reserve does not have a comprehensive monitoring program, it has engaged in the development of scientifically-sound monitoring data for biodiversity, fish stocks and changes in breeding bird populations (Francis and Whitelaw, 2001).

The use of scientific knowledge by the LPWBRF differs from its use in the environmental advocacy and conflict-ridden ORM case study. In the ORM, scientific knowledge was utilized by various parties to support arguments for or against new land use policy with legitimacy or "epistemic warrant" in judicial contexts such as the Ontario Municipal Board. In the Long Point case study, scientific knowledge has generally been generated outside of official, legalistic decision-making processes and more for the purposes of generic understanding and academic research. Biosphere Reserve/EMAN monitoring plots, for instance, have yielded scientifically-defensible evidence that 72% of the Eastern Flowering Dogwood *(Cornus florida)* has been destroyed by a fungus called *Discula destructive,* and if the fungus is left unchecked, dogwood populations in the LPWBR could be decimated in the next 5 to 10 years (LP-2; Parker and Brian Craig, 2004).

In addition, a rich understanding of the governance system and its inherent power relations and imbalances has been demonstrated in Long Point. Advocates for the biosphere reserve have had to learn through experience about the local power relations and especially the influence of local champions. It has been argued that, without the blessing of the influential local historian Harry B. Barrett, community support for a Long Point World Biosphere Reserve would have been much harder to garner (Francis, 2006). Even with Barrett's support, several interviewees noted that some members of the Long Point area community expressed strong misgivings about a UNESCO biosphere reserve designation for the Point, questioning the loss of local autonomy to an international agency (LP-1; LP-2; LP-3). Interviewees provided anecdotal evidence of heated conflicts among board members due, for instance, to an understandable misinterpretation of the power (or more accurately, the lack thereof) of the biosphere reserve to influence local land use and land use policy directly (LP-1; LP-2; LP-3). One interviewee noted that members of the local community "just didn't want anything to change, and they perceived Biosphere Reserve as having more power than it does, and they wanted to control it" (LP-2). Through a continuous process of social learning, as evidenced most recently through the results of the sustainability workshops, the board and the Long Point community have come to take pride in, and no longer fear, the prestigious UN designation. The sustainability workshops also demonstrated the Long Point community's understanding of the complex political economic system that governs the international agricultural markets and the profound influence this system has on its local economy.

7.1.4.3 Critical Reflection

Long Point community members posed questions that demonstrated all three levels of critical reflection. Workshop participants raised issues around how best to communicate and market the Long Point Biosphere Reserve and how to improve the education and agri- and eco-tourism programs in the Long Point Area (i.e. are we doing things right?). They also posed more normative questions around the issues of youth emigration from the area and rural poverty, noting that existing programs and policies were inadequate and suggested what else could be done to address these complex issues (i.e. are we doing the right things?). The fact that the LPWBRF board chose to reflect on its mandate and, by hosting the sustainability workshop series, explicitly made an effort to shift it from a conservation-focused to a broad notion of sustainability also reflects double-loop learning. Finally, misunderstandings around the power of the biosphere reserve, the influence of local champions such as Harry Barrett and the importance of interpersonal relationships within a board structure demonstrate the need for a keen understanding of local governance and power relations. One interviewee remarked that while it helped to have board members with relevant scientific background "the politics got in the way so that knowledge was not always tapped, or utilized" (LP-3). As well, issues around the collapse of the tobacco industry and the impacts of globalization of agricultural markets were raised several times in the context of this workshop series. Expressions of powerlessness due to lack of market control and questions around the ethics of global agricultural market standards clearly demonstrated Flood and Romm's (1996) third centre or loop of learning (i.e. an understanding of the relationship between a notion of "rightness" and broader power relations).

The evolution of the LPWBRF's mandate from strictly environmental conservation-focused to a broader notion of sustainability, demonstrated through its recent community workshop series, provides evidence of social learning. Social learning is a socially-embedded process of knowledge creation undertaken by individuals and groups with inherently limited and biased perspectives that results in changes to social structures (i.e. policy, mandate, social norms). This process appears to be fostered by the following three factors: an understanding of the importance of scale; critical reflection on various levels; and, the integration of scientific, local technical and governance knowledge.

7.1.4.4 SEE Systems Model of Social Learning

Just as three archetypical perspectives could be mapped on the SEE conceptual model of social learning in the ORM case study (Section 6.1.4.4), so too can the evolution of the LPWBRF's mandate (Figure 9). Representing the zone at the centre of the model (darkest blue), the perspective of the local residents who questioned and resisted the biosphere reserve can be argued to rely on local knowledge, single-loop learning and a focus on the local scale. The medium-blue circle on the diagram represents the environmental conservation-focused mandate of the LPWBRF. Here, scientifically-based knowledge is utilized in conjunction with local knowledge of the social and ecological system; policies and goals of the biosphere reserve are questioned in terms of environmental conservation and then sustainability. A third archetypical perspective, represented by the largest, lightest cube, can be related to the shift in mandate from environmental conservation to sustainability. Here local and scientific knowledge is considered in the context of governance systems; critical reflection occurs on all three levels, including considerations of the influence of power imbalances on traditional notions of "rightness"; and, interactions across scales from the local to the global are considered.

Figure 9: SEE Systems Conceptual Model of Social Learning Applied to the Long Point Case

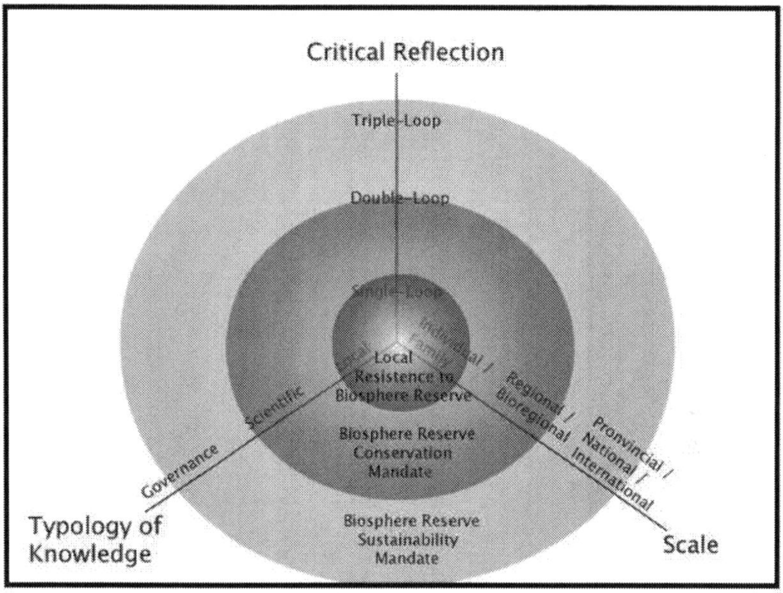

The LPWBRF Board, through the sustainability workshops, has begun to change the local community members' perception of the Biosphere Reserve as a solely environmental organization, to one also delivering on sustainability. Community members were engaged in thinking about the future of the Long Point area and this led to the generation of ideas that may lead to sustainability projects that benefit the community in the future. In three of the four workshops – business and industry, service, and agriculture – participants were individuals who had never had contact with the biosphere reserve before. This resulted in the emergence of new champions for the biosphere reserve. These positive outcomes appear to have resulted in large part from social learning processes that the LPWBRF initiated or tapped into.

When the LPWBRF Board decided to broaden its emphasis from environmental conservation to sustainability, it explicitly recognized the complexity of the issues involved and the importance of involving the local community. While promoting social learning through the sustainability workshops may not have been an a priori objective of the Foundation, it does appear to have made just such a contribution. Acknowledging this contribution and that of other related public processes can help focus attention on the importance of social learning in developing policy to address sustainability.

Social learning speaks to a process of knowledge creation and critical reflection on individual as well as group or organizational levels that foster a broad understanding of complex and politically contentious issues. For the LPWBRF and its goal of engaging the local community in considering the complex and contentious issue of sustainability of the Long Point area, this notion of social learning for policy making appears to be highly relevant. Through this series of public, sector-based workshops, the Foundation engaged in an iterative, collaborative process that demonstrated social learning and has provided many ideas for sustainability-focused projects in the Long Point area. As the result of social learning through this and previous public processes, future biosphere reserve projects may not only address policy-level issues but also broader institutional level issues such as the impacts of economic globalization on the agricultural industry.

7.2 Conclusions

Chapters 6 and 7 have applied a complex and critical systems-based approach to social learning to two case studies of environmental planning and governance systems in southern Ontario, and illustrate three key facets of the social learning process. From this perspective, social learning is an on-going, adaptive, communicative process of local, scientific and governance knowledge creation and synthesis undertaken by individuals and groups with inherently limited and biased perspectives that results in changes to social structures (i.e. policy, mandate, social norms) fostered by an understanding of the importance of scale (spatial and temporal) and critical reflection on various levels from the pragmatic to the ethical. The SEE systems conceptual model of social learning has emerged out of recasting narrative descriptions of the integrated land use planning process on the Oak Ridges Moraine and the evolution of the Long Point World Biosphere Reserve mandate through the SEE systems framework. The evidence presented from the instrumental case studies demonstrates that social learning is fostered by three key factors: an understanding of the importance of scale; critical reflection on various levels; and, the integration of scientific, local technical and governance knowledge.

What has also emerged from interpreting both the Oak Ridges Moraine and Long Point case studies through a systems perspective is the importance of a broad knowledge base supporting a strong stewardship network. In systems terms, both case studies demonstrated that in response to a stressor or perceived threat to the existing socio-ecological system, a specific type of SEE system emergent structure appeared to self-organize. This SEE system emergent structure can generally be said to represent the perspectives of civil society organizations, academic researchers and civil servants but can be characterized in more generic terms as reflective and open-minded, well-informed, and involving influential members of a community. Thus, these SEE system emergent structures that self-organized in response to a system stressor demonstrated all three factors that foster social learning.

In the ORM case study, STORM and its partner academic and government organizations and agencies emerged in response to the threat of development in the form of unchecked urban sprawl on the ecologically- and hydrologically-sensitive moraine. This SEE system emergent structure demonstrated evidence of social learning in the form of multiple levels of critical reflection, the use of scientific, local technical and governance knowledges and an understanding of the importance of scale and cross-scale interactions.

The Long Point World Biosphere Reserve Foundation has also demonstrated evidence of social learning through the evolution of its mandate. Interest in a UNESCO World Biosphere Reserve designation emerged from local civil society groups, academic researchers and government civil servants in response to environmental degradation in the sensitive Long Point geomorphological formation and associated ecological systems. Since the designation of the Long Point Biosphere Reserve in 1986, the mandate of the LPWBRF can generally be characterized as environmental conservation-focused. However, more recently the LPWBRF board has reached out to the Long Point community to engage it on the notion of expanding its mandate from environmental conservation to the broad goal of sustainability. The Long Point board in conjunction with its partners has demonstrated the use of scientific, local technical knowledge and knowledge of local to international, cross-scalar, power relations. There is also evidence that the LPWBRF has exhibited multiple levels of critical reflection from asking questions about how best to conserve the fragile ecosystems of the Point, to questioning the goals and mandate of the Foundation and ultimately to considering the power relations that reinforce the structures and dynamics of the Long Point SEE system.

These insights from the application of the SEE systems model of social learning to two empirical case studies have provocative implications for the related abstract and pragmatic fields of academic research and the practice of environmental planning and governance. More specifically, these insights may have direct implications for understanding social learning in the context of biosphere reserves and in particular for potential biosphere reserves such as the Oak Ridges Moraine. The final chapter explores these implications and provides recommendations for further research and for the exploration of an Oak Ridges Moraine World Biosphere Reserve.

Chapter 8: Conclusions, Implications and Recommendations

8.1 Introduction and Summary

This final chapter summarizes the key findings of this dissertation research as they relate to the goals and objectives in Chapter 1 (Section 1.2). The implications and recommendations for further research into the theory and practice of social learning in complex environmental planning and governance systems are also provided to address research objective #5 (Section 1.2).

My dissertation began with the assumption that complex and critical systems thinking is a useful approach to address phenomena that are too complex to be analyzed as machines and too ordered to be aggregated through statistical analysis (Weinberg, 1975) and that exhibit extreme uncertainty and high decision-stakes (Funtowicz and Ravetz, 1992; Funtowicz and Ravetz, 1993; Funtowicz and Ravetz, 1994; Ravetz and Funtowicz, 1999). Therefore, it is assumed that complex and critical systems thinking is a useful approach to address complex systems such as ecosystems, human social/institutional systems, and human knowledge and learning and especially systems that represent the integration of all three. The approach developed in my dissertation explicitly begins with generic critical, reflective, systems-based principles to problem solving, tailors these for use in the planning and policy domain, and finally illustrates their utility and begins to test them in two instrumental case studies of social learning in environmental planning contexts. Such a conceptual framework is not intended to replace existing, conventional rational comprehensive or participatory approaches but instead to complement them.

The overall goal of this research, as stated at the outset, was to illustrate and begin to test the utility of a complex and critical systems-based framework for research and intervention by describing and refining the contributions of environmental movement organizations to social learning in the context of complex environmental policy making and governance systems. This goal was addressed through work towards five key objectives:

1. to develop a complex and critical systems-based conceptual framework for research and intervention based upon an interdisciplinary literature review;
2. to develop a complex and critical systems-based methodological framework for research and intervention in the planning and policy domain;
3. to apply the frameworks to two instrumental case studies of innovative examples of social learning in environmental policy making and governance in Ontario to illustrate and begin to test their utility;
4. to develop a complex and critical systems-based conceptual tool for describing the contributions of environmental movement organizations to social learning in the context of environmental policy making and governance in Ontario; and,
5. to develop theoretical and practical research contributions as well as recommendations for further research and for the practice of environmental planning, policy making and governance.

The interdisciplinary literature review was intended firstly to establish the value of insights from critical, reflective and systems-based perspectives pervading fields of research related to environmental planning and policy making and secondly, to begin to synthesize some disparate fields of study into a reflective, systems-based framework for approaching research and intervention, and more specifically, for describing the process of social learning in environmental planning and policy making. The literature review identified a research gap and an opportunity to develop a socially-embedded view of knowledge and social learning for environmental policy, planning and governance using complex and critical systems-based heuristics. From this perspective, social learning is an on-going, adaptive, communicative process of local, scientific and governance knowledge creation and synthesis undertaken by individuals and groups with inherently limited and biased perspectives that results in changes to social structures (i.e. policy, mandate, social norms) fostered by an understanding of the importance of scale (spatial and temporal) and critical reflection on various levels from the pragmatic to the ethical. A complex and critical systems-based conceptual framework, a methodological framework and a conceptual model of social learning have emerged based upon this perspective.

The conceptual framework provides researchers and practitioners with three descriptive and three prescriptive principles for studying and intervening in complex socio-ecological, epistemological systems (objective #1).

The descriptive principles are:

- Co-Evolution and Self-organization – Social, ecological and epistemological systems self-organize and co-evolve.
- Uncertainty and Social Embeddedness – Perspective and Context-dependence – Systems are inherently complex and perspective-dependent.
- Cross-scalar Considerations - Holarchies and Structure-agent Interactions – SEE Systems are holarchically nested, exhibiting both top-down and bottom-up causality.

The prescriptive principles are:

- Critical Awareness and Experimental Boundary Critique – Within SEE Systems, research and intervention should be undertaken with a measure of critical awareness, reflexivity and openness to different perspectives.
- Pluralism (Knowledge, Perspectives and Methods) – Intervention within SEE Systems should incorporate a plurality of perspectives, methods and types of knowledge (e.g. epistemic, technical, phronetic).
- Enhancing Modes of Reflexivity – Intervention within SEE Systems should acknowledge issues of power in the form of structural constraints and opportunities for individual agents to reach their potential.

The methodological framework (objective #2) that has emerged through this research can be referred to as critical systems planning and policy research. Critical systems planning and policy research is a reflective, systems-based, participatory and action-oriented approach to the study of policy development and implementation. The goal of this approach to research and intervention is to explore the implications of a SEE systems perspective, describe the structures and process of SEE systems, explain the causal linkages within SEE systems, and provide action-oriented research outcomes.

This research contributes a theoretically-based and empirically-grounded conceptual framework for integrating knowledge and social learning into long-term, collaborative, systems-based descriptions of socio-ecological systems (Gunderson et al., 1995; Berkes and Folke, 1998; Kay et al., 1999; Gunderson and Holling, 2002; Berkes and Folke, 2003; Waltner-Toews et al., 2004; Berkes and Folke, 2003; Walker et al., 2006). The SEE systems framework was applied to two instrumental case studies of innovative, integrated land use planning to illustrate and begin to test it (objective #3). Through these empirical case studies, a conceptual model of social learning within socio-ecological systems emerged that illustrates the epistemological context for environmental governance and the requirements of social learning as defined along three axes:

Flyvberg's (2001) three-part Aristotelian, typology of knowledge; three levels of critical reflection based on Flood and Romm's (1996) triple-loop learning; and, a scale axis that highlights the importance of considering cross-scalar dynamics of complex systems (objective #4). The heuristic was developed as a descriptive tool to conceptually map perspectives of individual agents or organizations / institutions (structures) within an environmental policy and governance context or to trace the evolution of an individual's learning or an organization's social learning through time. It could also be tested as a prescriptive tool for designing environmental stewardship projects and programs that will foster social learning, such as existing or potential biosphere reserves like Long Point and the Oak Ridges Moraine, respectively.

The SEE systems conceptual model of social learning emerged out of the application of the conceptual framework to the two case studies. There appears to be evidence that social learning is fostered by three key factors: (1) an understanding of the importance of scale (spatial and temporal), (2) critical reflection on various levels and, (3) integration of scientific, local technical and governance knowledge.

What has also emerged from interpreting the Oak Ridges Moraine and Long Point case studies through a systems perspective is that, in response to a stressor or perceived threat to the socio-ecological system, a specific type of SEE system emergent structure has appeared to self-organize. This SEE system emergent structure can generally be said to represent perspectives from civil society organizations, academic researchers and civil servants but also can be characterized in more generic terms as reflective and open-minded, well-informed, and involving influential members of a community. These SEE system emergent structures that self-organized in response to a system stressor demonstrated all three factors that foster social learning.

8.2 Contributions and Implications

This research has implications on several levels, from the conceptual to the pragmatic. Implications for academic research in the abstract fields of critical social epistemology, social learning and complex and critical systems thinking will be described along with the more pragmatic fields of planning and environmental management. Implications for the practice of environmental policy making and planning will also be explored. In particular, this work contributes a conceptual framework and model for emphasizing the importance of and knowledge requirements for social learning within existing, and especially potential, biosphere reserves in Canada, such as the Oak Ridges Moraine.

8.2.1 Conceptual Contributions

This dissertation builds upon work applying insights from complex and critical systems thinking that explicitly integrates social and ecological systems for use in environmental planning and policy-making processes (for instance, Berkes and Folke, 1998; Kay et al., 1999; Holling, 2001; Gunderson and Holling, 2002; Mitchell, 2002). Other work that synthesizes insights from both complex and critical systems thinking and what, for the purposes of this dissertation, has been termed critical social epistemology begins to bring together socio-ecological as well as epistemological or learning systems for environmental planning and policy making (Funtowicz and Ravetz, 1992; Funtowicz and Ravetz, 1993; Funtowicz and Ravetz, 1994; Ravetz and Funtowicz, 1999; Fuchs, 2004; Forsyth, 2003; Healy, 2004). The main contribution of this work is that it explicitly integrates insights from complex and critical systems thinking and critical social epistemology into an understanding of the requirements for fostering social learning and attempts to ground this perspective in two empirical case studies. This work provides a generic complex and critical systems based framework in the form of descriptive and prescriptive principles for research and intervention. The research also tailors these principles into a methodological framework for planning and policy researchers. These conceptual tools provide researchers and practitioners with a perspective and heuristics to view learning as an explicitly social process (Fuller, 2002b) which, from a complex systems perspective, creates a new layer of uncertainty when developing policy in complex socio-ecological, epistemological systems.

These conceptual contributions also serve to buttress the philosophical and theoretical foundations of the concept of social learning. This research builds on Sinclair and Diduck's (2001) work on social learning in environmental assessment processes. Sinclair and Diduck (2001) use Mezirow's transformative learning theory to give theoretical shape to the concept of social learning. The SEE systems conceptual model further bolsters the theoretical basis for social learning by outlining and empirically grounding three key requirements (critical reflection, three types of knowledge, cross-scalar interactions).

On a more practical level, this research builds on work by Healy (2003), Yiftachel (1998) and Innes (2004) that applies a critical and reflective perspective to the discipline and practice of planning. Complementing these works, and more conventional approaches to planning, my dissertation provides a conceptual tool that addresses the complexity, uncertainty, power relations and plurality of knowledges involved in the process of social learning in planning processes. The framework and heuristics developed in this dissertation describe the types of knowledge, cross-scalar interactions and levels of critical reflection required for fostering social learning within planning and policy-making processes. This work also illustrates and begins to test the utility of this conceptual tool in two empirical case studies of environmental planning and policy processes. In addition, this research provides planning researchers and practitioners with a framework to study environmental policy development in the form of critical systems policy research.

8.2.2 Practical Contributions

The application of critical systems planning and policy research and the SEE systems framework and model of social learning to the ORM and Long Point case studies points to implications for and contributions to the practice of environmental planning and policy making. As noted, it would entail a collaborative process to integrate the systems dynamics operating in each area at different scales, but it is clear that local residents can be constructive and insightful participants in the process along with the disciplinary subject matter specialists. In the context of the Oak Ridges Moraine case study, the key findings could provide a framework for fostering social learning in preparation for the 10 year review of the ORM plan and act and for potential nomination of it as a World Biosphere Reserve. The Monitoring the Moraine Project (Section 4.5.1) is currently developing an environmental and policy monitoring program for the ORM, in part to prepare a sufficient and credible information and knowledge base to ensure the continued environmental protection of the moraine. This dissertation work could provide the Monitoring the Moraine project with a conceptual framework and model for structuring its program to ensure that it fosters social learning. As well, to be considered for UNESCO World Biosphere Reserve designation, a great deal of background research is required for both the nomination document and in considering the political issues surrounding the structure of biosphere reserve governance. While UNESCO does provide a structure for the required background research, my work could be utilized to help provide a framework for synthesizing the requisite scientific, local technical and governance knowledge necessary for the nomination process and development of the governance structure. The application of the SEE systems framework and model may result in generic lessons regarding the promotion of continuous social learning in biosphere reserves in Canada and around the world.

Regarding the Long Point World Biosphere Reserve, the findings from this research could provide useful insight for structuring the process of expanding its mandate from a conservation-focused to a broader notion of sustainability. In December 2005, the LPWBRF initiated a series of workshops to engage various sectors (business and industry, service, conservation, agriculture) of its community for their input on how to implement the concept of sustainability in the Long Point area. As part of this ongoing process, the LPWBRF is hosted a conference in the fall of 2006. The SEE systems conceptual model will be presented to the LPWBRF board and in conjunction with the results of the conference may be useful as a structure for fostering social learning in the context of attempting to realize sustainability in the Long Point area.

8.3 Limitations

As an initial phase of a broader research agenda, this exploratory research is intended to build a conceptual framework for illustrating and beginning to test a socially-embedded view of knowledge creation and social learning and to ground it empirically in two case studies. Subsequent research may be undertaken to adapt the SEE conceptual framework by testing it in a variety of other empirical cases, for instance, in other UNESCO

Biosphere Reserves in other parts of the world. On a more practical, action-oriented level, this work is intended to contribute to the exploratory research and documentation review required for recognizing the Oak Ridges as a World Biosphere Reserve. However, it represents only a first phase in a broader research agenda that will explore the tight connections between knowledge creation as a social process and the complex social and ecological systems.

Critical reflection and theorizing are often seen as divorced from action (Schon and Rein, 1994). The SEE systems conceptual framework, critical systems planning and policy research and the SEE systems model of social learning are attempts to build in a level of critical reflection into environmental policy and planning research and intervention while also requiring collaboratively defined, action-oriented outcomes. Patton and Sawicki, (1993: 25) note that "good policy analysis integrates quantitative and qualitative information, approaches the problem from various perspectives, and uses appropriate methods to test the feasibility of proposed options". The SEE systems perspective is intended to be pluralistic both in its use of methods and in its incorporation of multiple perspectives. While this particular application of the SEE systems approach does not utilize quantitative data, such use is not precluded. In fact, the use of various data and information sources developed using multiple methods are explicitly encouraged.

On a more pragmatic level, this study was limited due to its focus on social learning primarily within civil-society, non-government organizations. Subsequent phases could expand the scope to include a more extensive mix of government, private sector and other non-government organizations to reflect the broad notion of governance. However, this focus on non-government organizations involved in environmental and land use policy and planning was chosen for three reasons. First, given funding and logistical limitations, the empirical focus had to be manageable. This scope was justified as filling a research gap and as being based on the community-based nature of Canadian World Biosphere Reserves (Francis, 2004). In his recent work on the significance and role of environment movement organizations (EMOs), Whitelaw (2005) highlights a research gap on the role of EMOs, despite their increasing influence on land use policy and planning. My work on complex and critical systems-based approaches to social learning within non-government organizations as they attempt to effect change in environmental and land use policy will contribute to filling this research gap. Second, biosphere reserves in Canada have generally required a strong bottom-up, community-based commitment, as opposed to more top-down government initiated biosphere reserves in other parts of the world (Francis, 2004). And as this research is meant, at least in part, to contribute to an understanding of the knowledge and learning required for the Oak Ridges Moraine to be nominated for the UNESCO World Biosphere Reserve designation, the focus on social learning within non-government organizations is justified.

8.4 Recommendations

To address research objective #5 (Section 1.2), and based on the findings of this dissertation work, recommendations for further research and for the practice of environmental planning and policy making are as follows:

Further Research:

1. Apply and test the utility of the SEE systems conceptual framework and critical systems planning and policy research to other case studies of environmental planning and policy issues:
    a. across scales from the local to the global; and,
    b. in different areas of Canada and around the world.

2. Apply and test the utility of the SEE systems conceptual model of social learning to:
    a. policy-making processes in other existing and potential UNESCO World Biosphere Reserves in Canada and elsewhere
    b. other integrated land use planning processes
    c. environmental assessment processes

Due to the exploratory nature of this research, further refinement and testing of the SEE systems framework, critical systems planning research and the conceptual model of social learning is required. Testing these conceptual tools across a variety of scales and in different types of systems will verify their transferability to different planning and governance contexts.

Practice of Environmental Planning and Policy Making:

3. Use the SEE systems conceptual model of social learning within the context of landscape level environmental planning and governance processes, for example:
    a. to structure the Monitoring the Moraine environmental and policy monitoring processes to ensure the development of a comprehensive and reflective knowledge base
    b. to provide the STORM coalition with a framework for its transition from an advocacy coalition to a planning, implementation and research organization
    c. to foster social learning in the Long Point community as the LPWBRF attempts to address sustainability through biosphere reserve activities and network building
    d. to augment the UNESCO World Biosphere Reserve program to ensure that biospheres explicitly foster social learning

4. Use the SEE systems framework and model of social learning as organizational tools for the creation of an institutional structure or research institute to foster continuous social learning on the Oak Ridges Moraine. Such an institute could serve to formalize the SEE emergent structure that has self-organized in response to threats to the integrity and sustainability of the Oak Ridges Moraine (Section 6.1.2). This would foster the interchange of scientific, local technical and governance knowledges; various levels of critical reflection; and, critical awareness of cross-scale interactions.

Applying these critical systems-based heuristics in these planning and governance contexts will not only further test and refine the SEE conceptual tools, it will also provide the STORM coalition and the LPWBRF with a theoretically-grounded approach to knowledge and learning.

8.4 Conclusions

My interest in integrating learning or epistemological systems into an understanding of socio-ecological systems has emerged from an understanding of complex systems as inherently uncertain, perspective dependent, exhibiting internal causality, catastrophic and chaotic behaviour and exhibiting cross-scalar interactions. When applied to ecological systems, complexity thinking has posed questions that have jarred the ecological and biological sciences and the practice of environmental management and planning. Such questions have included: "is catastrophic behaviour such as fire or pest outbreak part of a healthy ecological system?", "ecological integrity according to whom and at what scale?", and "is disciplinary, scientific knowledge a sufficient basis upon which to make decisions when decision stakes and uncertainty are high?". Systems thinking has led environmental researchers and practitioners to begin to see the interconnections between systems across scales, sectors and disciplines. As a result, we have begun to discuss "socio-ecological" systems and the structures and dynamics linking global phenomenon such as climate change and economic globalization and local issues and initiatives. What has not yet been explicitly discussed is how tightly coupled are the ways we *think* about systems *vis a vis* how we interact with them.

Social epistemology challenges us to look at knowledge, not as a detached, unbiased, or divine secret to be unlocked or as an object to be acquired or managed, but as a very human, social and even political construction. The intent here is not to deconstruct knowledge and learning for the sake of deconstructing them but to promote continuous critical reflection that will continuously probe, question and critique the knowledge we use to make decisions, especially when the decision stakes and uncertainty are both high (Funtowicz and Ravetz, 1992; Funtowicz and Ravetz, 1993; Funtowicz and Ravetz, 1994; Ravetz and Funtowicz, 1999). We need to be critically aware of the social and historical context of our knowledge. We need to reflect on the implications of our knowledge and how it is used on others. We need to be open to a plurality of perspectives (Midgley, 2000; Jackson, 2000).

We should question how legitimacy or epistemic warrant is conferred within decision-making processes. What are the power relationships or imbalances imbedded in the process? Is legitimacy based on the proponent's adherence to a set of institutionally established protocols? Can the protocols be politicized through their institutionalization? Developers, environmental activists and government bureaucrats with interests on the Oak Ridges Moraine know that even science can be made into a political game.

There can be little doubt that scientific knowledge contributed greatly to understanding of ecosystems and landforms such as the Oak Ridges Moraine and the Long Point sand spit. As well, conventional planning approaches, such as rational comprehensive planning, have contributed to our understanding of many of the particular impacts and benefits of development on our social and ecological systems. Without scientific studies of these systems, we would not likely understand their significance or sensitivity. And there can be little doubt that scientific evidence brings with it legitimacy in decision-making processes. However, studies that overlook systemic behaviour tell only part of the story.

Moreover, environmental decision making is not simply a scientific process. It, like science or rational comprehensive planning, is a human, social and political process. Understanding or creating knowledge about environmental planning and policy making requires procedural, scientific knowledge but also requires local technical knowledge and especially political or governance knowledge. This dissertation has reinterpreted Flyvberg's interpretation of three key Aristotelian intellectual principles to emphasize the importance of, and dialectic relationship among, epistemic/scientific, techne/local technical and phronetic/governance knowledge.

The resulting conceptual framework, methodological framework and conceptual model of social learning were developed from insights gleaned deductively through an in-depth, interdisciplinary literature review and through an inductive, participatory research process and empirical case studies. As a result, the development of these conceptual tools was influenced by the experience and knowledge of members of volunteer, environmental movement organizations, civil servants and of course other researchers with interests in both the Oak Ridges Moraine and Long Point case studies. This resonance between the abstract, conceptual and the pragmatic, empirical is a key strength of these conceptual tools and this work and requires further research. The implications and contributions of this research consequently span the abstract-pragmatic divide from continued work exploring the implications of complex and critical systems thinking and critical social epistemology to working directly with STORM and the LPWBRF board to foster social learning.

To ensure continuous social learning, academic researchers, civil servants, politicians, environmental advocates and citizens alike need to continue to question the knowledge we use to make decisions and the learning that becomes embedded in social structures. We need to question and reflect critically upon our goals and the power imbalances imbedded into decision-making structures and institutions. We need to consider a wide variety of knowledges and perspectives when granting epistemic warrant. And we need to consider the implications of our decisions across scales from the local to the global.

References

Abel, N. A. L. (2001). Seeking Sustainability in the Western Division of New South Wales by Changing Laws, Policies and Administration. Canberra: LWA.

Ackoff, R. (1997). Strategies, Systems and Organizations. Strategy and Leadership, March/April, 22-27.

Agar, J. (2005). Before Critical Realism: Kantian Empirical Metaphysics . New Formations, 56, 27-39.

Ahl, V., and T. F. H. Allen . (1996). Hierarchy Theory: A Vision, Vocabulary, and Epistemology. New York: Columbia University Press.

Alexander, E. R. (1992). Approaches to Planning: Introducing Current Planning Theories, Concepts and Issues (Second Edition). Longhorne: Gordon and Breach Science Publishers.

Allen, J. (1996). Our Town: Foucault and knowledge-based politics in London. In: S. Mandelbaum, L. Mazza, and R. W. Burchell Explorations in Planning Theory. (328-344). New Brunswick, New Jersey: Centre for Urban Policy Research.

Allen, T. F. H., J. Tainter, and T. W. Hoekstra. (2003). Supply-side Sustainability. New York: Columbia University Press.

Allen, T. F. H., and T. W. Hoekstra. (1992). Toward a Unified Ecology. New York: Columbia University Press.

Allmendinger, P. (2002). Planning Theory. New York: Palgrave.

Alvesson, M., and Kaj Skoldberg. (1999). Reflexive Methodology. Thousand Oaks, California : Sage Publications .

Argyris, C., and D. A. Schon. (1974). Theory in Practice : Increasing Professional Effectiveness. San Francisco: Jossey-Bass.

Argyris, C., and D A. Schon. (1978). Organizational Learning : A Theory of Action Perspective. Reading, Mass.: Addison-Wesley Publishing Company.

Argyris, C. (1993). Knowledge for Action: A Guide to Overcoming Barriers to Organizational Change. San Francisco, California: Jossey-Bass Publishers.

Arthur, S., and J. Nazroo. (2003). Designing Fieldwork Strategies and Materials. In: J. Ritchie, and J. Lewis (editors), Qualitative Research Practice: A Guide for Social Science Students and Researchers.(109-137). Thousand Oaks, California: Sage Publications.

Bailey, R. O. (2005). Alternative Land Use Services (ALUS): An Opportunity for Agriculture to Lead in Conservation. Delta Wildlife Foundation.

Bandura, A. (1971). Social Learning Theory: Motivational Trends in Society. Morristown, New York: General Learning Press.

Bandura, A. (1986). Social Foundations of Thoughts and Action: A social cognitive theory. Englewood Cliffs, N J: Prentice Hall.

Bandura, A. (1991). Social Cognitive Theory of Moral Thought and Action. In: W. M. Kurtines; J. L. Gewirtz, Handbook of Moral Behavior and Development, Volume Theory. (45-103). Hillsdale, New Jersey: Erlbaum Associates Publishers.

Barrett, H. B. (1979). Lore and Legends of Long Point. Don Mills, Ontario: Burns and MacEachern Limited.

Berg, B. L. (1998). Qualitative Research Methods for Social Science (Third Edition). Toronto: Allyn and Bacon.

Berkes, F., and C. Folke. (1998). Linking Social and Ecological Systems: Management Practices and Social Mechanisms for Building Resilience. New York: Cambridge University Press.

Berkes, F., and C. Folke. (2003). Navigating social-ecological systems : building resilience for complexity and change . New York: Cambridge University Press.

Bhaskar, R. (1986). Scientific Realism and Human Emancipation. London: Verso.

Bhaskar, R. (1997). A Realist Theory of Science (Second Edition). London: Verso.

Blais, P. (2002). Inching Toward Sustainability: The Evolving Structure of the GTA: A report prepared for the Neptis Foundation. Toronto: Neptis Foundation.

Bobrow, D. B., and J. S. Dryzek. (1987). Policy Analysis by Design. Pittsburgh, PA: University of Pittsburgh.

Bocking, S. (2005). Protecting the Rain Barrel: Discourses and the Roles of Science in a Suburban Environmental Controversy. Environmental Politics, 14(5), 611-628.

Bouwen, R., and T. Taillieu. (2004). Multi-party Collaboration as Social Learning for Interdependence: Developing Relational Knowing for Sustainable Natural Resource Management. Journal of Community and Applied Social Psychology, 14, 137-153.

Boyer, M. C. (1983). Dreaming the Rational City. Cambridge, Massachusetts: MIT Press.

Boyle, M., J. J. Kay, and B. Pond. (1996). State of the Landscape Reporting: The

Development of Indicators for the Provincial Policy Statement Under the Planning Act . Waterloo: Ontario Ministry of Natural Resources.

Campbell, S., and Susan Fainstein. (1996). Introduction: The Structure and Debates of Planning Theory. In: S. Fainstein, and Scott Campbell, Readings in Planning Theory. (1-14). Malden, Mass.: Blackwell Publishers Inc.

Canadian Institute of Planners. (2000). Commission of Conservation, 1909-1921. Canadian Institute of Planners. [Web Page]. URL http://www.cip-icu.ca/English/plancanada/plan.htm [2005].

Canadian Man and Biosphere Committee. (1990). Biosphere Reserves in Canada. Ottawa, Ontario: Canadian / Man and the Biosphere Secretariat, Canadian Commission for UNESCO.

Cerny, P. (1997). Paradoxes of the Competition State: The Dynamics of Political Globalization. Government and Opposition, 32(2), 251-274.

Chapman, L. J., and Putnam, D. F. (1984). The Physiography of Southern Ontario (Third Edition). Toronto: Ministry of Natural Resources, Ontario Geological Survey.

Connell, D. J. (2003). Observing Community: An inquiry into the meaning of community based on Luhmann's General Theory of Society. Unpublished doctoral dissertation, University of Guelph, Guelph, Ontario.

Connick, S., and Judith E. Innes. (2003). Outcomes of Collaborative Water Policy-making: Applying Complexity Thinking to Evaluation. Journal of Environmental Planning and Management, 46(2), 177-197.

Conservation Ontario. (2000) Conservation Ontario Corporate Profile [Web Page]. URL http://www.conservation-ontario.ca/ [2003, November].

Cooper, K. (1998). Trashing Environmental Protection: Ontario's four-part strategy.[Web Page]. URL http://www.cela.ca/publications/cardfile.shtml?x=981 [2006].

Craig, B., G. Whitelaw, J. Robinson, and P. Jongerden. (2003). Community-based Ecosystem Monitoring: A tool for developing and promoting ecosystem-based management and decision making in the Long Point World Biosphere Reserve. Proceedings of the Fifth Science and Management of Protected Areas Association Conference [Web Page]. URL http://www.sampaa.org/PDF/ch4/4.4.pdf [2006].

Daniels, S. E., and Walker, G. B. (2001). Working Through Environmental Conflict: The collaborative learning approach. London: Praeger Publishers.

Daphne Brasell Associates Limited . (2003). Superb or Suburb? International Case Studies in Management of Icon Landscapes. New Zealand: Parliamentary Commissioner for the Environment, New Zealand.

Dean, K., Jonathan Joseph, and Alan Norrie. (2005). New Essays in Critical Realism . New Formations, 56, 7-26.

Delanty, G. Knowledge as communication: a review of recent literature on method and theory in social science. International Journal of Social Research Methodology, 5(1), 83-90.

Denzin, N. K., and Y. S. Lincoln. (2000). Handbook of Qualitative Research (Second Edition). Thousand Oaks, California: Sage Publications.

Dorcey, A. H. J. (2004). Sustainability Governance: Surfing the waves of transformation. In: B. Mitchell, Resource and Environmental Management in Canada: Addressing conflict and uncertainty (Third Edition). (528-554). Don Mills, Ont.: Oxford University Press.

Dunsire, A. (1996). Tipping the Balance: Autopoiesis and Governance. Administration and Society, 28(3), 299-334.

Eigen, M. (1979). The Hypercycle, a Principle of Natural Self-Organization. Berlin: Springer-Verlag.

Fainstein, S. S., and N. Fainstein. (1996). City Planning and Values: An updated view. In: S. Campbell, and S. Fainstein Readings in Planning Theory. (265-287). Malden, Mass.: Blackwell Publishers Inc.

Faludi, A. (1982). Toward a Combined Paradigm of Planning Theory? A Rejoinder. C. Paris (Editor), Critical Readings in Planning Theory (13-25). Oxford: Pergamon.

Fisher, J. R., and D. H. M. Alexander. (1993). The Symbolic Landscape of the Oak Ridges Moraine: Its influence on conservation in Ontario, Canada. Environments, 22(1), 100-104.

Fitzgerald, N. (1997). Harnessing the Potential of Globalization for the Consumer and Citizen. International Affairs, 73(4), 739-746.

Fitzpatrick, P., and A. J. Sinclair. (2003). Learning Through Public Involvement in Environmental Assessment Hearings. Journal of Environmental Management, 67(2), 161-174.

Fitzpatrick, P. (2006). In It Together: Organizational learning through participation in environmental assessment. Journal of Environmental Assessment Policy and Management, 8(2), 157-183.

Flood, R. L., and N. R. A. Romm. (1996). Diversity Management: Triple Loop Learning. Toronto: John Wiley and Sons.

Flyvbjerg, B. (2001). Making Social Science Matter: Why Social Inquiry Fails and How it Can Succeed Again. New York: Cambridge University Press.

Folke, C., Thomas Hahn, Per Olsson, and Jon Norberg. (2005). Adaptive Governance of Socio-Ecological Systems. Annual Review of Environment and Resources, 30, 441-473.

Fontana, A., and J. H. Frey. (2000). The Interview: From Structured Questions to Negotiated Text. In: N. K. Denzin, and Y. S. Lincoln (Editors), Handbook of Qualitative Research (Second Edition). (645-672). Thousand Oaks, CA: Sage Publications.

Forester, J. (1987). Planning in the Face of Conflict. Journal of the American Planning Association, 53(3), 303-314.

Forsyth, T. (2003). Critical Political Ecology: The Politics of Environmental Science. New York: Routledge - Taylor and Francis Group.

Foucault, M. (1977). Language, Counter-Memory, Practice: Selected essays and interviews . Ithaca, New York.: Cornell University Press.

Foucault, M. (1980). Power-Knowledge : Selected interviews and other writings, 1972-1977. Hassocks: Harvester Press.

Foucault, M. (2000). Power. New York: New Press.

Francis, G. R. (1985a). Biosphere Reserve: Innovations for Cooperation in the Search For Sustainable Development. Environments, 17(3), 23-36.

Francis, G. R. (1985b). Long Point Biosphere Reserve Nomination . Ottawa, Ontario: Submitted to the Man and the Biosphere Programme, Canadian Commission for UNESCO.

Francis G. R., and G. Whitelaw. (2001). Point World Biosphere Reserve Periodic Review. Canadian Biosphere Reserves Association, Reviewers on Behalf of the Canadian Commission for UNESCO and Canada/MAB.

Francis, G. R. (2003). Governance for Conservation. In: F. R. Westley, and Philip S. Miller Experiments in Consilience: Integrating Social and Scientific Responses to Save Endangered Species. (223-243). Washington D. C.: Island Press.

Francis, G. R. (2004). Biosphere Reserves in Canada: Ideals and Some Experience. Environments: A Journal of Interdisciplinary Studies, 32(3),

Francis, G. R. (2005). Nomination Submission from Canada for the Oak Ridges Moraine Biosphere Reserve. Waterloo, Ontario, Canada.

Francis, G. R. (2006). Waterloo, Ontario, Canada: Personal Communication. July, 2006.

Freire, P. (1973). Education for Critical Consciousness. New York: Continuum.

Friedmann, J. (1987). Planning in the Public Domain. New Jersey: Princeton University Press.

Fuchs, C. (2004). Knowledge Management In Self-Organizing Social Systems. Journal of Knowledge Management Practice, 5.

Fuchs, C., Wolfgang Hofkirchner, and Bert Klauninger. (2001). The Dialectic of Bottom-up and Top-down Emergence in Social Systems. INTAS Project "Human Strategies in Complexity.

Fuller, S. (2002a). Knowledge Management Foundations. Boston: Butterworth Heinemann.

Fuller, S. (2002b). Social Epistemology (Second Edition). Indianapolis: Indiana University Press.

Fuller, S. (2005). The Intellectual. Cambridge: Icon Books Ltd.

Funtowicz, S. O., and Jerome R. Ravetz. (1992). Three Types of Risk Assessment and the Emergence of Post Normal Science. In: D. Golding, and S. Krimsky, Social Theories of Risk (230-251). Westport, Connecticut: Praeger.

Funtowicz, S. O., and Jerome R. Ravetz. (1993). Science for the Post-Normal Age. Futures, 25(7), 739-755.

Funtowicz, S. O., and Jerome R. Ravetz. (1994). Uncertainty, Complexity and Post-Normal Science. Annual Review of Environmental Toxicology and Chemistry, 13(12), 1881-1885.

Gibson, R. B., S. Hassan, S. Holtz, J. Tansey and G. Whitelaw. (2005). Sustainability Assessment : Criteria and processes . Sterling, Virginia: Earthscan.

Giddens, A. (1984). The Constitution of Society : outline of the theory of structuration. Berkeley, California: University of California Press.

Giddens, A. (1996). In Defence of Sociology: Essays, interpretations and rejoinders . Cambridge, Massachusetts: Polity Press.

Government of Ontario. (2001). Oak Ridges Moraine Conservation Act. Ministry of Municipal Affairs.

Government of Ontario. (2002). Oak Ridges Moraine Conservation Plan. Ontario Ministry of Municipal Affairs.

Gowan, R. (2004). Norfolk at the Crossroads: Directions for a prosperous future in Norfolk County. Simcoe, Ontario: Norfolk County.

Gryzbowski, A. G. S., and D. S. Slocombe. (1988). Self-organization Theories and

Environmental Management: The Case of South Moresby. Environmental Management, 12(4), 463-478.

Gunderson, L., C. S. Holling, and S. S. Light. (1995). Barriers and Bridges to the Renewal of Ecosystems and Institutions. New York: Columbia University Press.

Gunderson, L., and C. S. Holling. (2002). Panarchy: Understanding Transformations in Human and Natural Systems. Washington: Island Press.

Haas, P. M. (1990). Saving the Mediterranean : The Politics of International Environmental Cooperation . New York : Columbia University Press.

Habermas, J. (1973). Theory and Practice . Boston: Beacon Press.

Habermas, J. (1984). The Theory of Communicative Action, Volumes 1 and 2. Cambridge, Massachusetts: Polity Press.

Haken, H. (1978). Synergetics: An Introduction. New York: Springer-Verlag.

Hanna, K., and S. Webber. (2005). Sustainability, Planning Practice, Housing Form in the Toronto Region's Oak Ridges Moraine: Project Report. Ottawa, Ontario: Canada Mortgage and Housing Corporation.

Harvey, L. (1990). Critical Social Research. Boston: Unwin Hyman.

Healy, P. (1997). Collaborative Planning: Shaping Places in Fragmented Societies. Vancouver, British Columbia. University of British Columbia Press.

Healy, P. (2003). Collaborative Planning in Perspective. Planning Theory, 2(2), 101-123.

Healy, S. (2004). Power, Knowledge and Sustainability. Proceedings of the 2002 Berlin Conference on the Human Dimensions of Global Environmental Change "Knowledge for the Sustainability Transition. The Challenge for Social Science" Berlin: Global Governance Project. [Web Page]. URL http://web.fu-berlin.de/ffu/akumwelt/bc2002/download.htm#H [2006]

Hessing, M., Michael Howlett, and Tracy Summerville. (2005). Canadian Natural Resource and Environmental Policy: Political economy and public policy . Vancouver: UBC Press.

Holling, C. S. (1973). The Resilience and Stability of Ecological Systems. Annual Review of Ecology and Systematics, 4, 13-20.

Holling, C. S. (1978). Adaptive Environmental Assessment and Management. New York: Wiley.

Holling, C. S. (1995). What barriers? What bridges? In: L.H. Gunderson, C. S. Holling, and S. S. Light, Barriers and Bridges to the Renewal of Ecosystems and

Institutions. (3-36). New York: Columbia University Press.

Holling, C. S. (2001). Understanding the Complexity of Economic, Ecological, and Social Systems. Ecosystems, 4, 390-405.

Holling, C. S., L. Gunderson, and D. Ludwig. (2002). In Quest of a Theory of Adaptive Change . In: L. Gunderson, and C. S. Holling (Editors), Panarchy: Understanding Transformations in Human and Natural Systems. (3-24). Washington: Island Press.

Howlett, M. (2002). Policy Instruments and Implementation Styles: The evolution of instrument choice in Canadian environmental policy. In: Van Nignatten D. L., and R. Boardman (Editors), Canadian Environmental Policy: Context and cases. (25-45). Oxford: Oxford University Press.

Hudson, B. (1979). Comparison of Current Planning Theories: Counterparts and Contradictions. Journal of the American Planning Association, 45(4), 3-36.

Hughes, M. (2002). Interviewing. T. Greenfield (Editor), Research Methods for Postgraduates (Second Edition). New York: Oxford University Press Inc.

Huxley, M. (1994a). Panoptica: Utilitarianism and land use control. In: K. Gibson, and S. Watson, Metropolis Now: Planning and the urban in contemporary Australia. (66-88). Sydney: Pluto.

Huxley, M. (1994b). Planning as a Framework of Power: Utilitarian reform, enlightment logic and the control of urban space. In: S. Ferber, C. Healy, and C. McAuliffe Beasts of Suburbia: Reinterpreting cultures in Australian suburbs. (148-169). Melbourne, Australia: Melbourne University Press.

Innes, J. E. (2004). Consensus Building: Clarification for the critics. Planning Theory, 3(1), 5-20.

Innes, J. E., and D. E. Booher. (1999). Consensus Building and Complex Adaptive Systems: A Framework for Evaluating Collaborative Planning. American Planning Association Journal, 65(4), 412-423.

Ivey, J. L., R. C. deLoe, and R. Kreutzwiser. (2002). Groundwater Management by Watershed Agencies: an Evaluation of the Capacity of Ontario's Conservation Authorities . Journal of Environmental Management, 64, 311-331.

Jackson, M. C. (2000). Systems Approaches to Management. New York: Kluwer Academic / Plenum Publishers.

Jamison, A. (2001). The Making of Green Knowledge: Environmental Politics and Cultural Transformation. New York: Cambridge University Press.

Jessop, B. (1993). Towards a Schumpeterian Workfare State? Preliminary Remarks in

Post-Fordist Political Economy. Studies in Political Economy, 40, 7-39.

Jessop, B. (1995a). The Regulation Approach, Governance and Post-Fordism. Economy and Society, 24(3), 307-333.

Jessop, B. (1995b). Towards a Schumpeterian Workfare Regime in Britain? Reflections on Regulation, Governance, and Welfare State. Environment and Planning, 27 (11): 1613–1626.

Jessop, B. (1998). The Rise of Governance and the Risks of Failure: The Case of Economic Development. International Social Sciences Journal, 155, 29-45.

Jessop, B. (2005). Critical Realism and the Strategic-Relational Approach . New Formations, 56, 40-53.

Jorgensen, D. L., (1989). Participant Observation: A Methodology for Human Studies. London: Sage Publications.

Kanter, R. (1990). Overview: Options for a Greater Toronto Area Greenlands Strategy. Toronto: Ontario Ministry of Natural Resources.

Kay, J. J. (1984). Self-Organization in Living Systems. Unpublished doctoral dissertation, Systems Design Engineering, University of Waterloo, Waterloo, Ontario, Canada.

Kay, J. J. (1991). A Nonequilibrium Thermodynamic Framework for Discussing Ecosystem Integrity. Environmental Management, 15(4), 483-495.

Kay. J. J., H. Regier, M. Boyle, and G. R. Francis. (1999). An Ecosystem Approach for Sustainability: Addressing the Challenge of Complexity. Futures, 31(7), 721-742.

Kay, J. J., M. Boyle, and B. Pond. (2002). Monitoring in Support of Policy: an Adaptive Ecosystem Approach. In: M. K. Tolba, Encyclopedia of Global Environmental Change. (pp. 116-137). Chichester: John Wiley and Sons.

Kay, J. J. and H. Regier. (1999). An Ecosystemic Two-Phase Attractor Approach to Lake Erie's Ecology. In: M. Munawar, T. Edsall, S. Nepsey, G. Sprules, and B. Shute, International Symposium: The State of Lake Erie (SOLE) - Past, Present and Future: A Tribute to Drs. Joe Leach and Henry Regier. (3-21). Netherlands: Backhuys Academic Publishers.

Kay, J. J. (1991). The Concept of Ecological Integrity, Alternative Theories of Ecology and Implications for Decision-Support Indicators. In: C. E. A. Council, Economic, Ecological, and Decision Theories. (23-58). Ottawa: Government of Canada.

Kay, J. J. (1993). On the Nature of Ecological Integrity: Some Closing Comments. In: S. Woodley, J. J. Kay, and G. Francis, Ecological Integrity and the Management of Ecosystems. (483-495). Delray, FL: St. Lucie Press.

Kay, J. J. (1994). Some Notes on the Ecosystem Approach: Ecosystems as complex systems. Waterloo, Ont.: University of Waterloo.

Keen, M., V. A. Brown and R. Dyball. (2005). Social Learning in Environmental Management: Towards a Sustainable Future. London: EarthScan.

Kickert, W. J. M. (1993). Autopoiesis and the Science of (Public) Administration: Essence, Sense and Nonsense. Organization Studies, 14(2), 261-278.

Klosterman, R. E. (1996). Arguments for and Against Planning. In: S. Fainstein, and Scott Campbell, Readings in Planning Theory. (150-168). Maldon, Mass.: Blackwell Publishers Inc.

Koestler, A. (1967). The Ghost in the Machine. Toronto: The MacMillan Company.

Kooiman, J. (1993). Modern Governance: New Government-Society Interactions. London: Sage Publications Inc.

Krause, P., A. Smith, B. Veale, and M. Murray. (2001). Achievements of the Grand River Conservation Authority, Ontario, Canada. Water Science and Technology, 43, 45-55.

Kuhn, T. (1970). The Structure of Scientific Revolutions (Second Edition). Chicago: University of Chicago Press.

Lewi, H. G. W. (1996). Modern Urban Government: A Foucouldian perspective . Urban Policy and Research, 14(1), 51-64.

Lewis, J. (2003). Design Issues. J. a. J. L. Ritchie (editors), Qualitative Research Practice: A Guide for Social Science Students and Researchers . Thousand Oaks, CA : Sage Publications.

Ley, D., and Tutchener, J. (2001). Immigration, Globalisation and House Prices in Canada's Gateway Cities. Housing Studies, 16(2), 199-223.

Lorenz, E. N. (1993). The Essence of Chaos. Seattle: University of Washington Press.

Luhmann, N. (1984). Social Systems. Stanford, California: Stanford University Press.

Majchrzak, A. (1984). Methods for Policy Research. Beverly Hills: Sage Publications.

Manuel-Naverrette, D., D. Dolderman, and J. J. Kay . (2002). A Historical Overview of the Ecological Integrity Concept. In: Ecological Integrity and Protected Areas. (113-122). Waterloo, Ontario: Parks Research Forum of Ontario (PRFO).

Maturana, H., and F. Varela. (1980). Autopoiesis and Cognition: the Realization of the Living. Holland: D. Reidel Publishing Co.

Maturana, H., and F. Varela. (1987). The Tree of Knowledge: The biological roots of human understanding. Boston: New Science Library.

Maturana, H. R. (1988). Reality: The search for objectivity or the quest for a compelling argument. The Irish Journal of Psychology, 9(1), 25-82.

Maturana, H. R. (Draft Manuscript). Autopoiesis, Structural Coupling and Cognition. [Web Page]. URL http://www.isss.org/maturana.htm [2003].

McCarthy, D., Graham Whitelaw, Paula Jongerden, and Brian Craig. (In Press). Contributions of Four Long Point Sustainability Workshops to Community Social Learning and the Logistics Function of the Biosphere Reserve. Environments: A Journal of Interdisciplinary Studies.

McCarthy, D. D. P. (2003). Post-Normal Governance: An Emerging Counter-Proposal. Environments: A Journal of Interdisciplinary Studies, 31(1), 79-91.

McCloskey, D. N. (1987). Responses to My Critics. Eastern Economics Journal, 13, 308-311.

McGuirk, P. M. (2001). Situating Communicative Planning Theory: context, power and knowledge. Environment and Planning A, 33, 195-217.

Mezirow, J. (1994). Understanding Transformation Theory. Adult Education Quarterly, 44(4), 222-232.

Mezirow, J. (1998). On Critical Reflection. Adult Education Quarterly, 48(3), 185-198.

Midgley, G. (2000). Systemic Intervention: Philosophy, Methodology, and Practice. New York: Kluwer Academic / Plenum Publishers.

Mingers, J. C. (1995). Self-Producing Systems: Implications and Applications of Autopoiesis. New York: Plenum.

Mitchell, B. (1997). Resource and Environmental Management. Toronto: Longman.

Mitchell, B. (2002). Resource and Environmental Management (Second Edition). Harlow: Prentice Hall.

Mitchell, B. (2004). Resource and Environmental Management in Canada : addressing conflict and uncertainty (Third Edition). Don Mills, Ont.: Oxford University Press.

Mitchell, B., and D. Shrubsole. (2001). Ontario's Conservation Authorities. Water News, December, 16-21.

Monitoring the Moraine. (2006). Status Report on the Implementation of the Oak Ridges Moraine Conservation Plan: Implications for the Greenbelt Plan. Toronto: Monitoring the Moraine.

Nelson, J. G. (2001). Retrospective on a Civic Approach: The Kitchener-Waterloo Urban Environmental Management Project. Environments: A Journal of Interdisciplinary Studies, 29(1), 113-122.

Nelson, J. G., and Kerrie Wilcox. (1996). Long Point Environmental Folio. Waterloo, Ontario: Heritage Resources Centre, Faculty of Environmental Studies, University of Waterloo.

Neuman, W. L., (1997). Social Research Methods: Qualitative and Quantitative Approaches. Toronto: Allyn and Bacon.

Norfolk County. (2003). Norfolk County in 2026: A scenario. Simcoe, Ontario: Norfolk County.

Norfolk County. (2006). Norfolk County Official Plan. Simcoe, Ontario: Norfolk County.

Nowotny, H., P. Scott, and M. Gibbons . (2001). Re-Thinking Science: Knowledge and the Public in an Age of Uncertainty . Cambridge, Massachusetts: Polity Press.

Oak Ridges Moraine Technical Working Committee. (1994). The Oak Ridges Moraine Strategy For the Greater Toronto Area: An ecosystem approach for long term protection and management. Toronto, Ontario, Canada: Ontario Ministry of Natural Resources, Oak Ridges Moraine Technical Working Committee.

Office of Research Ethics, University of Waterloo. (2005) Ethics Review Process [Web Page]. URL http://www.research.uwaterloo.ca/ethics/human/ethicsReview/reviewProcess.htm [2006].

Ontario Ministry of Municipal Affairs and Housing. (2002). Oak Ridges Moraine Conservation Plan. Toronto, Ontario: Government of Ontario.

Ontario Ministry of Municipal Affairs and Housing . (2005a). Greenbelt Act. Ontario Regulation 59/05.

Ontario Ministry of Municipal Affairs and Housing. (2005b). Provincial Policy Statement.

Ontario Ministry of Natural Resources. (1991). A natural heritage framework: a strategy for the protection and management of natural heritage in the Greater Toronto Area, Discussion Paper No. 1. Toronto: Greater Toronto Area Branch, Ontario Ministry of Natural Resources.

Ostrom, E. (1990). Governing the Commons: The Evolution of Institutions for Collective Action. Cambridge, Massachusetts: Cambridge University Press.

Ostrom, E., Joanna Burger, Christopher B. Field, Richard B. Norgaard, and David

Policansky. (1999). Revisiting the Commons: Local Lessons, Global Changes. Science, 284, 278-282.

Pahl-Wostl, C., and M. Hare. (2004). Processes of Social Learning in Integrated Resources Management. Journal of Community and Applied Social Psychology, 14, 193-206.

Pahl-Wostl, C. (2006). The Importance of Social Learning in Restoring the Multifunctionality of Rivers and Floodplains. Ecology and Society, 11(1).

Parker, B., and Brian Craig. (2004). Monitoring Ecosystem Change in Carolinian Forests and Oak Savannahs of Southwestern Ontario. Leading Edge 2004: The working biosphere. (1-8). Niagara Escarpment Commission.

Parliamentary Commissioner for the Environment. (2003). Superb or Suburb? International Studies in Management of Icon Landscapes. Wellington, New Zealand: Parliamentary Commissioner for the Environment.

Pattee, H. (1973). Hierarchy Theory, the Challenge of Complex Systems. New York: Braziller.

Patton, C. V., and David S Sawicki. (1993). Basic Methods of Policy Analysis and Planning . Englewood Cliffs, New Jersey. Prentice-Hall.

Pearce, D. W., G. D. Atkinson, and W. R. Dubourg. (1994). The Economics of Sustainable Development. Annual Review of Energy and the Environment, 19, 457-474.

Pierre, J. (2000). Debating Governance: Authority, Steering, and Democracy. Toronto: Oxford University Press.

Popper, K. R. (1972). Objective Knowledge. Oxford University Press: Oxford, UK.

Prigogine, I., and Isabelle Stengers . (1984). Order Out of Chaos: Man's New Dialogue with Nature. New York: Bantam.

Ravetz, J. R. (1999). What is Post-Normal Science. Futures, 31(7), 647-653.

Ravetz, J. R., and Silvio Funtowicz. (1999). Post-Normal Science: an insight now maturing. Futures, 31(7), 641-646.

Reason, P. (1994). Three approaches to participative inquiry. In: N. K. Denzin, and Y. S. Lincoln. Handbook of Qualitative Research. (322-339). Thousand Oaks: Sage.

Reason, P., and J. Heron. (1995). Co-operative Inquiry . In: R. Harre, J. Smith, and L. Van Langenhove, Rethinking Methods in Psychology. (122-142). London: Sage.

Reason, P. (1988). Human Inquiry in Action: Developments in New Paradigm Research.

London: Sage.

Reed, M. G., and Kirsten McIlveen. (2006). Toward a Pluralistic Civic Science?: Assessing Community Forestry. Society and Natural Resources, 19, 591-607.

Regional Municipalities of York, Peel and Durham. (1999). The Oak Ridges Moraine: Towards a Long Term Strategy. Toronto: Regional Municipalities of York, Peel and Durham.

Rhodes, R. A. W. (1996). The New Governance: Governing Without Government. Political Studies, XLIV, 652-667.

Richardson, A. H. (1974). Conservation by the People: the History of the Conservation Movement in Ontario to 1970. Toronto: University of Toronto Press.

Ritchie, J., J. Lewis, and G. Elam. (2003). Designing and Selecting Samples. In: J. Ritchie and J. Lewis (Editors), Qualitative Research Practice. (77-108). Thousand Oaks, CA : Sage Publications.

Robinson, J. (1996). Life in 2030 : Exploring a sustainable future for Canada . Vancouver, British Columbia: University of British Columbia Press.

Robson, C. (1993). Real World Research: A resource for social scientists and practitioner researchers. Cambridge, Massachusetts: Blackwell.

Rosenau, J. N. (1995). Governance in the Twenty-First Century. Global Governance, 1(1), 13-43.

Royal Commission on the Future of the Toronto Waterfront. (1992). Regeneration. Toronto: Royal Commission on the Future of the Toronto Waterfront.

Röling, N. G., and M. A. E. Wagemakers. (1998). A New Practice: Facilitating sustainable agriculture. In: N. G. Röling, and M. A. E. Wagemakers (Editors), Facilitating Sustainable Agriculture: Participator Learning and Adaptive Management in Times of Environmental Uncertainty. (3-22). Wageningen: Cambridge University Press.

Schneider, E. D., and J. J. Kay. (1994). Complexity and Thermodynamics: Towards a New Ecology. Futures, 26(6), 626-647.

Schon, D. A., and M. Rein. (1994). Frame Reflection: Toward the Resolution of Intractable Policy Controversies. New York: Basic Books.

Schon, D. A. (1983). The Reflective Practitioner : How Professionals Think in Action. New York: Basic Books.

Schwandt, T. A. (2000). Three Epistemological Stances for Qualitative Inquiry: Interpretivism, Hermeneutics, and Social Constructivism. N. K. Denzin, and Y. S.

Lincoln (editors), Handbook of Qualitative Research (Second Edition). (189-214). Thousand Oaks, California: Sage Publications.

Shields, P. (1999). The Role of Sense-Making in Critical Policy Research: Theoretical and Methodological Issues. San Francisco: International Communication Association.

Shor, I. (1993). Education is politics: Paulo Freire's critical pedagogy. In: P. McLaren, and Peter Leonard (Editors), Paulo Freire: A critical encounter. (25-35). London: Routledge.

Shrubsole, D. (1996). Ontario Conservation Authorities: Principles, Practice and Challenges 50 Years Later. Applied Geography, 16(4), 319-335.

Simon, H. A. (1973). The Organization of Complex Systems. In: H. Pattee, Hierarchy Theory, the Challenge of Complex Systems. (1-27). New York: Braziller.

Simon, S. (2004). Systemic Evaluation Methodology: The Emergence of Social Learning From Environmental ICT Prototypes. Systemic Practice and Action Research, 17(5), 471-494.

Sinclair, A. J., and A. P. Diduck. (2001). Public involvement in EA in Canada: a transformative learning perspective. Environmental Impact Assessment Review, 21, 113-136.

Skibicki, A. (1993). The Long Point Region: and Institutional and Land Tenure History and Examination of Management Needs. The Long Point Environmental Folio Series. Working Paper 3. Heritage Resources Centre, University of Waterloo, Waterloo, Ontario.

Skibicki, A. (1996). Land Management in the Long Point Area. J. G. Nelson, and Kerrie Wilcox (Editors), Long Point Environmental Folio . Waterloo, Ontario: Heritage Resources Centre, Faculty of Environmental Studies, University of Waterloo.

Slocombe, D. S. (1990). Complexity, Change, and Uncertainty in Environmental Planning: From the Great Lakes to the Kluane/Wrangells, PhD Dissertation. Waterloo, Ontario: Heritage Resources Centre, University of Waterloo.

Slocombe, D. S. (1993). Implementing Ecosystem-Based Management. BioScience, 43(9), 612-622.

Slocombe, D. S. (1998). Defining Goals and Criteria for Ecosystem-Based Management. Environmental Management, 22, 483-493.

Slocombe, D. S. (2004). Applying an Ecosystem Approach. In: B. Mitchell Resource and Environmental Management in Canada: Addressing conflict and uncertainty (Third Edition). (420-441). Don Mills, Ont.: Oxford University Press.

Solesbury, W. Making Social Science Matter: Why social inquiry fails and how it can succeed again. Planning Theory and Practice, 3(2), 250-251.

Stacey, R. D. (2001). Complex Responsive Processes in Organizations: Learning and Knowledge Creation. New York: Routledge.

Stewart, I. (1989). Does God Play Dice? : the mathematics of chaos. Oxford UK: B. Blackwell.

Stewart, J., and Russel Ayres. (2001). Systems Theory and Policy Practice: An Exploration. Policy Sciences, 34, 79-94.

Stoker, G. (1998). Governance as Theory: Five Propositions. International Social Science Journal, 155, 17-27.

Swyngedow, E. (2000). Authoritarian Governance, Power, and the Politics of Rescaling. Environment and Planning D: Society and Space, 18, 63-76.

Tartaglia, C. M., and Prasad Ramnath. (2005) Using Open Spaces to Resolve Cross Team Issues [Web Page]. URL http://agile2005.org/XR11.pdf#search=%22%2BTartaglia%20%2BRamnath%20 %2B2005%20%2B%22Open%20Spaces%22%22 [2006].

Taylor, S. J., Steven J., Bogdan R. (1984). Introduction to Qualitative Research Methods. New York: John Wiley and Sons.

Teubner, G. (1988). Autopoietic Law: A new approach to law and society. New York: de Gruyter.

Thom, R. (1975). Structural Stability and Morphogenesis: An Outline of a General Theory of Models. New York: W. A. Benjamin.

Thomas, M. J. (1982). The Procedural Planning Theory of A. Faludi. In: C. Paris (Editor), Critical Readings in Planning Theory. (13-25). Oxford: Pergamon.

Tippett, J., B. Searle, C. Pahl-Wostl, and Y. Rees. (2005). Social learning in public participation in river basin management—early findings from HarmoniCOP European case studies. Environmental Science and Policy, 8, 287-299.

Ulanowicz, R. (1997). Ecology, the Ascendant Perspective. New York: Columbia University Press.

Ulrich, W. (1987). Critical Heuristics of Social Design. European Journal of Operations Research, 31, 276-289.

Varela, F. J. (1992). Autopoiesis and a Biology of Intentionality. In: F. J. Varela. Autopoiesis and Perception. (1-11). Dublin: Dublin City University.

Wagner, P. (2001). Theorizing Modernity. London: Sage.

Walker, B. H., L. Gunderson, A. Kinzig, C. Folke: S. Carpenter, and L. Schultz. (2006). A Handful of Heuristics and Some Propositions for Understanding Resilience in Social-Ecological Systems. Ecology and Society, 11(1), 13-28.

Waltner-Toews, James J. Kay, Tamsyn P. Murray, and Cynthia Neudoerffer. (2004). Adaptive Methodology for Ecosystem Sustainability and Health (AMESH): An introduction. G. Midgley, and Alejandro E. Ochoa-Arias Community Operational Research Systems Thinking for Community Development. (334-339). New York: Kluwer Press.

Waltner-Toews, D., J. J. Kay, C. Neudoerffer, and T. Gitau. (2003). Perspective changes everything: Managing ecosystems from the inside out. Frontiers in Ecology and the Environment, 1(1), 23-30.

Watson, V. (2002). Do We Learn from Planning Practice? The contribution of the practice movement to planning theory. Journal of Planning Education and Research, 22, 178-187.

Webler T., H. Kastenholz, and O. Renn . (1995). Public Participation in Impact Assessment: A Social Learning Perspective . Environmental Impact Assessment Review, 15(5), 443-463.

Weinberg, G. M. (1975). An Introduction to General Systems Theory. Toronto: John Wiley and Sons.

White, G. F. (1945). Human Adjustment to Floods: A Geographical Approach to the Flood Problem in the United States. Chicago: University of Chicago.

White, L. (2001). 'Effective Governance' Through Complexity Thinking and Management Science. Systems Research and Behavioral Science, 18, 241-257.

Whitelaw, G. S. (2005). The Role of Environmental Movement Organizations in Land Use Planning: Case studies of the Niagara Escarpment and Oak Ridges Moraine processes. Unpublished doctoral dissertation, University of Waterloo, Waterloo, Ontario, Canada.

Whitelaw, G. S., and Daniel D. P. McCarthy. (2006). Exploring Sustainable Development Activities for the Long Point World Biosphere. Waterloo, Ontario: Long Point World Biosphere Reserve Foundation Board.

Whyte, W. F. (1991). Participatory Action Research. Newbury Park, California: Sage Publications.

Wilcox, S. (1993). The Historical Economies of the Long Point Area . The Long Point Environmental Folio Series. Working Paper 2. Heritage Resources Centre, University of Waterloo, Waterloo, Ontario.

Winfield, M. S., and A. Taylor. (2005). Rebalancing the Load: The need for an aggregates conservation strategy for Ontario . Toronto: Pembina Institute.

Wynne, B. (1992). Misunderstood Misunderstanding: Social identities and public uptake of science. Public Understanding of Science, 1(3), 281-304.

Yiftachel, O. (1998). Planning and Social Control: Exploring the dark side. Journal of Planning Literature, 12(4), 395-406.

Yiftachel, O., and Margo Huxley. (2000). Debating Dominance and Relevance: Notes on the 'communicative turn' in Planning Theory. International Journal of Urban and Regional Research, 24(4), 907-913.

Yin. R. K. (2003). Case Study Research: Design and Methods (Third Edition). Thousand Oaks, California : Sage Publications.

Appendix A: Oak Ridges Moraine Interview Questions

Your Story of the Oak Ridges Moraine

1. From your perspective what were the key events that contributed to and hindered the development and enactment of the ORM Act and Plan between 1988 and 2001?

2. Who were the key individuals / groups/ organizations / agencies that contributed to or hindered the development and enactment of the ORM Act and Plan?

3. What was your role and the role of your organization in these events?

4. From your perspective what was the role of knowledge and learning in these events?

5. Since the enactment of the ORM Act and Plan what do you see as your role and the role of your organization in Oak Ridges Moraine issues?

6. Since the enactment of ORM legislation what do you think has changed on the ORM?

7. Has the mandate of your organization changed since enactment of the ORM Act and Plan?

8. Who else should I speak to?

9. What are the key documents I should read?

Appendix B: Long Point Interview Questions

Interview Questions

Your Story of the Long Point World Biosphere Reserve:

1. From your perspective what were the key events that contributed to and hindered the 1986 designation of the Long Point World Biosphere Reserve? From your perspective what were the key events that have contributed to and hindered the continued evolution of the Long Point World Biosphere Reserve?

2. From your perspective how has the mandate of the Biosphere Reserved evolved since its designation? Why?

3. Who were the key individuals / groups/ organizations / agencies that contributed to or hindered the 1986 designation and the continued evolution of the Long Point World Biosphere Reserve?

4. What was your role or the role of your organization in these events?

5. From your perspective what was the role of knowledge and learning in these events?

6. Since the designation of the Biosphere Reserve in 1986 and more recently given the LPWBRF Board's efforts to address sustainable development as a complement to their conservation activities, what do you see as your role and the role of your organization in Long Point area issues?

7. Since the designation of the Biosphere Reserve what do you think has changed on the Long Point area? What do you think has or will change given the LPWBRF Board's efforts to address sustainable development as a complement to their conservation activities?

8. Who else should I speak to?

9. What are the key documents I should read?

45305584R00135

Made in the USA
Middletown, DE
30 June 2017